FINDING
Daniel Boone

Finding Daniel Boone

His Last Days in Missouri & the Strange Fate of His Remains

Ted Franklin Belue

Published by The History Press
Charleston, SC
www.historypress.com

Cover: Chester Harding (American, 1792–1866); Portrait of Daniel Boone *(1734–1820), 1820; Oil on Canvas. Gift of Mr. and Mrs. Arthur H. Almstedt. Conservation funded by the Honorable Order of the Kentucky Colonels, 2015, 1957.7. Collection of the Speed Art Museum, Louisville, Kentucky.*

First published 2020

Manufactured in the United States

ISBN 9781467145886

Library of Congress Control Number: 2020938498

Also by Ted Franklin Belue

The Long Hunt: Death of the Buffalo East of the Mississippi
The Hunters of Kentucky: A Narrative History of America's First Far West, 1750–1792

Edited

Peter Houston's *A Sketch in the Life and Character of Daniel Boone*
Lyman C. Draper's *The Life of Daniel Boone*

This book is for
Lavina Turbeville Belue

When he moved from that country that he left every promise to himself that he never would return to Kentucky again owing to Some mistreatment he had Received there—in consequence of that promise I objected to his Remains being Removed to Kentucky.

—James Boone to Lyman C. Draper, October 11, 1855

My father and mother were sadly out of fix when they thought he had been so badly treated about his land titles to come and dig his old bones up after Picking out the Place for his wife and telling them all to lay him by her side. Carrying them to Kentucky—laying some Old Stumps around their graves.

—Eviza Coshow to Lyman C. Draper, March 1, 1883

Boone was soured against Kentucky.…If Boone's bones could but speak the real feelings the old man cherished in his lifetime, they would have protested indignantly against their removal to Kentucky.

—General Edward Coles to Lyman Draper, circa 1850s.

Daniel Boone requested his body should not rest in Kentucky. He never got over the feeling that Kentucky had treated him unjustly.

—Mrs. A.K. Weir, circa 1880s

Contents

PREFACE

Daniel Boone died September 26, 1820, near Marthasville, Missouri. He was interred beside his wife, Rebecca, who had died seven years earlier, on a grassy rise above Tuque Creek in David Bryan's family cemetery. Twenty-five years later three Kentuckians representing the Frankfort Cemetery Company returned to the Bluegrass on a steamer named *Daniel Boone*, bearing their remains. Amid much pomp and ceremony, and attended by a crowd nearly twenty thousand strong, the famous frontier couple was reinterred in the capital's new garden cemetery.

Despite rumbling thunderheads, drizzling rain and a damp slog up Frankfort's Main Street the procession that Saturday went remarkably well. Reinterring the Boones was the city's ultimate groundbreaking ceremony to herald its fancy necropolis's grand opening, the singular event coinciding with the FCC's newspaper advertisements to sell burial plots.

Many years later, Missourians charged that the commonwealth had retrieved Rebecca but not Daniel, claiming that the FCC had reburied an unknown enslaved person of African descent, sparking a long simmering debate: Where is Daniel Boone buried?

FEW ATTEMPTS AT UNTANGLING the enigmatic fate of Boone's bones are as quixotic as the one told to me by a late-night caller who, with his wife, had driven to Frankfort to sit by Boone's tomb and chant invocations to summon Dan and Rebecca from eternity's abyss. (One hopes it was a low-attendance day and that the cemetery superintendent was elsewhere.) After waving sacred crystals overhead they dropped a plumb bob on a thread, inviting the Boones to stir. Presently, Daniel hearkened and signaled back, the enigmatic voice in my receiver said, by causing the bob to sway. Nothing was heard from Rebecca.

Likewise in Missouri, a psychic was summoned to Boone's Tuque Creek grave. Hunting for some trace of Dan—no one was sure what the medium was looking for; she never said and puzzled onlookers were too polite to ask—she shuffled among the weathered gray stones and towering walnut, hackberry, persimmon and cedar, her divining rods bobbing and sidewinding. After a few laps of the cemetery she frowned, stared at nothing for a while and left, leaving her L-shaped brass rods in a bystander's hands.

In 1856 when the austere bibliophile Lyman C. Draper, the State Historical Society of Wisconsin's corresponding secretary, interviewed Nathan Boone and his wife, Olive, in Missouri, there is no hint that the reburial rumor about Nathan's father was mentioned. Today that is the one question a Boone speaker can depend on getting. Neutrality on Colonel Boone's whereabouts is not an option on either side of the Mississippi, as I learned.

Booked for a speaking engagement one night at a venue deep in the Bluegrass that shall remain nameless, I strode to the podium and launched into my Boone talk, rambling through Colonel Dan's forays and ending with his last Missouri sunset and legacy. Afterward were questions, including, of course, the dreaded warhorse: Where is Daniel Boone buried?

I gave my pat response: The documents say so and so; Kentuckians argue this and that; Missourians claim that and this; historians argue the matter.

My articulate dodge had never failed me. Except this time.

As the crowd filed out, a tall, elderly man in a black suit walked toward me with resolution, his darkly patinaed cane poking ahead and gold watch chain dangling from a silk-lined vest pocket. He fixed me in his sights, elevating his hickory parallel to my nose. Peering past its rubber toe I took him to be in his eighties as he began our row with, "Sir, the Daughters of the American Revolution put that monument up in Frankfort. My dear departed mother was part of that outfit. We all know Daniel Boone is under it."

In truth, the DAR's founding came thirty years after Boone's tomb was built. No matter, he was armed and ready to throw down over his mother's good name, which I had unknowingly besmirched. I mumbled something like, "Yes, sir, likely, you're right." Glaring but honor satisfied, the old Kentuckian lowered his cane, donned his fedora with a dignified flourish and left, tap-tapping off in the night like Captain Ahab.

I packed with haste and fled to the safety of Motel 6.

How did this begin? Was there any truth to it? Why did it matter where Daniel Boone was buried? What elements sustained these tales as they mutated from racist lore into canonical decrees in history books? Why were folks so protective of Boone's body parts, even his memory?

There was more to this tale than a hunt for a man's bones. I would begin where Daniel's biographies end—on his death bed. Working forward, I'd juxtapose his vanished realm with what it became in my day. This was not hard to do east of the Mississippi where many of his trails are marked; a few, like U.S. Highway 25-E, which began as Boone's Wilderness Trail, are highways.

But across the Big Muddy few have breached the historical force field where he sojourned the longest. Confronted by a frontier Midwest now gone, to hear his death song and defray the rumors plaguing its coda I'd be forced to immerse myself in the life and times of his last days—and in those caretakers' lives acting as stewards, present and past, of his memory, complicating my already daunting task.

I did not know where the frontiersman's last trail would end or what detours I'd face as I plunged into the chiefest of his mysteries. Wary of creating new myths and heedful of the old Kentuckian's rebuke that fateful night, I approached with trepidation my journey—Daniel Boone's last journey—from his Missouri grave and back to his Kentucky grave.

—Ted Franklin Belue
Murray, Kentucky
July 17, 2020

A Selected Two-Hundred-Year Daniel Boone Postmortem Chronology

1820 **September 26**, Daniel Boone dies and is interred beside his wife, Rebecca, who died seven years earlier. Their graves are marked by head- and toe-stones.

1836 David Bryan commissions new inscribed tombstones for Daniel and Rebecca's graves.

1837 Nathan Boone sells Femme Osage home and seven hundred acres for $6,120; moves to Ash Grove.

1842 **April 12**, Colonel Ambrose W. Dudley acknowledges that Frankfort has no cemetery.

1844 **February 27**, Mason Brown forms the Frankfort Cemetery Company (FCC).

April 30, The *St. Louis New Era* reports David Bryan cemetery overgrown.

1845 **January 28**, The FCC receives proposals to develop innovative garden cemetery.

February 16, The FCC buys Hunter's Garden for $3,801; hires famous Scottish landscaper.

April, Bill unsuccessfully submitted in Missouri Legislature for $500 for Boone monument.

April 17, The FCC forms retrieval committee to go to Missouri to exhume the Boones.

April 21, The FCC drafts letters to Nathan asking for parents' remains; mails to wrong address.

April 24, The FCC vows to spend $10,000 for garden cemetery.

(1845, continued)

June 3, William Boon informs Missouri's ex-governor L.W. Boggs of FCC's designs.

July 17, FCC envoys meet in Missouri with Harvey Griswold; unearth Boone coffins.

July 23, Wednesday, the Boones' remains arrive at Frankfort on the steamer *Daniel Boone*.

August 26, The *Frankfort Commonwealth* announces Boone reburial/cemetery dedication.

September 12, Philip Slater Fall and Henry C. Davis cast Boone's skull in plaster.

September 13, Reburial of Daniel and Rebecca, crowd estimated up to twenty thousand.

October 28, The FCC advertises sale of burial plots in the *Frankfort Commonwealth*.

1860 **March 2**, Kentucky Legislature authorizes $2,000 for Boone Monument.

1862 The Boones are re-exhumed; coffin and bone fragments taken by souvenir hunters; monument erected.

1862–65 Civil War occupiers deface monument for souvenirs.

1876 William S. Bryan's *Pioneer Families of Missouri* published; causes doubt that Daniel Boone moved.

1906 Kentucky Legislature's Spence Bill allows $2,000 to replace the monument's vandalized panels; Rebecca Bryan Boone Daughters of the American Revolution (DAR) chapter donates $500 toward restoration.

1909 Marthasville citizens conclude Daniel Boone still in original grave.

1910 **May 26**, DAR unveils Frankfort's restored Boone monument.

1911 John S. Jones letter casts more doubt on location of Daniel's remains.

1913 Centennial of Rebecca Boone's death.

1915 Warren County, Missouri's DAR unveils Boone memorial in Bryan graveyard.

1917 David Gardyne's Alonzo Callaway story published; promoted by Jesse P. Crump.

1934 Descendants from across the United States gather at Frankfort monument to celebrate Daniel Boone's 200th birthday.

1935 Kentuckians rebuff Missouri's lieutenant governor Frank Gaines Harris's efforts to return Rebecca.

1937 Missourians again request Rebecca's remains.

1939 John Bakeless's *Daniel Boone* becomes first credible Boone biography to mention burial controversy.

1940s Frankfort Boone monument damaged by falling tree and is repaired.

1955 St. Charles Chamber of Commerce seeks to have Rebecca's remains returned. Kentucky governor Lawrence Wetherby notifies Missourians that her bones will remain in Kentucky.

1975 Dr. Thomas D. Clark, University of Kentucky History Department chair, suggests getting "a reputable physical anthropologist" to examine Frankfort's Boone cast.

1977 Richmond-Madison County Chamber of Commerce proposes moving Daniel and Rebecca's remains to Fort Boonesborough State Park. Plan rejected.

1983 **June**, Dr. David Wolf, Kentucky's state forensic anthropologist, examines Boone skull cast; concludes it may possess African American characteristics; AP spreads news.

1985 Dr. David Wolf reexamines Boone cast for *National Geographic* magazine's "Daniel Boone: First Hero of the Frontier"; reopens controversy.

1987 **September**, Missouri state representative Russell Brockfield, Warrenton, demands that Kentucky's house of representatives officially declare Daniel Boone to be in Missouri.

1988 Missourians pressure Governor John Ashcroft to declare Daniel Boone in Missouri.

1995 Dr. Emily Craig, Kentucky's state forensic successor, reexamines Boone skull cast.

August, FCC sesquicentennial Boone funeral reenactment; Boone declared to be in Frankfort cemetery.

2008 **June 24**, Thief steals bronze DAR Boone plaque from Bryan Cemetery; replaced by black marble plaque.

2009 David Bryan's cemetery claims newly contested.

2011 Two authenticated Boone plaster skulls rediscovered at Louisville's Filson Historical Society.

2012 **September**, Missouri University of Science and Technology conducts Ground Penetrating Radar survey at the Bryan Cemetery. About thirty marked and unmarked graves are delineated. Anomalies detected around Boone graves indicate disturbance.

2020 **September 26**, Bicentennial of Daniel Boone's death.

Acknowledgements

A thousand-mile journey begins with one step, and this journey of thousands of miles over several states careened into a lot of fine folks who more than once salvaged this weary traveler, humbling him with their generosity, knowledge and expertise. I can't thank them all personally but will name as many as I can; my sincerest apologies to any I missed.

I first cannot forget those who sadly passed on before I finished this book, notably Warren "Hawk" Boughton, Mountain Man mentor; Dr. David J. Wolf, Kentucky state forensic anthropologist; William Strode, superlative photographer; Ralph Gregory, historian and delightful human being; Dr. Thomas D. Clark, virtuoso historian and friend; Paul Harp, friend.

I appreciate the warm openness of interviewees Russ Hatter, William Ray, David Wolf, Thomas Shelby Watson, Marc Houseman, Bernardo Brunetti, David Knotts, Wheelock Crosby Brown, Elizabeth Moize, James Holmberg, Jim Richardson, Ken Kamper, Ralph Gregory, Grady Manus and others I met along life's highway, including diligent researchers like Kathy Schoppenhorst and, via email, Margie Miles.

William Ray, Kristine Madras and Meredith Rau unstintingly put up with my repeated intrusions, often for days at a time, at the Historic Daniel Boone Home near Defiance, Missouri, and never treated me like anything less than family. Their kindness and hospitality in every way remains overwhelming. I'm awed.

The same is true with Ken Kamper, Missouri's Lyman C. Draper incarnate, and his superior half, Bernice. Thank you for tolerating my rambunctious freeloading and late-night Boone chats for more than twenty-five years with charitable humor. Ken's in-the-trenches work on Daniel Boone is amazing. Ken, Russ Hatter and Bill Ray deserve an extra-special mention for their selfless yeoman service on my behalf.

For their energy and forbearance in coming through so stupendously with photographs, illustrations, research and critical advice, I'm indebted to Hannah McAulay, Speed Art Museum, Louisville, Kentucky; Anne Cox, State Historical Society of Missouri, Columbia, Missouri; Lauren Sallwasser, Missouri Historical Society, St. Louis, Missouri; Heather Potter and James Holmberg, Filson Historical Society, Louisville, Kentucky; Cheri Daniels, Kentucky Historical Society, Frankfort, Kentucky; Russ Hatter, Capital City Museum, Frankfort, Kentucky; Kate Hesseldenz, Liberty Hall Historic Site, Frankfort, Kentucky; Meredith Rau, Historic Daniel Boone Home, Defiance, Missouri; Bob Lanham, Frankfort, Kentucky; Gene Burch, Frankfort, Kentucky; David Wright, Pathfinder Press, Gallatin, Tennessee; and Jason Gatliffe, *MUZZLELOADER* magazine, Gallatin, Tennessee.

Ken Kamper, Dr. Jerry A. Herndon, Russ Hatter and Lavina Belue read over portions of the text and made invaluable comments. Yancey Madison Courtney's landmark congener studies spared us all many a headache, and her GPS rescued me more than once.

At Murray State University I used a vanload of books, quarterlies and the Draper Manuscripts in the Pogue Special Collection Library. My ex-bosses and History Department chairs, Dr. Terry Strieter and Dr. Kathy Callahan, never turned me down in securing funds from slim budgets for my multitudinous forays across the wide Missouri. Again, my deepest appreciation.

John Higginbotham of FPB-TV-Frankfort Kentucky supplied me with a DVD of Frankfort's August 1995 reenactment of the city's sesquicentennial Boone reburial.

Others who assisted in various ways include Mike and Kim Courtney, Versailles, Kentucky; Dr. Emily Craig, Georgetown, Kentucky; Dr. Nelson L. Dawson, Kentucky Historical Society, Frankfort, Kentucky; Exeter Society of Friends Meeting, Douglassville, Pennsylvania; Nicki Hughes, Capital City Museum, Frankfort, Kentucky; Jim Lewers, Daniel Boone Homestead, Birdsboro, Pennsylvania; Dr. Kevin Qualls, Murray, Kentucky; Greg DeLancy, Murray, Kentucky; State Historical Society of Wisconsin, Madison; Black Swan Books, Lexington, Kentucky.

This book required unusual care and tending and received it from The History Press. I much appreciate commissioning editor Chad Rhoad's efforts on my behalf and equally thank copy editor Hayley Behal for her patience, concern and sharp eyes.

And lastly, I could not have stuck this out were it not for my wife, Lavina, the metronome of my world. It's been a whirlwind so far, hasn't it?

Part I

Missouri, 1820–44

1

First Light, Tuesday, September 26, 1820

"I am going. Do not grieve over me—my time has come" were the last words he uttered. His bed was close to the east wall near the door. Ladder-back chairs by the west wall braced his cherrywood coffin. Opposite the door the fireplace warmed the hearth and the dark, walnut mantle. Beeswax candles and an oil lamp dripping lard illumed his wan features. Dawn was breaking—the sun half an hour high when Daniel Boone slipped into eternity.

He was a month shy of the eighty-sixth year of his birth. Rebecca, his wife of fifty-six years who'd borne ten children, died seven years before. He had outlived three daughters and three sons. Shawnees killed James and Israel. William died at birth. Levina and Rebecca passed of natural causes in Kentucky. Susannah was buried in the Missouri's bottoms.

Jemima Callaway, his surviving girl, and Nathan, his youngest boy, held their father's ashen hands as his face paled, a gasp escaped and his wide mouth creased into a scowl. It is a profound thing in a child's life to watch a parent die.

Boone's "good death" was his last accomplishment. He'd chosen not to lull himself into a stupor induced by Dr. John Jones's alcohol- and opium-based tonic proffered upon his arrival with Minerva and her mother, Jemima. Happenstance, likely, had brought them; no word had gone out about the patriarch's sudden failing. He assembled them around him "to bid them goodbye—told them he was going to a world of happiness; for them not to grieve." Like Jacob, the Old Testament patriarch, gathered his progeny at the last, so too did Boone.

Nathan's son-in-law Reverend James Craig, a blacksmith and Baptist circuit rider, walked in the narrow doorway with his wife, Delinda, in time to agree to do his eulogy. Boone was to be buried next to Rebecca at David Bryan's cemetery on Tuque Creek. He had moved from Nathan's to Jemima's home to tend her grave and "marked a Place by her side for himself and always seemed to long to lay by her side; was willing to be called anytime."

And so he was this dawn.

He'd called the family's slaves near to bid them "a fond adieu" and then he asked to be "made ready." Harry, one of the enslaved, shaved him. Delinda brushed his teeth. Jemima plaited his white hair, snipping off a lock. Olive took his last request: "I have not heard you sing in a long time. Please sing to me." And so she did, plaintively, as kith and kin hearkened, peering in his room.

Nearby—across the wide oaken floored hallway in the southwest sitting room—sat Olive's widowed mother, Margary Bounds Van Bibber, who was two months older than Daniel.

Hours before, the dying man had checked his polished, darkly burled cherry coffin one last time, thumping it with his cane to hear its resonant thud. The grave held no fear. There was peace. There was acceptance.

Symbolically too it seemed that as the Great Spirit gathered the last Long Hunter present in his death room were two future Mountain Men, America's new generation of pathfinders. There were Daniel's grandson, Albert Gallatin Boone, who within five years signed on with William Ashley's brigade, trapped the Green with Kit Carson and Jim Bridger and became an Indian agent and Isaac Graham, who would attend the 1832 rendezvous at Pierre's Hole, hunt with George Nidever and Joe Walker and distill Kentucky bourbon in Santa Cruz. John Coulter Boone was there too, born four years earlier to Olive and named for Lewis and Clark's illustrious hunter who, near their trek's end, turned his face back to the Shining Mountains where he trapped beaver by the bale and outran a murderous Blackfoot horde on the Three Forks.

Sophocles himself could not have scripted it any finer.

Daniel Boone was old and worn out—his life spent and his race run. Three days before he'd felt poorly from overeating venison, sweet potatoes and walnut dainties the children cooked for their doting grandpa. Lingering chills and fever from exposure during last winter's hunt on Loutre Lick returned. Deep, throbbing stabs pierced him from shoulders to sternum. He rebounded enough to be helped up to go out to look off the porch facing Femme Osage Creek. After his last sunset he spooned corn mush and milk from his porcelain china bowl. He rested. Hours later, his vital signs plummeted, and his heart failed.

The death watch ended. The family ceased all labors, save for the essentials. Neighbors and the enslaved tended the livestock and gathered provisions in such times. For the Femme Osage community to do less would have shown disrespect to the dead.

Nathan Boone. *State Historical Society of Missouri.*

Major Nathan Boone, discharged from Missouri's Mounted Rangers, was thirty-nine and Olive two years younger. They would get word out around the Femme Osage—Nathan to his brothers, Jesse in St. Louis and Daniel Morgan in the Pineys near the Gasconade on the upper Missouri.

Jemima and Flanders lived in Marthasville, the American town's sprawl subsuming its colorful French and Indian predecessor, La Charette. On Sundays, their spacious log home and then, after its construction, their freshly built pine barn near the crumbling Callaway's Fort perimeter served as Friendship Baptist Church, the first local Protestant fellowship, where Pastor Craig preached (as did circuit riders Timothy Flint and John Mason Peck, who would go on to write their own Boone biographies) to those gathered to worship.

Flanders's home was a mile, thereabouts, from David Bryan's burial ground. Thursday was sure to be memorable for the close-knit community. Two centuries later the burial of America's first frontier hero would still be Marthasville's most significant event.

2

Crossing the Big Muddy into Boone's World

Five hours from my Kentucky home and heading to I-270, west of St. Louis's spaghetti junction and townships—Florissant, Kirkwood, Creve Coeur…lost count after that—I crossed the wide Missouri (not so wide due to drought this early March day) and took Exit 17 at Boone's Crossing toward Defiance on Highway 94 South, dodging another wad of brown pulp and translucent zinc-gray bands; seven dead armadillos so far.

Would that I could yank up St. Louis's Arch and replant it here, I thought, skirting the land of the West's fabled trailblazers. Signs along 94 designate it Lewis and Clark Highway. I fast closed in on Daniel Boone country—his last far western spate of it. Pennsylvania, North Carolina, Kentucky and Virginia boast their own Boone countries. Even Florida, near Pensacola, where he purchased his southernmost English land grant after the French and Indian War but never returned to occupy it after Rebecca put her foot down—she wasn't leaving the Blue Ridge for the Land of Flowers.

I passed over Femme Osage Creek; three hundred years ago a voyageur canoeing past its banks named the rivulet for an Osage woman who drowned in its turbid waters. Meriwether Lewis left no word on this May 22, 1804, when he and the Corps of Discovery tented on the "Osage Woman R, about 30 yds wide" and came upon roving Kickapoos hunters, their ebony hair roached into scalp locks aflutter with hawk feathers, sterling silver and red and yellow porcupine quilled strips. The corps swapped the men two quarts of whiskey for "4 Deer as a Present."

Across at Wild Horse Creek—an hour from Daniel by river and thrice that by horse—thrived San Andre del Misuri, where a few dozen expat Kentucky families grew corn, wheat, tobacco, hemp, cotton and boiled maple sap into sugar to barter to travelers. New Orleans's governor Gayoso de Lemos appointed James Mackay as San Andre's leader, his ragtag militia patrolling from present-day Chesterfield to Washington.

In 1795, Mackay—a Scotsman turned Canadian turned American—and John Thomas Evans journeyed upriver past Mandan land, mapping Spain's empire from the Big Muddy to South Dakota's White River. At New Orleans, a facsimile of Mackay's "Indian Office Map" was passed to U.S. consul Daniel Clark, who told President Thomas Jefferson that "this survey is the best that was ever made in that Part of the world." Indiana territorial governor William Henry Harrison gave William Clark the copy he and Lewis followed "to the Mandane Nation."

By 1811 San Andre was in ruins, flooded out. James Mackay—proto-Mountain Man, cartographer and land baron—died in 1822. His role in the West was relegated to four entries in the Corp of Discovery's diaries, like the one William Clark logged on a rainy Friday, September 14, 1804, near Brule City, South Dakota: "I walked on Shore with a view to find an old Vulcanoe, Said to be in this neighborhood by Mr. J. McKey of St. Charles." Clark never sighted Mackay's "Vulcanoe." Today, I-55 has obliterated his grave south of the arch, and his name survives as Mackay Place, a two-block gentrified stretch bordering St. Louis's posh Lafayette Square.

Closer to Highway F's turnoff was once the six-hundred-arpent Spanish grant of Captain William Hays. (An arpent is a French colonial surveyor's term equaling .08507 of an acre.) Hays, a weaver, was a good hand in a fight but was quick to anger and a strong drink exacerbated his prickliness. Word was that he was abusive to his wife, Susannah, Daniel and Rebecca's eldest girl. Daniel dealt with his son-in-law but he knew of the talk alleging Susie's infidelity in Kentucky. Her death in 1800 ended the troubled marriage. James Davis, Hays's son-in-law, shot him four years later. As Hays was fool enough—drunk enough maybe—to charge Davis with a pistol while he wielded a rifle, his slaying was ruled a suicide.

No one is sure where William and Susannah Hays are buried. The murky, churning Missouri erased their graves, along with much of their original Spanish grant, long ago.

I turned right from Highway 94 and on to F at the Historic Daniel Boone Home corner sign. In truth, it was Nathan and Olive's home. (Recently owned by St. Charles's Lindenwood University, its proprietorship has transitioned to St. Charles County.) Daniel and Rebecca lived for eight years on their youngest son's estate but also dwelled with sons Daniel Morgan and Jesse and with daughter Jemima and her husband Flanders Callaway. Daniel's sons raised their parents' cabin at Nathan's—their sole Missouri home—before their father died in Nathan's stone house, dooming it to being misnamed in ads, brochures and on billboards to lure in tourists as the state has perennially neglected this one of its architectural crown jewels.

Segments of F corkscrewing in slow ascent to New Melle five miles away overlap parts of Boone's Trace, Daniel's wagon route beginning on his Spanish grant in Big Muddy's bottoms near Matson. Past the rolling terrain and scrub were pruned grape vines candelabraed along taut wires behind the sign for Chandlar Hill Vineyards. Rumbling semis hauling log-heavy flatbeds and pushing past fifty-five miles per hour reminded me of this asphalt ribbon's slim shoulders.

Leafless red maple, white oak and black walnut closed in along F's curvy two-lane, along with invasive sugar maples and cedar understories. Old surveys and hand-sketched plats refer to white oak, hickory, mulberry, elm, ash and dogwood stands. Red oak, burr and black oak are mentioned. Towering maples grew in the Big Muddy's bottoms where Daniel and Rebecca during February's sunny days decamped to render sap into sugar. Closer to the shoreline, paralleling its banks, grew stout cottonwoods and shaggy, sun-bleached sycamores.

Low, stubby limestone ledges up ahead, rightward, are vestigial gray remnants of a primeval glade—a dry, open grassy islet set in a forested ocean. Warmed by the sun, the stony outcroppings shelter yellowish scorpions, hairy tarantulas and collared lizards, which are as rare as the secretive ring-neck snakes sharing their shrinking habitat. Purplish prairie cone flowers and pale shooting stars dot the veldts, flecked by yucca and prickly pear. The Boones journeying this path in 1799 saw Missouri, like Kentucky of old, as America's new Canaan land.

Onward. Past Old Colony Road, the Femme Osage, barely flowing after days of hard rain, gradually appeared alongside the two-lane. A long-vanished gristmill—a ubiquitous sign of Anglo occupation—once ground flour and corn here for the Boones, Bryans and Callaways.

The elevation lifted, gradually.

In the haze a tractor disking the black soil into a furrowed chiaroscuro creates a rippling landscape that might make Master Basho smile. I'd wager the Deere's pilot has never heard of Micajah Callaway. Nor does he care that he's plowing his 680-acre Spanish grant. Nor does he know that

Shawnees seized him (with Boone and thirty-four salt-boilers) on Kentucky's Licking and whisked them to Fort Detroit. The warriors adopted Micajah; with Joseph Brant's Wyandots he waylaid Colonel Archibald Lochry's flotilla snaking down the Ohio. "Callaway was the worst savage amongst them," said a Pennsylvania fighter. After George Rogers Clark freed 'Cage, Boone hired him to mediate parleys and "Macagy Callaway served twenty days as an interpreter." He came here with his wife, Mary Arnold. When she died, he returned to Kentucky and wed Franky Hawkins.

Passing another pre-1812 gristmill site, I slowed for Callaway Fork Bridge, named for Flanders and Jemima Boone Callaway. Today the creek bed of fist-size orange and white rocks is parched, chalky; the unseasonable warmth boded ill, adding to it the dearth of March rains. Flanders, 'Cage's older brother, came to Kentucky from Virginia as a lanky runaway, a pock-faced smallpox survivor. By way of matrimony he stepped onto history's pages.

In 1776 on a summer Sunday following an Anglican brush arbor service, Shawnees seized Jemima and Fanny and Betsy Callaway's (Flanders's nieces) canoe on the Kentucky River. Jemima's father formed a posse and dashed out Boonesborough's gates. After two days on the trail, Boone, switching to warrior mode, left it to take a buffalo path shortcut. After a bloody dawn skirmish they freed the girls. Flanders escorted Jemima back to the fort and married her.

John Filson tells of the girls' capture in *The Discovery and Settlement of the Present State of Kentucke*. *Kentucke* sold well in America, England, France and Ireland, inspiring James Fenimore Cooper to flesh out the saga into *The Last of the Mohicans*. Boone morphed into the redoubtable Natty Bumppo. Jemima, Fanny and Betsy were revived as Alice and Cora Munro. The Shawnees became Hurons. Cooper's Leather-Stocking Tales became, copping a line from Richard Taylor's elegiac *Girty*, America's first "eastern westerns."

Flanders and Jemima rest near Marthasville in what's left of David Bryan's one-acre burial ground. "A Golgotha of Unknown and Forgotten Graves," William S. Bryan called his family's graveyard atop Tuque Creek's knoll; and it is just that, barely. Souvenir hunters carted off the Boones' and Callaways' original headstones.

In 2008 a vandal pried Daniel's bronze marker off his monument that the DAR erected in 1915, netting himself $100 for scrap metal plus 120 days in jail. Jemima's parents' markers—their second, set sixteen years after Dan's death and sparking speculation about their placement's accuracy—are housed at Central Methodist University's Stephens Museum in Fayette. A fitting epitaph for Jemima might read "Rebecca & Daniel Boone's Daughter: Muse of America's Western Literature."

I veered from F westward onto Stub Road, braking to ease my tires in and out of clay potholes and gravelly washouts. A red-tail hawk hunting over a fallow field tucked its wings in a *V*, dipped and sheared leftward, rending the air with *Tseeearr*—a warning?

This being my third jaunt on Stub I was alert to folks around here not liking strangers poking around. The three-story stone house of Boone's grandson Daniel Hays and wife, Mary Bryan, and Hays's cemetery is a half mile past three blaze-orange signs—"PRIVATE PROPERTY No Trespassing." After camouflaging under a blue-striped white point blanket my gig bag with its old Martin and travel bag, and latching the doors, my ball-capped head bowed to look for deer and turkey sign, I trudged along on foot.

Leftwards, ten feet down a steep bank, was what remained of a leaf-cluttered, earthen leg of Boone's Trace, marked by Dan himself. The huntsman had a lifelong penchant for blazing animal and native paths—called "traces"—by tomahawking deep slashes into the trees lining the way to mark the path for fellow sojourners.

A conduit that, miles later, splinters into the first nondescript legs of the Santa Fe, Oregon and Great Salt Lake Trails, and the first American road in this region, this slice of Boone's Trace cuts toward Nathan and Olive's place, hugging Femme Osage Creek six hundred yards southward. "From Stub Road westward," says Ken Kamper, a local Boone historian, I'd be "traveling along the old 'Boone Trace' or Trail, which came out of the hills at Stub Road and headed west along the near side of Femme Osage Creek."

To most around here this hint of a two hundred-year-old trail is a shaded, shallowly rutted ATV path strewn with beer cans, napkins and pop bottles, yet it speaks of nothing less than a nation's push from Jamestown to San Francisco, from Plymouth to Taos, and of America's first frontier hero and its original pathfinder.

Suddenly, deep-throated barks ahead halted my trek, hastening my retreat to my car.

I regained F, turning left. After two more bends was Nathan and Olive's Home. A buzzard devouring a hard, flattened rabbit lifted from the road. So immersed in Boone land that it seemed karmic and strangely ironic, I turned left onto the asphalted drive.

The parking lot was empty except for a motorcycle, a few cars and a Winnebago; closing time was nearing. At the Boone Carriage House, the gift shop and the home's entrance, I perused Boone T-shirts, mugs, toy rifles, authentic Native American wares from China, faux coonskin caps Daniel never wore, Boone books and pamphlets and Lindenwood University brochures.

Rear of Historic Daniel Boone Home, built by his son Nathan. In Daniel's time this was the house's front. *Historic Daniel Boone Home.*

Leaving word for Grady Manus, site coordinator, and Bill Ray, lead interpreter, I exited to the sidewalk leading to the home one hundred yards away. The Boones would be amazed to see this pre-industrial urban sprawl, Boonesfield Village, around their old homeplace, "comprised," said an LU leaflet I read along the way, "of more than a dozen historic buildings…and a school, the Old Peace Chapel, a carpenter's shop…a general store, and a grist mill."

In his day Nathan's place evolved into a community, with cabins, barns, outbuildings and slave quarters. Hammering away in his blacksmith shop, Daniel repaired guns and farm tools and shoed horses; when brother Squire, a smithy and silversmith, visited, maybe he fired up the forge. Deputy sheriff Anthony Palmer, a shy schoolmaster deemed "excessively polite," felted beaver plews into hats as the enslaved stirred a rank slurry of rotting oak bark in the tannery's vats. During the War of 1812, Hannah Cole—no slouch with a rifle, knife, trap or axe—put up a cabin here for her and her brood. Perishables were stored in the spring house.

Newlyweds Nathan and Olive, on January 10, 1800, secured 680 acres from Robert Hall for a horse, bridle and saddle (worth $120) for Survey No. 1794 and put up a shack and burned off enough scrub to plant corn—the usual settling procedure enacted by westering Americans. Between sowing and

BOONE'S CABIN IN ST. CHARLES COUNTY, MISSOURI.
From photograph in possession of Wisconsin State Historical Society.

Daniel and Rebecca Boone's cabin near Nathan's home, circa 1880. *Missouri Historical Society.*

reaping and hunting and trapping, the soon-to-be parents readied to build a "sturdy log house" near their bubbling spring, which today is barely a trickle.

Daniel and Rebecca moved here within six years of their arrival, leaving Dan Morgan's farm ascending from the Big Muddy's bottoms to the hilly hamlet of now Matson. Army life kept Nathan patrolling Osage land bordering Kansas with his Ranger Company of Dragoons. The War of 1812 fueled Sac and Fox raids against U.S. forts and settlements.

When a fragile peace was brokered, Nathan went home. Often there would be a new baby to greet his or her absentee father and then, weeks later, when he'd bid Olive adieu to return to his soldiers, another baby on the way. So it went every even year for twenty-eight straight years until there were fourteen babies in all.

Daniel, nearing seventy, surveilled the homeplace during Nathan's absences. And though he left here in 1813 to reside nearer to what became Marthasville, still, his frequent visits made him ubiquitous in Nathan and Olive's world.

To decipher the puzzling events occurring after his death required understanding his trans-Mississippian world, starting here—where he spent many of his last years and said his last words.

3

Where the Hunter Lived and Died

Walking on Boone turf elicited an array of feelings as I trudged up the rise to the home where Daniel "passed off gently." William Ray intercepted me. We shook hands but we'd met once before, he said, at a Bluegrass Alliance and New Grass Revival bluegrass jam at Rudyard Kipling's, a pub located at "Mile 604 on the Ohio River."

I went blank. "What's 'Mile 604'?"

He smiled, brown eyes crinkling behind his wire-framed glasses. "Louisville. Starting up at Pittsburgh at Mile 0. The river is 981 miles long."

Bill—tall, lanky, dark-haired under his dirty green Boone Home cap—is a true "Kaintuck," as Frenchmen called boatmen. For six years he plowed the Ohio as a deckhand or manned the *Belle of Louisville*—"I've been as far down as Henderson and as far north as thirty miles past Marietta." Like most riverboat men he's a free-spirited, engaging fellow. He trains guides, researches and plans events. He's an old-time fiddler and plays banjo, talents that go well here or on the Ohio. We made plans to pick some Boone-era tunes after hours.

A long rock wall bordered our left. Remnants of a well and Nathan's once-gurgling spring—these days barely a trickle—were to our right, once considered the property's rear. "We've found evidence of cabins right about here." He pointed a few yards away. "Maybe three, close in proximity. It makes sense that their cabins would have been close to the source of water." One structure may have been slave quarters.

Nearby lay the gray masonry core of a giant American elm (*Ulmus americana*), Daniel's so-called Judgment Tree, looking like a derelict Cecil B.

DeMille movie set prop, circa 1935. Here, legend has it, Boone—of stout build and ruddy faced, with white hair queued and attired in earth-toned homespun or a linen ruffled shirt, buckskin coat and weskit or wearing a woolen regimental pulled over a walnut-dyed shirt and breeches—prevailed over his shade-tree court.

It's a romantic image, an untutored woodsman acting as magistrate under a splattering of sunlight filtering through shimmering, saw-toothed foliage. Such "council elms" soared 150 feet or more. At thirty feet the trunk splits, forks leafing skyward above billowing, dappled shadows. In 1775, beneath Boonesborough's Divine Elm, Boone and other assembly delegates doffed their hats as an Anglican minister preached the gospel in the Bluegrass.

As "Commandant of the District of the femme osage," he sentenced lawbreakers, signed documents and brokered peace between brawlers like James Meek who "bit off a piece of Bery Vincent's Left Ear," governing "more by *equity* than by *law*." Spain's lieutenant governor Carlos Delassus, who handed rule to Americans, called him "a respectable old man, just and impartial" and advised that "in view of my confidence in him for the public good," he should stay at his post. "Whipped and cleared" was a usual sentence or fines paid in cash, livestock or labor.

One hothead displeased at his verdict vowed he'd fight him if he were not so old. Boone threw down: "Let not my gray hairs stand in your way. I am old enough to whip the likes of you." Swift justice kept men out of jail to provide for families. His was an equitable system.

In 1925 when Francis Marion Curlee bought the home the Judgement elm was showing the ravages of two hundred years. Curlee excised its dead wood, fertilized and concreted its decaying trunk and limbs—standard remedy for languishing hardwoods. Like a "dentist when cleaning a tooth for filling. If all the decay is not removed, it will continue as if the filling had not been placed."

Photos prior to Curlee's era show the elm leafed out. G.H. Pring, horticulturist for Missouri Botanical Gardens, stands by the trunk, its girth making five of him. He estimated it at "sixty-five feet high, forked about three feet from the ground, each branch measuring nine feet in circumference at the fork. The main trunk is sixteen feet six inches in circumference two feet from the ground."

When the defoliated crown crashed to earth, workers jammed rebar down its erect trunk and pumped in more concrete. As its pith rotted around the concrete and the scaly bark peeled away (to be scooped up by tourists), it

THE DANIEL BOONE JUDGMENT TREE.
(ULMUS AMERICANA).

G.H. Pring, Missouri Botanical Garden's horticulturist, stands by the second Judgement Tree near the Historic Daniel Boone Home. *Missouri Historical Society.*

left a duplicate stone elm sprouting steel spikes. Dan's ominously leaning Judgment Tree was roped off to keep it from toppling over on someone.

"I've seen a photo of it standing in the 1970s," Bill Ray said. "It was stripped. No green, no bark. With the rebar it looked pretty foreboding—like something out of a Tim Burton film." He sighed. "One of the misconceptions we get from people is this was 'Boone's Hanging Tree.'"

Actually, there were two Judgment Trees. Nathan's elm was the second. How often Boone held court here is speculative, though it was less than on his land near Matson where he lived and presided until 1805. By the time he moved here this was U.S. territory evolving to statehood. As Governor William Henry Harrison of the Louisiana Territory was appointing district judges, any Boone-arbitrated decisions would have dubious legal standing.

"This is one of the more exciting finds we've had." Bill pointed to an archaeological test pit exposing a tight vertically laid stone phalanx. "We found this cobblestone path. Theoretically, you could be looking as early as 1810, but it's more probable you're looking at the 1820s or so."

Maybe by this route (or the river) Nathan got word of their father's death to his brother Jesse, serving in St. Louis's legislature. The fourth-born son survived Boonesborough's siege, inspected salt-works in Virginia and Greenup County and was a Kentucky judge. He married Chloe Van Bibber and came here after his parents did. To honor Dan's memory, Missouri's Constitutional Convention adjourned for twenty days, yet Jesse missed his pa's funeral. Maybe he wasn't well, as consumption killed him by year's end, leaving Chloe with five sons and four daughters. Chloe died the following year.

St. Louis's *Missouri Gazette* published her father-in-law's obituary. Riddled with errors, it still captures the spirit of the man beneath the buckskin—its length confirming Boone's stature:

DEATH OF COL. DANIEL BOONE

DIED—At Charette village, in the state of Missouri, on the 26th September last, Col. Daniel Boone, the first settler of Kentucky, in the 90th year of his age. He was a native of Buck's County, Pennsylvania; he left that state at 18 years old, and settled in North Carolina. He was one of the few men of our country whose enterprise led him to search into the wilderness for the best tracts of land for man to inhabit. As early as the year 1775, he removed with his family, and settled on the Kentucky river, (with the loss of his eldest son, killed by the Indians,) at a plain now called Boonesborough, then an Indian country, where he remained until the year 1799. During this period of time, although most of his life had been spent in agricultural pursuits, and he had been frequently honored by his countrymen, as a member of the Virginia Legislature, and lived, at the close of the Revolutionary war, in peace and plenty, yet, such was his delight in hunting—such his devotedness to it, that, in the year 1799, with a numerous train of followers, he removed from Kentucky, and settled on the Femme Osage River, which empties itself into the Missouri River, about 50 miles above its mouth, then a wilderness. The year after he discovered the Boon's Lick country, which now forms one of the best settlements of the state. In that year he also visited the head waters of the Grand Osage river, and spent the winter upon the waters of the river Arkansas. At the age of 80, in company with one white man and a black man, whom he laid under strict injunction to return him to his family, dead or alive, he made a hunting trip to the head waters of the Great Osage, where he was successful in trapping beaver, and in taking of other game.

Colonel Boone was a man of common stature, of great enterprise, strong intellect, amiable disposition and inviolable integrity—he died universally regretted by all who knew him; and such is the veneration for his name and character, that both Houses of the General Assembly of this state, upon information of his death being communicated, resolved, to wear crape on the left-arm for 20 days, in token of regard and respect for his memory.

Bill Ray and I stayed on the walkway up to Nathan and Olive's front door; in their day it was their home's backdoor. The home fronted the creek six hundred yards southward and was bordered on the northern shore by Boone's Trace, Daniel's wagon route circumambulating the Femme Osage.

On my right was a stone wall marker set by the DAR's St. Louis Chapter.

This tablet marks
the Daniel Boone home
where colonel Daniel Boone lived
and died on September 26, 1820

I stooped to peer into a slot by the door frame; the slots were blocked off on the interior end. I shoved my fist in, stopping three inches past my wrist. Using the door as a center point to divide the home's face, between it and four window frames were three slots per side, each five and a half inches across by eight and a half inches high and fifty-five inches from the ground. Home lore deems these as "gun ports" or "loops"—fashioned so that Nathan and kin could poke guns out to blast away. Perhaps this tale was birthed by Curlee, whose construction crew, while "working on the walls of the house… found at the front six stones practically identical in size, evenly spaced and at the same height from the floor. Curiosity prompted investigation, and it was found that they filled what appeared to have been portholes. The conclusion that these openings were designed for portholes is natural, for at the time the house was built, it was surrounded by a wilderness through which Indians lurked and wandered."

To me (I'm five foot eight, same as Dan), these ports seemed a mite low to shoot out of unless the home's defenders were hobbits. Gun ports typically flare at the sides for aiming and side-to-side mobility; these were rectangular, sharply edged and compact. And why ports just to the northeast?

I nodded to my kind host who I suspected didn't buy the story either.

Others say the holes held scaffolding—an explanation less thrilling than whooping, war-painted apparitions circling on dashing ponies shrouded from flintlocks blazing away. Such skirmishing happened up the road a few miles at Jonathan Bryan's. Not here.

On entering, the first door on the right opens to narrow stairs—thirteen steps, not counting the landing—leading down to the basement. A grandfather clock occupied a hall corner by Karl Bodmer and Jean-François

The Capture of the Daughters of D. Boone and Callaway by the Indians, by Jean-François Millet and Karl Bodmer. *Washington University Gallery of Art.*

Millet's lithograph, *The Capture of the Daughters of D. Boone and Callaway by the Indians*. Above the mantle in the parlor—the wide, open-air sitting room leftwards where the Boones greeted visitors—was a finely done oil-on-canvas bust of Daniel reminiscent of John James Audubon's *Boone*.

The darkened timbers above the smoke-stained hearth told of many fires. Between the two windows on the north-south walls hung portraits of Francis and Ursula Curlee across from the first official presidential lithograph, *The Courtship of Washington*, suspended above an old chair and couch. The parlor was light federal blue and trimmed in walnut. Its patinaed floors were hammered with square-headed nails and the room smelled of age and smoke.

"We can head into the death room," Bill said.

4

The Bed Stood in the N.E. Corner of the N.W. Room

Fifteen steps from the main entrance, Bill and I turned to go in the small room off to the right. He pulled back the rope looping off the doorway from the hall to keep tourists out. I stepped in, feeling a shiver of otherworldliness.

Bill followed, speaking as if the colonel had just breathed his last. I was curious how he presented "the death room," his words, to sightseers with children in tow. It seemed a little grim.

"I just say this is the room Daniel Boone lived in and passed away in. If it's a lighter crowd I might say 'this is where it was the end of the trail for Daniel.' While I don't want to make this an exercise in mourning, this is where an American legend died. I'll set the narrative up in the hall and let the room speak for itself."

The room afforded the hunter privacy and access, sunshine and breezes. Its two large windows have four panes side to side and five panes bottom to top, and they are draped in ivory curtains. The trundle bed, with ropes underneath cinched to firm the tick, sat below the chair rails, head posts to the wall. A Quaker-like hunter's hat—black felt, low-crown with a blue jay feather in its band—was on the spread. Dan's death room was tastefully appointed—simple, poignant, evocative.

"Do people ask why it's not a coonskin cap? I guess you don't get that much anymore."

Boone hated them, deeming them uncouth. Fur caps are hot, reek when wet, don't deflect ice and snow or shed rain (except down one's back) and

Daniel Boone's room, where he died. *Historic Daniel Boone Home.*

are practical only in the coldest winter. Some backwoodsmen wore them. Indians did too. Boone did not.

"No, no. You get it all the time. I'll beat them to the punch. I'll say, 'The hat you're going to see is not going to be the hat you're expecting to see. And the hat you're expecting to see is not the hat he really wore.' And sooner or later, I'll have to answer questions about Daniel dying at the Alamo." I thought he was kidding. Really?

"Oh, yes. Sometimes I bring it up, saying something like, 'You'd be surprised, many people are convinced Daniel died at the Alamo.' That way, if someone was thinking it, I've corrected it. Same with the coonskin caps people show up wearing. It doesn't help that the actor Fess Parker played both Davy Crockett and Daniel Boone on television."

Parker, a tall, dark-haired, handsome Texan who died in 2010 at the same age as the real Dan'l, starred in such notable Hollywood films as *Old Yeller* (and less notable ones, like *Them!*, featuring humongous atomic-infused ants threatening to overrun civilization) and attained celebrity in Walt Disney's 1950s ABC mini-series *Davy Crockett*. Davy-mania swept the land—trappers reaped a bonanza to get a coonskin cap on every little Boomer's head—unleashing a mercantile of Crockett lunch buckets, toy guns, thermoses, powder horns, fringed jackets and more.

Such canonizing of a dead folk hero had never been seen before—or since. The hubbub—succinctly put, a $300 million hubbub in 1954 bucks!—stunned Parker and grubstaked Uncle Walt's Disneyland.

In 1964 it was Boone who was reborn—as runner-up. Parker had proposed rekindling Crockett's flame (and his career after missing out on *The Searchers*) with his own backwoods serial. When the well-lawyered lord of Sleeping Beauty's Castle (and copyright holder to Davy's merch) got wind of the half-horse/half-alligator's rising phoenix he threatened to sue NBC. "Disney didn't want any further Davy Crockett films—especially from me." So, the star obligingly changed his show's title, thwarting litigation by two words: *Daniel Boone*.

Pretty slick this malleability of history. Parker's Dan'l wore coonskin and acted and talked like his Davy. He barnstormed Kentucky and stopped in Missouri. "I visited his Boone's home near St. Louis where he died. I was really quite surprised. It was a nice little house."

Did Bill Ray know anything about Fess's stopover?

"I'd heard he visited here in the late '60s or so. I've never heard anything but glowing things about him." Parker's show helped Bill contrast the myth with the real man.

"If it weren't for the popularity of Fess Parker, we'd have a generation who might not know about Boone. About once a day, I get the 'where is he buried' question, so I start with a timeline of Rebecca's and Daniel's death. Most folks are curious; a few get confrontational."

Musing, I tried to take in his last ephemeral moments. Dawn's muted light bringing to life cardinals and wrens, robins and jays, his chest barely moving as the short, inward-cutting gasps eased, the family watching, seconds ticking, his spectacles near and his Bible at hand—he diligently searched the scriptures. He'd lie with his eyes closed, opening them to peer at the blurred, talking forms hovering over him. These were cramped quarters.

"When he calls for his coffin to be brought in, do you think it was brought in here or put out on some chairs in the main hall?"

"We don't know for sure. Traditionally, it's always been thought that the coffin was in here, but you're looking at a pretty tight room. There's not a lot of wiggle room."

I gazed at the carved walnut mantles, rubbing their dark, tight vertical grooves. The designs, Bill thinks, are reminiscent of brother Squire's woodwork, though "who knows," he said, countering himself. Oak and walnut appointments predominated. By northeast to southwest, the oblique alcove measured eleven feet, nine and a half inches, and from southeast to northwest, we stretched the tape to fourteen feet six inches.

A small wooden desk against the eggshell white wall had twin candleholders. Andirons sat on the fireplace's floor. George and Martha Washington's portraits gazed from the hearth at a chamber pot under the bed.

On the opposing wall hung a watercolored engraving, *Col. Daniel Boon.*, in a knee-length indigo linen hunting shirt edged with goldenrod fringe and a dog at his moccasined feet. He was standing by the Missouri leaning on a rifle. Italicized font above the matte read "*C. Harding*" and "*J. O. Lewis.*"

C. Harding is Chester Harding; *J. O. Lewis* is James Otto Lewis. In June 1820 when Harding arrived in La Charette, Boone lived next to Jemima in one of Fort Callaway's blockhouses. As if scripted by James Fenimore Cooper, the artist found *La Longue Carabine* seated before a hearth roasting a deer filet on his ramrod's tip and sprinkling the back strap with salt and pepper. After some prodding, Boone, modest and unpretentious to the last, agreed to sit.

As he sat posing, the two chatted. Had he ever been lost? "No," said Boone. "Can't say as ever I was lost, but I was bewildered once for three days." When Harding brushed in the last stroke, Boone was "astonished at seeing the likeness."

From this oil (and a lost pencil sketch) Harding painted two busts and a full-length. He left the latter in Frankfort, sure that the commonwealth would buy it. Instead, the Kentuckians rolled it up and stashed it in their capitol's cupola. Ignoring the artist's plea for $200—"This is the only painting of the old hunter ever taken from life"—the legislature spent $250 on William C. Allen's *Daniel Boone*, portraying a dark, brooding goth leather-stocking with Elvis sideburns seated in J.R.R. Tolkien's land of Mordor.

James O. Lewis engraved Harding's full-length to release as *Col. Daniel Boon.* The home's *Boon.* is a Kentucky bicentennial reprint true to James E. Welch's glimpse of him just prior to his death: "He was rather low of stature, broad shouldered, high cheek bones, very mild countenance, and fair complexion."

Daniel Boone's 1820 unfinished oil portrait, rendered from life by Chester Harding. *Massachusetts Historical Society, Boston.*

"It took several letters from Draper to Nathan to get his description of this room," Bill said. We have Nathan's letter with the little map he drew out showing where Daniel's bed was situated."

I glanced at a copy, deciphering Nathan's high-ended, upward-cutting scrawl so like his father's, "The bed stood in the N.E. corner of the N.W. room." Decades after the old man's death, Nathan sketched from memory where we stood, dotting in the bed flush against the wall.

"Do you think this was how the room was originally configured?" I asked.

"Maybe so in the summer. In the winter, the bed may have been more perpendicular to the fireplace. Another thing: when Nathan is writing Draper, is he hurrying through it or is he taking his time? He wasn't a young man when he was writing this."

Nathan's narrative is straight-forward—typical of a plain-spoken generation that loathed heaping praise on themselves. He began corresponding with the historian in 1851, when he was seventy-one, and died five years later. He enjoyed his dealings with Draper and tried to be concise in recounting his memories.

Bill opened a case in the hall and turned on a light. "Here's a priming horn."

I held the flat little cow horn in my palm and tugged my wire frames down my nose to peer over them. I couldn't read the folksy motifs scrimshawed in the yellowed patina.

"D.Boone 1818." He put a finger by a brass tack. "I'm not sure the strength of our provenance. I just say it's a primer that has 'D.Boone 1818' on it." Near it was a stone war club suggestive of Mississippian culture vaguely attributed to Jemima's rescue from the Shawnee. There were other such Boone artifacts; given time and wishful nostalgia, these objects have attained holy grail status, making the home a reliquary of fabricated Booneiana not unlike similar motherlodes in Kentucky and Pennsylvania.

"One approach I take when we look at objects like these, we'll talk about what provenance they have, but more importantly, about their context: What would they have been used for? What was their role in the family?"

He stepped in the south hall and looked back in the death room. "You make him alive as best you can. Though no doubt he was throughout this house, this is where he lived and died."

Bill got a call to meet a tour group. Hearing voices coming up from the narrow door by the death room, I took the basement's steps to meet Grady Manus.

He's about the same height and build as Boone and fair-skinned and soft-spoken, with blue eyes behind wire frames. Boone's tawny hair had more auburn tints than Grady's blond locks—left unshorn to fit the *dramatis personae* he portrays on-site. One day he's a hunter; then Drouillard, Lewis and Clark's consort to the Shoshone teen Sacajawea who secured horses for the corps; or he's with Nathan's Rangers. He's been here five years.

We ambled by herb and dye gardens, passed Squire Boone's limestone home, stepped into a one-room school and walked to the carpenter's shop, smokehouse and blacksmith's shed. We perused generations of Booneiana in the yellow-sided Staake House (built 1828), from Bibles to creepy human-hair art of mousey-brown wreaths and flower petals woven from locks shorn from heads of the dead—just the thing for a stylish Victorian fashionista.

In 1816 when Samuel Grant visited Daniel he asked the old man to snip off a silvery lock. "He was then living with Nathan Boone…eighty years of age and hale and active and had just returned home after being absent on a hunt for several months on the Missouri." Grant sent Boone's hair to Boone's granddaughter Delinda Craig. Later, James Henderson mailed it to Lyman Draper at the State Historical Society of Wisconsin; the talisman was as close to the woodsman as he ever got. It has never been found.

I told Grady about Bill saying how tourists asked about Daniel's dying at the Alamo.

"I get it at least twice a week," he said. "When you explain it was Crockett, sometimes they get confrontational. Most folks are just embarrassed. Our typical comeback is, 'That was Fess Parker.'" Do tourists ask where Boone is buried?

"Daily. That's the first thing they'll say: 'Is he buried here or in Kentucky?' It's standard around here. Visitors from Kentucky always take the Frankfort side. If they're from Missouri, they'll take Missouri's side."

Some visitors get upset at the thought of husband and wife separated in death. Confronting the "where is Daniel Boone buried?" issue left Grady curious about the Kentucky investigative report done in 1983 on an alleged plaster cast of Boone's skull. "Look, I don't understand science, but I believe in it—kind of. When you have a forensic scientist examine the skull and determine it's not Caucasian..."

"You mean Dr. David Wolf, Kentucky's official state forensics guy?"

"Yeah. I mean, how do you argue with science? People will ask, 'Where do you think he's buried?'" After years of daily interrogation about Colonel Dan's whereabouts, Grady's repertoire of answers was well developed. "I tell them it doesn't matter—Daniel and Rebecca are together somewhere. But it shows how his bones are almost considered to be holy relics."

We ended our tour at a tiny fenced-in cemetery occupied by Rolla Andréa and his wife, Gertrude—the home's owners for thirty years—and Rolla's parents, Alexander and Mary Alice. In 2007, Elsa Hansen—a relative and home worker—was interred.

Looming before us was the Old Peace Chapel, which served as New Melle's saloon before being remodeled into a high-flown church with New England appointments to rent out for weddings. The chapel's rear door led to the front. Twin black granite slabs etched with the Ten Commandments framed the altar. The pine floors were a satiny brownish-red. Its walls were copied from Thomas Jefferson's Monticello. The timber ceiling was sky blue.

Up the glossy spiral stairs to the loft was a pipe organ; an auto-play computer made the organ organist optional. The steeple, topped by a dove perched on a vane, was no small thing. For a country church, such a display would have astonished the frugally minded, largely Calvinist Boones, though Dan's grandson Albert Gallatin, a Roman Catholic convert and Jesse and Chloe's son, might have approved of this Boone basilica.

In the front, under the chandelier, Grady and I stood before nine empty white pews with red armrests and brass fixtures. It seemed that we'd missed the rapture.

Grady broke our reverie, "Acoustics in here are great." Without warning, he launched into "Wayfaring Stranger." The effect was ethereal, otherworldly. Inspired by this backwoods Caruso at my elbow, as his sonorous baritone rose to "I'm going there to meet my mother," I, too, lifted my voice to make a joyful noise, my strident cat tenor rising and falling in search of the harmony.

He shot me a hard glance, cutting short our duet. We headed over to Jemima and Flanders' home, rescued from a Marthasville cornfield some twenty miles away and pieced back together on-site to serve as administrative office space.

I had seen all but what I wanted most to see—the mysterious ballroom at the top of the stairs that is not part of the tour and is off-limits to visitors. This is where Daniel kept his coffin.

5

Coffin in the Ballroom

The compound's administrative facility, once Flanders and Jemima's home and trucked here from Marthasville, housed the site's overseer, Dr. David Knotts's office on the top floor. He narrated as I swigged tepid coffee worthy of any truck stop at 2:00 a.m.

"One of the two most asked questions we get is, 'Where is Daniel Boone buried?' The other is, 'Did he really die at the Alamo?'"

I poured the coffee down the drain. Bill started a fresh pot. What drew Knotts to Boone?

"He never stopped. He always had another hilltop to look over," he said. "You know, he brought families here before Lewis and Clark. Kids don't know what role he played in our history."

My thermos replenished, I swirled in creamer and asked if it was okay to walk down to Femme Osage Creek where Nathan's land abutted Boone's Trace, Daniel's last blazed trail that became his funeral processional route.

"Be careful. Copperheads are out. I ran over three last night and backed over 'em to be sure. They're beautiful, even for a snake, but I hate snakes."

A smile crept across my face.

Snake hook in hand, hopeful in my quest to catch an Osage copperhead—I've never seen one of the gorgeous, reddish-brown banded pit vipers of the genus *Agkistrodon* in the wild—I circled the home's lot, staying clear of skylarking schoolkids freed from a flotilla of yellow buses and unwilling to yield to portly chaperones chugging behind them. Bill queued up two lines of the kids to show them how to fire a flintlock. The rest invaded cabins and the blacksmith's shop, explored gardens, chased hoops with sticks and bobbed like jack-in-the-boxes in sack races.

The blue, cloudless sky was bright. It was nearly seventy degrees, unseasonably warm and humidity high. The grass had little spring to it, having relinquished its green. Golden red leaves budded on the young maples.

On past a jade green canebrake twice my height, billowing windward as if spirit possessed, I walked to a tangle littered with construction flotsam, my hook flipping boards, bark, busted cinder blocks and tin. Finches flitted in the copper-tinged canopy searching for buckshot-sized hackberries. Rotting black walnuts littered the understory.

Then, off behind me, *Fffiitt…Ka-boom*, followed by faint shrieks, clapping, laughter. Bill's firelock was performing to a lively crowd.

The land rose slightly. A great blue heron put out its gray wings to lift itself skyward to join a crow. Buzzards circled. A garter snake slithered past, its three stripes a bluish-yellow blur from neck to tail. A sprinkling of muddy tracks revealed rounded dew claws and wide, chiseled hooves; the buck, six months past rut, did not appear. Nor did any coons; their tiny, eerily human-like prints ran hither and yon near their chunky dung of purplish persimmon seeds and corn and thatched with frayed, translucent crayfish hulls and frog bones.

Six hundred yards from the home I gazed at the Femme Osage where long ago Dan's death cortege merged with his path to Marthasville. There was no hint of wagon ruts, just cottonwoods and walnuts full of robins, grackles, cowbirds and jays. Beyond lay gray fields of dead cornstalks.

The creek, twenty yards across and running clear, whirled with water beetles, hatchling bass and bluegill. Mosquito fish (*Gambusia*) nipped at water skimmers scooting herky-jerky over the top. With my sleeves rolled, feeling under the rocks unleashed goggle-eyed dragonfly nymphs. On the banks, crayfish had erected fist-size mud turrets. No Boone's Trace.

The only sounds more abundant than woodpeckers hammering were the buzzing mosquitoes forcing my retreat.

NEARING DUSK I MET Bill to swat out fiddle tunes and see the home's uppermost floor where Daniel kept his fancy casket. We rendezvoused in Flanders and Jemima's parlor, where Daniel would have lain in state (and Rebecca seven years before him). Walking over to the home, we took the southwest steps up a flight and sat midway on the south porch.

From here, Boone's blue eyes beheld his last sun, fall's fallow fields and yellow cottonwood leaves dropping. "The next morning, he went out upon the porch, looked around the farm, and said if he felt as well the next day as he then did, he would ride horse back around the farm," Nathan wrote. "He was brought back in and lay down on the bed and slept." Nathan sketched the death room.

"Thank goodness we have that porch reference," Bill said. "We don't get many specific references on this house. He wasn't feeling well, went back in and died the next morning."

Bill's bluesy fiddle evoked the land's lonesomeness—the stark bluffs opposite the creek and bare cottonwoods, and Daniel's race nearly run. Wind rustled the grassy bottoms like the swish of heavy skirts as he fine-tuned a droning D string. "I'm sure he heard 'Leather Britches.'" He bowed open G. Holding first position G on the second and third strings and sawing a four-count Georgia shuffle, he kicked it off slow, bluesy and steady, playing the head and singing the melody:

Oh, leather britches, oh, leather britches,
Daddy killed a 'bar and ma sewed the stitches.

Left hand easing to second position on the rollicking melody, grinning and red-cheeked in the sinking sun, Bill took it on home, his wrist jigging the bow in figure eights. I drove him on the two and four, my guitar's G-runs landing as exclamation points.

Were Daniel here he'd be enjoying himself, I hoped, buck-dancing like Papaw Belue did when I was a kid hammering on the five-string banjo hanging off my right shoulder threatening to tug me to the ground. The banjo goes back to a West African import that Thomas Jefferson called a "banza," a Caribbean word hearkening to the Middle Passage. British traveler Nicholas Cresswell saw slaves in Maryland in 1774 "dancing to the Banjor. This Musical instrument…is made of a Gourd, something in imitation of a Guitar…and play'd with the fingers."

Bill reached for his replica fretless slave banjo—gourd resonator, gut strings, friction pegs. We settled into "Soldier's Joy," a tune from the British Isles. On Sundays, the slave's day off, maybe from right here Daniel heard a banjo's barbaric yawp and thrum.

"In 1817, according to the tax books," Bill said, "there were at least three enslaved here," quartered, ironically, near the Judgment Tree. Maybe they saw Dan on his last day.

When he asked for his coffin, they likely shouldered it downstairs. Jemima's daughter, Susan Howell, said he was "buried in a coffin… which he had helped the children pick full of cotton before he died. This sickness was very sudden, after eating heavily of Baked Venison and Sweet potatoes—only lasted three days." Albert Gallatin stored apples in his grandfather's cist "made of boards." His gothic fruit bin might have been the black walnut coffin Daniel gave to a friend, giving him an excuse to commission a fancier one.

The ballroom where they frolicked (after hauling out, again, Boone's ambulatory catch-all coffin to make room) was not part of the home tour, lacking proper OSHA access and egress codes for sightseers. It was the room I'd most wanted to see.

We cased our instruments and went into the stairs, climbing. The seventeen steps steepened and creaked. It was echoey. The walls closed in as the steps took a bend leftward. The steps ended at a narrow wooden door that was locked. I felt like Mary Lennox in *The Secret Garden*.

"Take a deep breath," said Bill, sorting through the keys in his hand, turning the knob. "This is it, the existential room where Colonel Boone kept his coffin." Click.

I took a deep breath. We stepped in. My first glance was less than existential.

The sanctum sanctorum had been modified: partitions nailed in; rooms added; and closets, lights and plumbing installed. The ballroom was a cramped, skunky-smelling attic fitted with a toilet. Workers had installed windows and removed the fireplace. Fires had ravaged the masonry, leaving fist-sized soot smudges. After a second blaze in 1960, carpenters laid a new oak floor to match the third floor's tongue and groove and replaced the roof.

"It was really a mess." The newspaper reported smoke and water damage clear to the first floor. I could see the old stains.

Propped against the wall was a faded sepia sketch of a nondescript woman, its cutline reading "Rebecca Boone—from a painting by Peale now in possession of Col. Boone, of Colorado." This "Col. Boone" was her grandson Albert Gallatin Boone.

Charles Willson Peale died seven years after Daniel. Rebecca's head is hatless, and ringlets wreath her face—a hairstyle in vogue by the Civil War. Mrs. Boone lacked these fashion prospects when mobcaps were the day's order. Her neckline is open, when women of her estate wore scarfs to hide any décolletage. Her wide-eyed, impassive face typifies idealized mid-nineteenth-century portraiture, like the Madonna-like Rebecca in George

C. Bingham's *Daniel Boone Escorting Settlers through the Cumberland Gap*. Maybe a Peale descendant familiar with Bingham's iconic painting sketched this later image. It is not a from-life image.

Dan came up here to feign naps in his coffin and as the kids crept in, gramps lurching up to send them darting out, screaming and then tippy toeing back. He'd set his cane aside and buff it with a red silk scarf, peering through his specs for worm holes. He'd "lie down in it to see if it would fit—whistle, sound it with his cane to see if it had sprung, or any repairs wanting." Susan "Sooky" Howell shuddered seeing "him thump around his coffin and whistle so happy and content."

Andrew Jackson Coshow witnessed what made cousin Sooky shiver so, recalling memories of more than three score and ten years before when he was four. "My father was on his way up the Femme Osage Creek to visit his stepfather, Jonathan Bryan, with me riding behind him on horseback. As we were passing in front of Nathan Boone's house, Daniel Boone came out and asked father to come and see his new coffin. We went in and Daniel Boone led the way upstairs and into the west room, took the lid off the coffin and pulled the cotton out on the floor and lay down in the coffin to show how well it fit him. It was made of wild cherry."

Was this the cotton Susan Howell referred to her grandfather picking just before he died?

Bill paced off the room, forty-five feet or so by twelve, long and narrow—fine for face-to-face contredanses—with space for the fiddlers, good acoustics and conviviality. There was something charming about America's first pioneering family blazing trails, salt-boiling, farming and hunting, raising cabins, ranging the West and staking out a town, Missouriton, all while building their dream home, complete with a little ballroom.

The last dance documented here, Bill said, was in 1836. Delinda Craig, married to James Craig, who preached her granddad's eulogy, told how "family entertainment" enlivened this much-lived-in place. Her niece Eviza Coshow was four when her great-grandfather died and was at Nathan's that night.

"You will have to excuse my bad spelling and printing and grammar," Eviza writes. "I have only one Eye and lost my Specks in the Snow," the ink darkening after a fresh dip. "I was raised a spinner and a weaver of flax and wool. Could play the violin, dance all Night, and work all next day—suppose there is some of the Boone in me."

She reminisced about life at Nathan's. "They were kind, affectionate, light-hearted, gay people, great fiddlers and dancers." Eviza's brother Amazon

Ballroom circa 1930s, top floor of Historic Daniel Boone Home, where Daniel Boone kept his coffin. *Historic Daniel Boone Home.*

once "swam the Missouri, hat on his head," holding aloft his fiddle, shirt and moccasins to play for a party. Four more brothers played, as did her son and Nathan's boy John. Cousins Howard and Nancy joined their ensemble, bows rising and falling, rising and falling to "Fisher's Hornpipe," "Arkansas Traveler" and lilting 6/8 jigs like "Haste to the Wedding," composed in 1750 by English playwright Thomas Arne.

Cross-legged on the floor I tried to see them in my mind's eye—young and old—dancing as ten keening violins filled the night, singing; clapping time; eating; aromatic whiffs of clove, nutmeg, vanilla and cinnamon in the air; and illuminated by whale oil and crackling fire. Rhythmic thuds were accompanied by creaking beams and stairs, squeaking oaken flooring and joists, gaiety and laughter as children flitted in and out past bedtime, the Boones and Bryans, Howells and Coshows, Hays and Van Bibbers, Callaways, Shobes and Lammes with knees bobbing, elbows lifting, heel-and-toeing, buck-and-winging in kid slippers across the waxed floor. In their midst the white-haired patriarch took a turn before retiring to a corner, perhaps with a hot toddy in one hand and a spicy tart in the other.

The famously hospitable Boones could throw a serious shivaree, complete with backwoods wall-of-sound music.

Voices a floor below vaporized my dancers and fiddlers as the ballroom rematerialized to its musty storage room self. Bill and I went out to the parking lot and got in our cars to leave. I turned left onto Highway F to head to James Van Bibber's home and, hopefully, a cup of coffee and an improvised supper.

A mile-long horse trail once connected Van Bibber's to Nathan's and the old colonel had to have spent many a night there. Tonight I would too.

6

On His Last Trail

Graying skyline, twilight.

I hearkened to the Femme Osage's encroaching night sounds. *Hoo—hoo—hoohoo*, sounded a barred owl, warning mice of the death angel's variegated wings whooshing from tree to tree. *Whippoorwill* (emphasis on the last syllable) was a muffled response, an omen of loss. Then, a long muzzle's furtive flash, a soldierly gait and a bushy tail as a coyote, guard hairs in tatters, trotted near the cottonwoods down toward the creek.

The Boone Home folks had lodged me in James Van Bibber's stone home, built in 1817 a mile adjacent to Nathan's when he and Olive were building theirs; the rutted horse path linking them is now Highway F. I'm humbled to stay where Boone shared fireside chats. Van Bibber's features the rarity of indoor water—a tiny spring gurgling in the basement vanishes under a south wall to empty into a pond behind the house.

One cannot help but marvel at the pioneers' resourcefulness, their huge families, sprawling estates and tight-knit clannishness—the spine of westering settlement. James was Olive's brother and Nathan's brother-in-law. Cousin Chloe's marriage to Jesse made them first cousins to Isaac Van Bibber, who at thirteen was a scout during Virginia's Indian wars. He later married Elizabeth Hays, Daniel's granddaughter. A mile west is Jonathan Bryan's home; his father, James, was Rebecca's uncle.

For one said to always be in need of elbowroom, Dan certainly did not have it here. Far from being a recluse, he was an optimistic fellow, a traveler said, who "had a bright florid countenance expressive of cheerfulness and great good nature; and that as little of the savage was apparent in his manners and appearance as in those of any man he had ever met with."

Sitting on James and Chloe's back steps I nursed a steaming cup of instant coffee with milk—poor man's Starbucks, high cotton all the same. I am centered, between sips thumping guitar to melancholy Celtic tunes: "Crested Hens" (E minor) and "Cuckoo's Nest" (A minor).

Quiet descends. Nathan and Olive's lights blink out. A growling stomach, rain, cool breezes and an empty blue speckleware cup send me in for a cornbread and buttermilk nightcap.

I awoke before dawn, drank an improvised café au lait and set out for the western end of Boone's Trace to La Charette. Part of the trail meeting his funeral processional route now winds through farms and pastureland along the Femme Osage—serious Boone land.

Driving out of Van Bibber's I turned left on F (odometer: 476.5 miles) passing the Fuchs-Wessler house bordered by dormant vineyards. German immigrants bringing Old-World vintner skills were arriving as the Boones were leaving. Veering onto Femme Osage Creek Road, I paused on a tiny bridge. The creek's oases swirled with hatchlings bream, bullheads and bass. Hardwoods and sycamores shaded a scraggly canebrake. It is hard to see this branch as a usable watercourse but beaver frolicked here until trapping out their colonies emptied its backwaters. Now only a hard rain will fill it but not for long.

Powerlines on the opposite side dotted a sea of lilting cornstalks and brown mats of last year's soybean crop. Angus and Hereford nibbled what was left. Dust from passing combines powdered the cottonwoods. Late winter–early spring's deadness offered little.

On the right past the bridge a path once led to Jonathan and Mary Bryan's walnut dogtrot. Jonathan, along with his widowed father, James, and brothers, David and Henry, came here with Daniel. Thirty years before in North Carolina when James's wife, Rebecca Enox, died, her niece Rebecca Boone took the six Bryan kids—three boys and three girls—to raise with her own half dozen children.

Bryan's was the first mill here; its stones, spun by a lateral waterwheel, ground six bushels a day. St. Charles's tax rolls show he owned "1 slave, 12 horses and 18 cattle" and had a family of eleven. "Daniel spent as much time at my grandfather's as he did at home," said William Bryan. "There was hardly a day they did not visit back and forth." When he wasn't there, Cuff, his hunting dog, was, gobbling up the meal spinning into the basin. Cuff darted off once with his head wedged in the pewter bowl and the men in pursuit.

Nearby are humps from Bryan's fallen chimneys. Up the rise are James, Jonathan and Mary's graves. Daughters Mary and Alsey lay nearby but not the two Indians Mary shot. James Bryan's may be the earliest American grave west of the Mississippi. Boone's death route led on past silos, junipers and leaning fences strapped with rusted wire. A sweep left over a bridge is the red-hued farm complex where James Morrison's place once was. He was co-owner of Nathan and Daniel Morgan's salt operation 150 miles west.

Odometer: 479.9. Beautifully spare land. Rabbits dash along shoulders and fox squirrels roam trees alert for kestrels, descending for corn. Angus lay gazing, jaws in perpetual cud chewing. A huge Charolaise bull sat aloof from the gray brahmans, their melon humps heaving with each breath, lank pale ears flickering.

Twin avian hulks of regal bearing perched on a limb above Indian Creek Lane's road sign eyed me eyeing them. I slowed. Glowering at my intrusion the eagles swooped off, screams rending the air. One majestically spiraled over, heading, perhaps, to his aerie. The other banked left to a sycamore to preen and stretch his talons, puffing out his snowy hackles like the presidential seal, contemptuous of the pleb below staring up through a camera.

At 483.2 miles Femme Osage Creek Road bisects Cappein Osage Road. Still on Daniel Boone's death route, I crossed, gaining speed. After a right onto Highway T then a left on D was a gigantic seven-story tower of split firewood. "Every man," claimed Thoreau, "looks at his woodpile with a kind of affection." Henry's neighbors never saw anything like this.

Four miles later was Emmaus Institute. It was the Missouri Evangelical College and German Lutheran College when founded in 1850, later becoming Emmans Asylum for Epileptics. A longhair in a MIA-POW T-shirt—WE WILL NOT FORGET—limping over Wolf Creek Bridge didn't return my wave. But a cowboy-hatted driver of a road-hogging dump truck farting soot did. Then a sign:

Welcome to Marthasville Home Area of Daniel Boone
Marthasville City Limit

Slowing by a bluff crowned with a stately red-brick home, I peered beyond ivy-choked cedars and Norway spruce at Harvey Griswold's old place. In July 1845 Kentucky envoys of the Frankfort Cemetery Company—Philip

Swigert, Thomas Leonidas Crittenden and William Boon—came here to retrieve Daniel and Rebecca. Harvey, who'd bought David Bryan's farm figuring the Boone graveyard added value to his land, tried to circumvent their efforts. In failing Harv became a cantankerous historical footnote.

I eased left of city hall, wary of a constable's radar cone hanging out his window, to drive on to Wessel Park, parking in a lot fronting a cabin encircled by a rail fence, its marker's inscription written by my old friend Ralph Gregory (who at 105 really is old) commemorating Lewis and Clark's arrival. In a pavilion across from the park was another DAR marker:

THE DANIEL BOONE TRAIL: CA. 1799

Here was Boone's role opening the West: The Trailblazer. Here was where he lived out his last days and was buried on the cutting edge of America's Great West. Fitting.

Back on Highway 47 I upped my speed east for a mile to turn right into black loam guarded by a "No Trespassing" sign, an added caveat penned in metallic script: "VIOLATORS WILL BE PROSECUTED." I reined in, mileage 491.7, facing a galvanized shed sitting where Flanders and Jemima's home once sat. A combine parked in its bay loomed in my binocs.

My rebellious, historically metaphysical side ached to drive one hundred yards more to sink my feet into the turf of the lost village of La Charette. Flanders Callaway's cabin was here. His fort was here. Lewis and Clark and Zeb Pike visited. Charles "Indian" Philips lived nearby. John Colter mustered here with Nathan's Rangers. The Boones lay in state here.

I longed to scale the levee to see Big Muddy roll as Daniel saw it.

But no, it was all gone. My Camry wasn't mud-worthy anyhow. Drivers were slowing to check out the unknown guy in the fedora and Ray-Bans in the car with Kentucky plates. So much history lost with so great an indifference.

And what of La Charette, where Daniel lived next door to daughter Jemima?

LA CHARETTE'S HUNTERS HIRED out to St. Louis fur moguls like August Chouteau. Their Native wives mediated alliances, tutored the men in Native protocol and acted as linguists. After Rebecca died, Dan, to be near her grave, moved to this polyglot caravansary on the cusp of Anglo civilization.

Today, La Charette's legacy is mostly forgotten (except at New Haven's Grill and Levee Bar where the John Colter Burger is the house specialty).

On 47 I zoomed over to Washington. William Owens auctioned off lots here in 1829. After his murder his widow Lucinda began the town where Johann Busch brewed Busch beer. Adolphus, his brother in St. Louis, married Lily Anheuser and brewed Budweiser—"that slop," he called it, preferring wine.

Barreling along Highway 100 during noon's rush I spied the sign "La Charrette Trading Post" and turned onto a long, forested drive. The land lifted. City sounds filtered away. I idled past cabins, a cottonwood bateau, a blockhouse and a blacksmith's shed to arrive at Wheelock Crosby Brown's palatial log home built by James Greene in 1798 and worthy of its own exhibition at St. Louis's Museum of Western Expansion. Missouri's retired chief of State Historic and Archaeological Sites waved me past his drive on a picturesque bluff, the Big Muddy three hundred feet below.

Brown was a handsome, towering oak of a man with a flaxen beard and a rack of shoulders, though in his seventies his hair curled past his collar. Reminiscent of a Viking-sized *voyageur* in jeans and a khaki shirt, antique silver crucifix about his neck, beads, turquoise ring and Navajo concho belt buckled with an antler clasp, Buffalo Bill Cody could have used him as a stand-in.

His home was an eighteenth-century fur trade diorama with a twenty-first-century sensibility. William Raney's *Trapper's Last Shot* hung on the left. On the right was David Wright's *Wind River Man*. Glass beads dangled from the ceiling. War clubs, hawks, buffalo horn rattles, quilled bags, guns, knives and traps decorated walls. Thomas Jefferson stared from a hearth. A sterling Lewis and Clark peace medal hung over the dining table. Fiddles jutted from corners.

Even cyberspace yielded to Brown's antiquarian eye: "1608," his email's last four digits, marks the year of Quebec's and Santa Fe's founding. Such incongruities are omnipresent in his curious neo-frontier world; every glance is a moveable feast.

"It's a personal passion. It's equity for my retirement, and it gave my parents a place to live." After sixty-two years of marriage his parents died within a month of each other. He interred their ashes out back on the bluff and wrote their epitaphs.

"Really, this is my place to escape from this horrible society we are living in, which has become such a morass—morally, ethically and value-wise." He lit a Marlboro. As a frontiersman born out of due season when one's word was his bond (except to Indians and Africans), he's got a point. April through August, he welcomes sightseers and only asks for donations. "I do it to teach history," he said. Down at his lavishly outfitted trading post he handed me a flyer.

Welcome to Fort Charette museum. This log building stood across the river from the French Village of La Charrette, west of Washington, MO. The fort is authentically restored and furnished as a 1700s French-Indian trading post.

Forty Osages once happened by and got his impromptu talk proclaiming Thomas Jefferson the father of Native American disenfranchisement. His thoughts on Daniel Boone?

"He didn't come until '99. Too many chimneys in Kentucky, too many people—this was the frontier, the jumping-off place." How much time did Dan spend here?

"Boone visited Flanders's house more than he was visiting Nathan's. He was upriver hunting. He just happened to be there when he died." He scoffed at ideas that the first-floor apertures at Nathan's Home were for shooting. "They're holes left over from scaffolding. I've seen them a hundred times in houses earlier and later." What about Flanders's fort where Daniel lived?

"The first story was about ten feet by ten feet, the second story sixteen feet by sixteen feet," he said. It was used for "forting up" during the War of 1812 conflict in Missouri. How bad was the fighting around here?

"Bad. Six hundred killed in eastern Missouri by Sauk and Fox. British up north riled them up, arming them against Americans." He walked to his home's window fitted with thick, hardwood shutters. Clapping them shut, he slammed in a bolt and looked at me, muskets, knives and axes on the wall behind him framing his eagle profile: frontier homeland security.

"My crew saved Callaway's house, putting it on the National Register of Historic Places." It went through several owners before being restored. "Missouri has been slow to preserve pre–Civil War historic and archaeological sites. I don't want to offend anyone, but that is a fact." Few historians would disagree. Brown also believed Boone was still buried a mile away in David Bryan's old cemetery.

"This rumor that the slave knew where he was buried and showed them the wrong grave. I believe this is true, that he is still here. No exhumation here has ever happened. Was there another grave next to Rebecca's? And if so, who is in it?" We walked to my car.

"Who cares, really, where Daniel Boone's buried?" he said. "Once people are dead, they're dead until Christ comes, supposedly, then everyone gets up and there's a judgment."

I wasn't sure what to say. Brown lit another Marlboro.

Flanders and Jemima Boone Callaway's home in Marthasville, with later siding and porch, prior to removal to the Historic Daniel Boone Home site in Defiance. *State Historical Society of Missouri.*

We exchanged waves as I looped his drive. Meandering through scraggly thickets leading down Wheelock's trace, past his smithy's shop, blockhouses and La Charrette Trading Post, I turned right into Old Highway 100's rush-hour traffic. Back to the twenty-first century.

LESS THAN A MILE east of Marthasville on Boone Monument Road I pondered Brown's words as I neared Tuque Creek: who cares where Boone is buried?

Frankfort's Cemetery Company delegates cared. The many thousands thronging to his two graves care. That his resting place is debated shows that it matters to lots of other folks.

I clambered up the ten steep concrete steps and stepped over the seven rotting wooden erosion beams. Someone had mowed. The poison ivy was down. I was sweating.

David Bryan, three years after getting a grant in 1800, bought this plot from Jeremiah Groshong, a Huguenot who arrived in Pennsylvania via the

Queen of Denmark and trekked to Missouri. Rebecca Boone—who died March 13, 1813, "aged 74 years, 1 month and 11 days"—was the first interred here. Walter and Grace Stemme, the site's stewards through the 1990s, kept a donation box and visitor's register, prompting darkly humorous entries. "Dear Daniel, I saw you last at Frankfort, KY," scribbled one signee. "Happy Haunting! Rest in Peace," said another.

Three big barren persimmons rose from behind the Boones' stone. Between knobby hackberry and scraggly cedar were scattered gnawed walnut hulls. There was no sign of life westward at the Bryans' farm. Doffing my cap, I knelt to pray and left some tobacco, my heart full.

WHEN DANIEL BOONE DIED it seemed logical that his body was laid out at Nathan's. Things were ready and the procedure was not complicated. The right people were present but they would have to work with efficiency.

Was it possible to conjure any hint of the moment when he passed into eternity on that September 26 two centuries ago?

7

Sitting Up with the Dead

Nathan and Olive's front gates shone in my Ram's headlights on this predawn anniversary of Daniel Boone's death. Clicking off high beams and moving the gear shift lever to PARK, I got out to recycle coffee on a bush and then walked to the gate's bars, swigging another slug of Super 8 brew. It was cool—high fifties. A big dog bayed in the dark, its chugging, raspy howls swelling to falsetto to end on an abrupt *woof*; it was Sunny, the resident bloodhound. The groundskeeper was warned I'd be out front before first light. I got back in my truck.

Bill Ray's SUV eased off Highway F and in behind me, re-arousing Sunny's doleful bawling as Roger Guernsey emerged from the murk jangling a key lanyard—the ghost of Christmas past in a pale golf hat like a lamp shade. We drove in to park. Talking softly and tugging my bag's strap on my shoulder, I walked behind Bill's flashlight past the gift shop and the fresh, piney-smelling lumber and concrete blocks near the new visitor's center and through a wooden gate, latching it. We cut up the grassy bank to the right of the Judgment Tree to a brick walk curling to the home's glass-paneled doors in back. Bill had the key.

Inside it was dark and cool. Bill went up to shut off the alarm, his steps resonating overhead. I stood at the basement's hearth squinting at the dry twisted herb bundles and fake bread rolls all glazed and shiny and set out for tourists to see. I reached for the fire tongs and felt of the bellows' wooden sides and the powder horn tied to the shot bag on the wall peg. Above the mantle my hand slid along the flintlock's octagon barrel to the lock on half-cock. Past the dim outlines of steel support poles, tables, chairs and door jambs I could not see the far wall or the adze hash cuts on the wide joists overhead.

Such calm would not have existed on this day in 1820. Livestock would be stirring, cattle lowing; roosters heralding dawn; the enslaved stoking fires, splitting kindling, drawing water; women cooking; footsteps assaulting the creaking stairways; hushed voices; children scurrying.

The home smelled of the honest stink of verity and age. The same was not so on this day two hundred years ago when planed oak, walnut and pine freshened its interior. Dust flecks hung in a beaming sliver through the glass from a light outside as I heard Bill and saw a descending halo from a pewter candle holder, the beeswax taper flickering his face yellow blue. We went on up, our shadows creeping wraith-like along the stair walls to the death room's door. At Daniel's passing, this tight corridor resounded with foot traffic from the visitors here the day before. More would arrive.

He would have been saying his last words, Olive singing, kith and kin drawing near and the dying patriarch drinking a bowl of milk and mush as we gained his room's threshold. Bill lifted the low wood gate used to keep tourists out from its pins and stepped in, parting the pale curtains. He set the candle on the stand west of the bed, its wavering light illuminated Harding's and Lewis's *COL. DANIEL BOON.* enough to where I could barely, on the facing wall, make out the old man's white hair and goldenrod hem bordering his hunting shirt's indigo cape.

Bill lit a candle on the mantle, its wax droplets clinging and turning milky. We sat between the andirons on the floor by the hearth—Bill on my right, chest of drawers to his right and nightstand to my left. I poured coffee in my thermos cap and motioned. Bill shook his head.

Thirty minutes later, sunup's first slow lightening through the window silhouetted a branch. Umber brown leaves skittered in the wind as a yellow beam pierced the wavy glass. In the painting the colonel's long coat had paled. His golden hem was gone and his dog was fading. I could no longer see his knife. Dan's head vanished as the sun topped the trees just past seven. Daylight flooded in, bringing a twinge of historical time travel.

Bill hunkered in a half lotus—elbows on knees, palms clasped, fingers steepled as a chin rest—his doe eyes fixed ahead, reminiscent of the Buddha admonishing his disciples to pay attention.

We sat another hour not speaking.

Pay attention!

Col. Daniel Boon. Hand-watercolored reproduction of the Harding-Lewis engraving released after Boone's death and the first true rendering of an American frontiersman. *Pathfinder Press.*

HIS BURIAL BY NECESSITY would be handled according to that day's traditions and ceremony. A week into fall at Colonel Dan's homegoing, the days had likely not yet turned cold. Normally interments were done within two days in accordance with weather and circumstances.

Those gathered at Nathan's leaned toward Baptist, Methodist or Presbyterian traditions and understood, in a literal way, apostle Paul's admonition in his first epistle to the evangelist Timothy, chapter five, verse eight: "But if any provide not for his own, and especially for those of his own house, he hath denied the faith, and is worse than an infidel." To such plainspoken people, this New Testament precept went beyond temporal needs. Last rites were private matters—a chance to "provide for one's own." Transgressing social and family mores at such a time would have been unconscionable. Laying out bodies at home was as natural as delivering babies.

The first hours were critical. After the heart ceases to beat, blood drains into the veins. The body cools, voiding itself of gas and fluids. Cellular enzymes dissolve, rupturing body cells.

This would preclude notions of Dan's unprepared corpse loaded on a wagon and hauled to Flanders and Jemima's home in La Charette and the stiffening cadaver unloaded and the laying out done there. Rigor mortis, discoloring and intensifying smell with the day's rising heat would have made the task more unpleasant and results less than satisfactory.

In American households, it was usually the women—the host's daughters or the *paterfamilias's* next-of-kin—who lovingly cleansed and shrouded corpses for coffins. It was considered a domestic errand with profoundly spiritual overtones; older women taught the younger ones the ritual. Jemima was fifty-seven and was Rebecca's and Daniel's last daughter. Maybe she assisted laying out her father, aided by her girls.

Did Nathan help or the other men? An army man who'd seen death from the Indian wars, likely he'd prepared bodies and assisted in doing so with due formality.

Preachers comforted the bereaved and readied corpses. Did Reverend Craig do it? Physicians like Dr. Jones were adept in "rendering the last offices." Boone was his patient, so did Jones and Craig take charge to allow Nathan and Jemima to plan the event and notify their loved ones? At this busy time ritual and ceremony were paramount.

As the laying out commenced, the women stitched a dark linen or cotton shroud. The nineteenth-century New England novelty of interring the dead fully dressed was seen as radical—a faddish break with custom that Quakers condemned as "disguised pomp"—and might not have been in vogue among westerners. Many rich and poor were buried clothed but barefooted; shoes, being of practical value and hard to come by, were passed on.

Death shrouds were long-sleeved, open-backed and pinned with straight pins about the head and torso and pelvis and feet; they were especially used for children. Winding sheets—simply wrapping corpses in a blanket—required no pins and was done too. Especially on the frontier.

Boone had taken about three days to die, so maybe a burial garment was ready—*if* he was put in one. Evidence from his exhumation proves that he was wearing a shirt with buttons. As the women picked out the funereal garments, likely Jemima, as eldest Boone matriarch, selected his.

Perhaps his shirt was worn over a shroud. Maybe he was arrayed in homespun—doubtful—or, more properly, in his finest attire befitting a man of stature. William Bryan's dubious account says he "was dressed in his hunting suit." On the trail he went native, dressing as the poorest of woodsmen. It is inconceivable that he would have been sent to his maker clad in greasy buckskins, ragtag shirt, filthy breechclout and moccasins.

Did Daniel, a practical man and lucid to the last, lay out his own garments? Possibly.

When a death watch had begun, if it had not already been done, the men hammered brass tacks to fasten a dark cloth—silk velvet or cotton velveteen—to his cherrywood coffin's interior; plainer boxes lacked padding. Boone's likely had a quilted batten. Some coffins had handles and were six- or nine-sided. Caskets—meaning "jewel box," a case for something precious—were squared off, rectangular, cruder and of simple design and made of pine or poplar.

As Boone took pride enough in his coffin to show it to friends and care for it, his was well made and aesthetically pleasing. Likely it was built by a professional coffin maker and came lined. Furniture carpenters made custom coffins on commission.

Now his cherrywood coffin was readied. So was his corpse.

After undressing him, they laid him on his back to bathe his tightening body with a brine, soda and vinegar wash for the preservative qualities it offered and to suppress the acrid odor sure to intensify within the next thirty-six hours—a stench so overpowering that when the lid was raised, it might cause attendees to faint; it happened. They swabbed about the eyes, nose, mouth and lower body orifice, perhaps plugging it with cotton, as was custom.

After drying the corpse, "streeking" came next before rigor mortis set in, folding his arms below his chest, binding feet and legs, weighing limbs with clothes irons to limit spasms as muscles stiffened and relaxed, his legs straining. They cinched a strip under his wide jaws and knotted it atop his head, checking its tension until his thin lips clamped shut on their own.

Thumbing his pale eyelids over his eyes they settled a heavy coin (perhaps a Spanish gold dollar or a draped American dime) on each one; the custom goes back to the ancient Greeks—a staring, open-eyed corpse was unsettling to viewers. Less affluent folks and the enslaved used circular flat rocks or octagon metal discs.

To suppress the spreading discoloration they rewashed Dan's face, or kept a vinegar-saturated rag over it, staving off liver mortis's purplish stain. As muscles stiffened, the rigor tugged at Boone's eyelids, neck and jaw, the tightening striations visible even when powdered.

In eight hours the rigor would peak and smells would intensify. In three days, tissues began to bloat and putrefy as blisters tinted the skin from a pinot noir to a greenish tinge. By then Daniel would rest alongside Rebecca as decomposition and drying returned his body to its simplest form—ashes to ashes, dust to dust.

Nathan likely dispatched someone to David Bryan's cemetery to dig a grave alongside his mother's and a rider took a wagon of tools for the enslaved to do the shoveling. It would have been hard to do this on his own; the solemnities were just beginning. Maybe Jemima was en route to Marthasville to ready for her father's wake and funeral service, as formalities would shift from Nathan and Olive's to Flanders and Jemima's.

Much was on the last-born son's mind. But this day of dying marked, ironically, a day of living. Some there would have known about it and were empathetic. Nathan and Olive hardly had time to acknowledge it. But likely they spared a passing moment for soft words, a sustained hug and a deep, longing look into each other's eyes.

Today was their twenty-first wedding anniversary.

THE MEN LIFTED DANIEL'S stiffening corpse to settle him onto his coffin's batten—tucking him in, checking bindings, touching eye coins and securing him—for the nearly twenty-mile ride to Jemima's in La Charette. Three years before, Dr. John Young had re-platted La Charette, renaming it Marthasville after his wife.

Did Reverend Craig offer prayer or a scriptural flourish? Maybe he read from the Bible and led a hymn. Their voices, joyously melding in acapella psalmody, hewed to the melody and harmonies of fourths and fifths, their plaintive slurs bending into modal thirds to end on the root—ancient tones hearkening of Appalachia. The natural reverb created by this stark chamber—wide halls, stone walls, open rooms, bare floors—confirming, truly, that the most sublime musical instrument remains the voice, unadorned and unaccompanied. Such was their hymnody.

Neighbors came, including James Van Bibber, Jonathan Bryan and James Morrison, Nathan and Daniel Morgan's partner in their Howard County salt works; Morrison lived off the trace a mile past Jonathan's. Their wives might have lingered to cook and tend to details. Grandson William Hays's land bordered Nathan's acreage; likely he and Mary had come as the women stayed busy. Children were subdued. Men mingled. As they talked, death's tensions eased, foreshadowing closure's coming. It was a good day, considering all.

Stew pots warmed on the basement's hearth. Perhaps on the table across from the fire the girls piled pewter plates with smoked ham, bear, venison, sweet potatoes, hoecakes, wheat and cornbread with butter. Honey or maple sugar was by the milk pitchers and teapots hovered on the cranes swung into the firepit. A dram of smooth Kentucky bourbon or a shot of brandy, peach maybe, would have been fortifying and thought proper.

Nathan and Olive directed these rites, aware that their home was on display. Folks filtered inside and out, filling the grounds with horses and buggies, carriages and wagons.

"THE FOLLOWING DAY HE was conveyed to the Flanders Callaway place near the old cemetery on the hill," states William Bryan.

Those of age grasped the singular moment on Wednesday as the men fitted his cist's dark lid tightly. Gathering along its sides and ends, on signal and with the enslaved lending hands, they hefted it from the chairs and, angling right and back, straightened into the hall, turning and leveling leftward toward the north door. The hall's ten-foot width made lugging it wieldy. Family and friends stepped into the adjoining south room and Olive's parlor—about twenty-five feet front to back, sixteen feet side to side—to let them pass.

The north doorway, ground-level, was the best way out. The horses were harnessed or an ox-team was hitched to a wagon by a path to Femme Osage Creek. Maybe Derry Coburn stood by, securing halters to keep the animals still.

To convey his body they used his double-spring carriage that Lorna Damon, wife of David Darst, rode in with Grandmother Jemima and her mother, Tabitha Callaway. "I was with great granddaddy Boone up to his death," Lorna recalled. "I remember him well as he would take all the grandchildren out and take his seat in the woods, and amuse us every way he could. I remember when he was buried, and used the same wagon to carry him to his grave."

The men emerged with the coffin, raised it to the wagon bed and slid it against the buckboard for support and roped it in. Riders readied to escort the caisson. Rifles were laid over the saddles. Powder horns, knives and shot bags were strapped on. Hostilities had ceased but one never knew if a velvet buck sensing rut's itch might show.

Did the cortege slip black crepe bands onto their arms, pushing them to their biceps? The rein's snap roused the team southward to Boone's Trace by Femme Osage Creek—this leg to Flanders and Jemima's nearly twenty meandering miles of twin ruts curling westward.

Black gum leaves were reddening and falling. Buckeye limbs were bare. Golden rod was hanging lank.

Was it a warm day or cool, with northwest winds? Was it sunny? Cloudy? Was the Femme Osage bone-dry, its rocks dusted white? No one mentioned these details.

Nor did anyone note what time that Wednesday Daniel Boone's funeral procession reached Marthasville.

8

News of His Decease Had Spread Rapidly

Crowds walked alongside the stout, slow-rolling double-spring wagon as news spread that the white-headed old man who lived in the bottoms that people came from all over to see, had died. In a day when celebritydom as a concept did not exist, Daniel Boone was a celebrity.

The carriage's entourage reined at the Callaways' two-story walnut home of Federal design that was five bays wide with chimneys on each end and facing southward toward the Big Muddy. Its first floor had served as trading post of the War of 1812 complex Callaway's Fort. Larkin Barnes, Flanders's grandson, described the fortification. The Callaway home was its focal point: "T'was built after the manner of other Forts with a blockhouse in each corner with portholes to shoot through. It covered about three acres and was a quarter of a mile from the river. Daniel Boone and Grandfather Callaway owned the Fort."

Eviza Coshow, Dan's great-granddaughter, described "the Old Marthasville Fort" as built of logs "20 inches in diameter…set 3 feet deep in the ground and extended 12 feet above the ground." Flanders lapped timbers between the gaps to "make the fort bullet-proof," which housed a blacksmith shop, a well and two other cabins. Rising waters swept away most of it.

There's a sketchy account of the fort being fired on; Sac warriors camped along its spiraling buffalo paths en route to fight the Osage. Rebecca died here in Jemima's home. Dan lived in one of the fort's blockhouses. Every day he visited his wife's grave.

From here, he'd watch for canoes, keelboats and flatboats; chat with the fur-takers mooring in at the wharf—Indians, French, mixed-bloods—and inspect peltry, fluff the beaver hair, thump hide bundles, buy jerk and bear bacon, trade and barter, gossip. Baptist circuit rider James M. Peck, who published *The Life of Daniel Boone, the Pioneer of Kentucky*, said that Callaway's Fort by 1818 had dwindled to "a cluster of cabins."

Boone's wagon arrived at the Callaways'. The pallbearers bore the cist in to the parlor, about eighteen feet square. Jemima and Flanders readied things as the ceremonial focus shifted to their home. On removing the lid to freshen her father's corpse, she would have detected the tang of ash, lye, vinegar and the death smell's pungent beginnings

His face was re-wiped with vinegar as they gazed upon his pallid countenance—jaws bound, his pale neck giving way to a burgundy tint. They touched; probed; removed the eye coins, straps and irons; powdered away purplish stains; unbound his jaws; combed his hair. (Other than William Bryan's memoirs—which are always interesting, rarely reliable but quoted as gospel—there's varying proof that the body was exhibited.)

Rosemary, tansy's late golden blooms, cedar and pine sprigs set out in the house cleansed the air. The women placed a black fringed pall over Daniel's face to block the sun and keep out flies. They shrouded any mirrors to obscure the living's images for fear they might soon be called to their eternal homes.

Neighbors came with baskets, sweets, bounty from fall's harvest, beef, chicken, pork and wild meat. Reverend Craig shook hands and consoled. Nathan, back from campaigning against the Sac and Fox, perhaps was attired in his dragoon worsted regimental coatee festooned with gold braids and epaulets, his red silk sash knotted above his gaitered trousers and knee boots. Most attendees dressed in black. Women kept their heads covered.

Custom dictated that the body was not to be left unattended. As the colonel lay in state, Nathan and Jemima—and Daniel Morgan, if word reached him—sat with him. Maybe their spouses and Derry Coburn joined in praying, weeping and reminiscing. In the wavering light they lifted the shroud to shoo off any mice gnawing the cadaver (which is why sitting up with the dead began) and reset the veil to block moths drawn to the corpse candle's glow at his head.

Creepy tales abound about these somber night vigils—bones creaking and snapping; the body's last aching moans; eyelids gaping open; limbs rising in spasmodic jerks above the casket; unfettered feet thwacking its sides; and groaning, grunting corpses convulsing upward to a half-sit-up and breaking wind. Loudly.

Hopefully the Boones were spared such distractions. No one thought much about such things or shielded children from life's lessons of mortality and brevity. Dying was as natural as birthing.

Death's stench intensified as Boone's pallor grayed to mottled purplish. They reapplied vinegar and readjusted his pall. Come night, a soda-soaked rag left spread over his hard face and thin lips staved off splotches. Cooler months were better for dealing with the unembalmed.

The men and the enslaved walked to Flanders's new two-story barn fifty yards behind the Callaways' home to shovel it out; put away plows, ox collars and tack; and realign buckboards. They laid timbers over barrels and kegs, shifted split-log benches, added cedar and pine funereal trimmings. The spacious barn with its soaring loft was veneered with aromatic planking that Flanders's brother-in-law Dan Morgan floated down from his Pineys sawmill.

On Sundays the barn served as Friendship Baptist Church (the sole Protestant fellowship in the Roman Catholic community). Attendance was twelve to twenty, mostly foot-washing Calvinistic Hard Shells and one unaffiliated ex-Quaker. Friendship Baptist Church would become the ex-Quaker's chapel.

A crowd was expected. Two centuries later, it would still be the most noted event of this community. Yet it was far from a tragedy: Daniel Boone, at four score and five, had gone home.

> *Thursday, September 28, 1820*
> *The news of his decease had spread rapidly, and a vast concourse of people collected on the day of the funeral to pay their last respects to the distinguished and beloved dead.... The coffin was carried to the large barn near the house, into which the people crowded to listen to the funeral services.*
> *—William Bryan*

Bryan was born twenty-six years after the day he's writing about. He knew many of the attendees and was kin to a lot of them. Reconstruction of events tied to Daniel's death must be woven of disparate threads from many spools and often are inferred.

"There was a very large funeral," Nathan said, in understated Boone fashion. "The house would not hold a hundredth of them," said Bryan. It would not have taken many to fill Jemima's. Her father's attendants would have occupied the parlor and filtered into the main hall. His offspring's offspring—three generations—packed the lower rooms.

Jemima and Flanders now had three sons and five daughters, Jesse and Chloe had five sons and five daughters, Nathan and Olive had three sons and five daughters and Daniel Morgan and Sarah ten sons and two daughters. The late William and Susannah Hays had five daughters and four sons. After Levina Boone Scholl died in Kentucky, her husband, Joseph, moved here with their eight children. Their eldest daughter, Rebecca Goe, had died and so had her husband, Phillip Goe, sending Daniel Morgan back to Kentucky to retrieve their parentless brood—some of them would have been at the funeral. This is not counting the rest of the considerable offspring.

How many attended? Writing to John Coburn in Maysville, Kentucky, Jesse, writing from St. Louis, implies that he missed his father's funeral.

> *Dear Sir—this morning an express arrived in time that my Father was buried on yesterday...at Sharett Village in presence of a numerous and respectable concourse of people. You will be so kind as to make such statements in your papers....I have probably got myself in the State Legislature and shall be confined here until the 1st Dec. There will I presume be a resolution in the House this day that the members were in crepe for 30 days as a testimony of respect.*
>
> *My best wishes to your family. J.B. Boone*

Aside from Jesse's absence, add great-grandchildren and extended family, as well as friends, townspeople and arrivals from the Femme Osage. Add the enslaved and those drawn by the spectacle of a true American celebrity's passing—a novel thing. For all those there who sensed being a part of history, why did no one think to describe the event or pen letters of remembrances or later, at the behest of someone like Lyman Draper or John Dabney Shane, reminisce about Colonel Dan's homegoing?

Daniel was a Mason, as were many men of his day. The Boone family, one correspondent reported, delayed his funeral to allow his St. Louis lodge brothers to arrive. Nathan said there "were no Masonic honors...as there were then but very few in that region of the country." Some did attend and wore their embroidered aprons and distinctive accoutrements.

Nearby, many old Shawnees lived in Roger's Town. Did any elderly Shawanoes, who'd spent their youths crossing the Beautiful River sundering Ohio land from the Bluegrass, attend brother Sheltowee's funeral? Their presence might have created a stir but peace had been ratified by President Madison in 1815. Did a few Shawanoes, like old

La Charette Area – Early 1800s

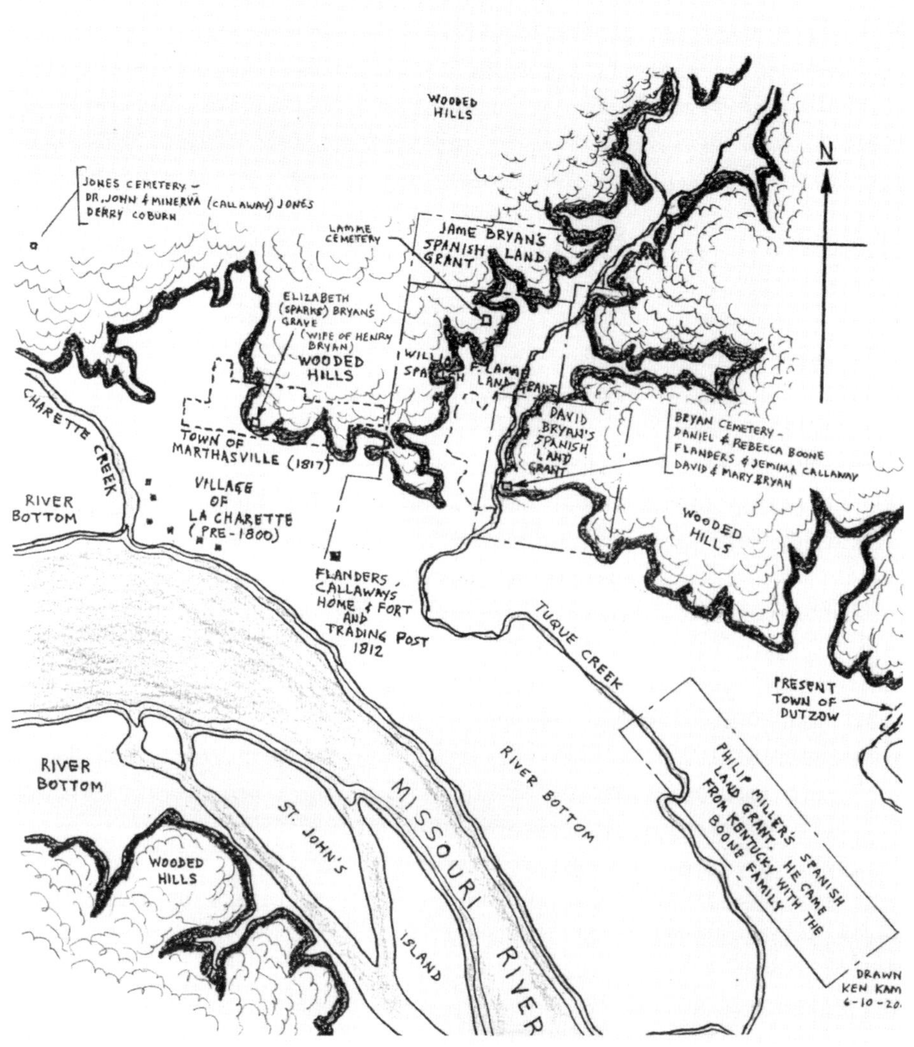

La Charette, early 1800s, showing location of Bryan Cemetery. *Ken Kamper*.

Kishkalwa, come? His portrait, as rendered by Charles Bird King—his slit auricles are bedazzled in silver and he's wearing a blue, ruffled trade shirt and nose ring—appears in the McKinney-Hall collection. One snowy day in 1778 he captured Boone hunting buffalo on the Upper Blue Licks. In Missouri forty years later he defended Boone's Lick from the Osage.

Was Charles "Indian" Philips there? The warrior who fought Sheltowee at Boonesborough but decades later, past the Ozarks and into Kansas, was Boone's camp-hand—a perfect escort for the old colonel. Charles wore a tattered mix of Anglo and Indian attire and alarmed Boone's kin when he came unannounced with his Shawnee family (and pony as a gift) to Nathan's to visit Black Fish's white son. Philips had moved from La Charette to Le Beouf Creek's mouth—an hour's ride and near Daniel's original Spanish land grant.

There's no mention of any of Boone's adopted Native kinsmen's attending.

PERHAPS DANIEL BOONE'S FUNERAL service went something like this.

The Boones, Callaways and Pastor Craig left Jemima's to go out to the barn. Maybe they'd ringed the bier with flowers, rosemary or tansy, Queen Anne's lace, goldenrod, pine and cedar wreaths, "where the body lay in state while the people filed through doors and looked for the last on the beloved features," wrote William Bryan, whose father, Elijah, likely attended. The coffin's lid was slid into place, a sour, caustic reek hanging in the air.

Ushers escorted older folks. The family sat in front. Many stood in back. The enslaved, maybe, were out beyond the eaves.

One could smell animal dung, the fallow soil's muskiness, smoke from the house and drying tobacco and hear cattle lowing. Roosters crowed, horses whinnied and stomped. Black skirts rustled as the ladies fingered mop-caps tied under their chins. Men doffed beaver hats and thumped pipe bowls on strait-last shoes, snuffing out embers on the hard dirt floor.

There were a few coughs, bawling babies and sobs, muted voices and whispers. Heads were bowed and shoulders quivered. From outside came the shuffle of more feet, low talk, whispers, a clatter of hooves, hacks, wagons and buggies all in a line—the late arrivals.

Craig conducted his service without pomp. Dan Boone's life overlapped King George's War, the Seven Years' War, America's Revolution and the War of 1812. Though he'd mustered in many militias, "there were no military honors," Nathan recalled. Such a display would have fitted George Rogers Clark, not Daniel. "I have been but a common man," he once said.

Was there any retelling of his hairsbreadth escapes—of Braddock's killing field, Blue Lick's grinding carnage, James' and Israel's brutal slaying, Boonesborough's harrowing siege, G.R. Clark's laying waste to Ohio? Was there talk of Boone's trailblazing—his hunting, opening Kentucky, coming to Missouri? What about his service and sacrifice for God and country?

Most here had endured the same. Surely Craig touched on *some* of this.

Or on Dan and Rebecca's fifty-six years together, maybe the pastor naming their dead children—Levina, Susannah, Rebecca, Israel, James and baby William—and recognizing aloud their living children, the adopted Bryans and their children and grandchildren seated in the assembly. Funerals are for the living anyway.

Did the assemblage lift their voices in song?

Quakers then had no hymnody tradition. Daniel wasn't a Friend—not outwardly—though their quietist spirit forever imprinted him; he remained a seeker of the Inner Light. Many unchurched counted themselves as Christians. Attending were Presbyterians, Methodists and Roman Catholics, maybe Cane Ridge Stoneites, Campbellites and Hard Shells. The austere sects, heirs to Scottish Psalter acapella traditions and of Scots-Irish and English stock, would have known "The Lord Is My Shepherd" and Isaac Watt's "Psalm Twenty-Three." Both were sung at such times, as was Charles Wesley's "Jesus, Lover of My Soul":

> *Jesus, Lover of my soul, Let me to Thy bosom fly;*
> *While the nearer waters roll, While the tempest still is high:*
> *Hide me, O my Savior, hide, Till the storm of life be past;*
> *Safe into Thy haven guide, O receive my soul at last.*

Abner Bryan, Jonathan's son and grand-nephew of Rebecca, was eighteen and wrote about the funeral years later, after he'd opened the area's first grocery. Craig "was only an ordinary preacher," but he "did pretty well."

Craig would have recited, "Blessed are they that mourn: for they shall be comforted" and talked of Daniel's love of the Golden Rule, "Therefore all things whatsoever ye would that men should do to you, do ye even so to them," as well as his reputation, "A good name is better than precious ointment; and the day of death than the day of one's birth." He'd testify of assurance to the bereaved—how Dan had "placed his hopes in the Savior." "Let not your heart be troubled: ye believe in God, believe also in me. In my Father's house are many mansions: if it were not so, I would have told you. I go to prepare a place for you."

He'd pray a powerful prayer. Amen!

There would be a rustle as they filed out, hands patting skirts, men donning hats. A driver pulled the wagon near. Teenaged Jimmie Bryan mounted and lifted an American flag, trotting to the van to lead southeasterly along Boone's Trace paralleling the Big Muddy. They advanced three quarters of a mile. On crossing Tuque Creek, the land lifted—the path bending left and the crowd passing David Bryan's farm. On a shaded knoll a few hundred yards farther and near the creek's fork he'd sectioned off an acre for burials. Rebecca Boone was the first interred there.

They jostled in for a benediction—a prayer, a hymn, recollections, parting words. Departees swept the contour below the rise after "all that was mortal of Daniel Boone was lowered into the grave by the side of his wife," wrote William Bryan. His head was pointed west so that on resurrection morning he'd greet the sun. After they tossed in handfuls of dirt, wildflowers and juniper, they shoveled the grave full.

Perhaps someone set a rock and laid a red cedar bough on his grave. Rebecca's head- and toe-stones were set years before. Daniel's came soon. The throng dispersed easterly past Bryan's orchard and back to the trace leading to Flanders's to share a meal.

For Rebecca and Daniel, the circle was unbroken.

In pace requiescat!

9

In the Heart of Boone Country

I returned to the Boone Home during Murray State's spring break. After a quick hi to Bill and Grady, I headed for Nathan and Olive's digs to fall in with some well-fed Latter-day Saints escorted by a youthful, slightly built man in a War of 1812 tunic and sporting enviably cool rockabilly sideburns. The LDS were a polite bunch, inquiring about the Boones' pedigrees and pondering their eternal state. The puzzled guide kept mum, evincing a straight-lipped smile. As Zion's faithful departed down the walk to a van, I left to patrol the grounds.

Winds north by northeast swept the valley, flexing the cottonwood's bare branches, the mercury falling as the sun's rays glowed orange against stray lilac wisps of fleeting cirrus. Sprinkles moistened my glasses. "Weather moving in," a lady said as we hurried to our cars.

Wheeling out of the gravel lot onto F, I drove the descending five miles to Highway 94 and then turned right toward Hermann, fifty miles west, to visit Ken Kamper, a Boone historian whose ardor for the hunter borders on cultic. Getting there required traversing serious Boone territory.

Past Femme Osage Bridge and into Defiance, Darst Bottom Road bisects 94. David Darst, who fought in the Revolution, gained a Kentucky grant and later moved here. His son Jacob died at the Alamo; five grandsons rode with Sam Houston's avenging Texicans at San Jacinto. His survey nudges Boone's Settlement, a seventeen-mile stretch from the colonel's land near Matson to Marthasville. Dan's kin owned much of this historically drenched swath.

At Tavern Rock Cave on a bluff facing the Missouri opposite Boone's land, Lewis and Clark's trek nearly ended just as it was starting when Captain Clark spied the cavern as the corps drifted by. "We passed a large *Cave*…120 feet wide 40 feet Deep & 20 feet high." Lewis bade them halt. Scaling the cliff, he slipped, skidding downhill and stabbing his knife at the rubble until it snagged, saving him. Clark's Hemingway-esque entry compressed his partner's death-defying plunge into sixteen words: "Capt. Lewis near falling from the Pinecles of rocks 300 feet, he caught at 20 foot."

Three miles past Defiance the road flattened as the land opened to reveal Boone's 1799 Spanish grant of 850.702 acres (U.S. Survey No. 1646). I veered left into a narrow common of faded, bug-gnawed posters showing Boone's life in maps and images. Past a Pabst can, a purple flip-flop and ATV ruts, a wooden sign dangled from a level 4x4.

DANIEL BOONE
JUDGEMENT TREE MEMORIAL
IN THE HEART OF BOONE COUNTRY

The Boones lived about three hundred yards due northeast with son Dan Morgan from 1799 to 1804 before decamping to Nathan's. His original Judgment Tree was near here. Ken Kamper, Peggy Bradbury and others planted a sapling in this park to honor Boone's arrival. Bounded by decrepit rail fence, this Stonehenge of warped plexiglass placards seemed like more of a metaphor of his foiled dreams. Like his lost one-hundred-acre town of Missouriton, maybe under this earthen sea are vestiges of Daniel's Atlantis. No archaeologist has ever looked; two hundred years of plowing and flooding would give one little reason to now.

A rock's throw away is Matson. Alice Street runs 150 yards westerly past shuttered store fronts and houses resembling an *Our Town* Hollywood set. Paralleling 94 is a way station with Matson's biggest draw: a unisex flush potty. Off Matson Hill Road, a gravel driveway girded by redbrick piers fronts a bluish frame house; beneath its tatty façade is Dan Morgan Boone's cabin. Next to it was Boone's Fort—the strongest 1812 outpost in St. Charles's district.

Snapping pictures from afar, I parked to hike Matson's formidable forest. Its primeval topography has kept its dense woods intact. Riven by plunging ravines, rocky creek beds and undulating bluffs, its unharvested soaring oaks and hickories offer a glimpse of this terrain's flora in Boone's day.

Near the way station the easterly side of a black granite DAR historical marker read:

The Boone Trace
Eastern Trailhead
CA. 1805

The Boone Trace was an important westward trail for American settlers. The Boone Trace probably followed a trail used by American Indians. In the early 1800s it was used by Daniel Boone's sons Nathan and Daniel Morgan Boone for travel to the Boone salt lick in present-day Howard County. Nearby this marker was the Boone settlement composed of Spanish land grants given to Daniel Boone and the Boone family. The trace ran from the Boone settlement through Charette (near present-day Marthasville) and westward along the Missouri River to the Boone Salt Lick.

Boone's Trace started here at the Missouri, proceeding westward; nearer Marthasville, it overlaps Daniel's funeral route. Folks tailed it to Booneslick Trail (shown in Louis Houck's *History of Missouri*) arching to Cooper County, where Nathan and his father, before Lewis and Clark's foray, "located and surveyed the 10,000 arpents of land on the north side of the Missouri opposite Boonville…and made maps" they filed in St. Charles. Afterward, the Louisiana Purchase Congress rejected Boone's claim, giving him back a tenth of it as a consolation prize.

In 1819 his grant here looked promising enough to Abraham Shobe, who gave him $5,000 for it, proving Boone did not die penniless. Maybe he used the cash to pay off debts. Relatives said he died poor but happy, forsaking real estate ventures to return to what he knew best: the woods. Stephen Hempstead saw him, his son-in-law and Derry Coburn nearing a St. Louis landing after a successful hunt. The old Long Hunter's canoe, Hempstead told historian Lyman Draper, "was covered with bearskins. And they landed first the stern and the sterns man got out and the bowman rowed her around and they landed; this done to enable them to land and not disturb the cargo—the whole middle being full and covered. Flanders Callaway and the Negro rowed in front and Colonel Boone steered in the river. The value of their furs and their skins I cannot state, but it was considerable.…Boone, I should suppose, then to be eighty years of age or upwards."

It is a remarkable image of vigorous living for a man who'd endured a long life of camp and trail, still taking his plews to market. To the end Boone looked to the future.

And so too must I. My gnawing gut reminding me of Bernice Kamper's supper on the stove.

Throttling southwesterly through rugged hills, I spiraled around curves, piloting speed zones and dizzying hairpins. Travel safe yelled a sign near wildly bent guardrails—galvanized veterans of inebriated hell-bent-for-leather driving. The convoy on my bumper seemed less concerned along this winery-saturated leg of 94, the *Weinstrasse*, "Missouri's Rhineland." Its lush arable bottoms still sustain the Midwest. It is little wonder Boone settled here.

On to Hermann. Shadows were darkening, storm clouds were whipping about and the horizon portending of things worse. I eased through Dutzow's tight bends to go left at the light. On crossing the Missouri—its chocolate turbidity roiling into miniature whirlpools tugging and vanishing and the marbled sky darkening from indigo as thunderheads rolled in—I entered Washington on 47 and four intersections later I turned right on 100.

Tired and heading to parts unknown with neither map nor GPS, I pulled into a ZX gas station that doubled as a liquor mart and grocery. I was down to a soured cornbread wedge and was tolerably sharp set. Inside I asked the tattooed, multi-pierced cashier yakking on his iPhone if the ZX sold buttermilk. The sign at his arm by the Zigzag 1.25 rolling papers demanded customers "PLEASE REFRAIN FROM USING CELL PHONES WHILE BEING WAITED ON."

The attendant pulled his cell phone from his ear. I repeated my question. He frowned.

"Is that like regular milk?"

"Sort of. Except clabbered."

"Never heard of it. You from out of town?" He eyed me while making change for a PayDay, coffee, cheese and crackers. He set his cell down. Customers queued up behind me.

I said I was from Kentucky, researching Daniel Boone. I looked legit in jeans and sneakers, a Daniel Boone Blazers Athletic Dept. T-shirt and Daniel Boone Homestead Berks Co. Penna. ball cap logoed with a powder horn—gifts from my Birdsboro, Pennsylvania jaunts to Daniel Boone Middle School where I gave two talks that bombed (my first PowerPoint attempts). Peering through my nerdy Balrim 51 specs, I was a twenty-first-century Boone hipster fashion statement in full dweeb.

"Where *is* Daniel Boone anyway?" an inquiring voice over my shoulder demanded to know. I turned, startled, to find a middle-aged, thick-built fellow with a majorly receding hairline grinning defiantly, eyebrows arched in expectant Show-Me-State mode above aviator wireframes.

"That seems to be the big question around these parts," I allowed, returning fire. We paid and took our discussion outside the ZX. Where did he think Boone was buried?

"If you ask me, Kentucky's got him. All this talk about wrong bones, switched bodies, the Black dude—that's all crap, but it's all we're known for around here. There are articles in the newspaper about Boone's grave all the time."

"Which newspaper?"

"The *Washington Missourian*. This old guy writes a column in there—Ralph Gregory."

I knew Ralph and for years had clipped his work. I had plans to stop and see him.

My newfound pard was up on Boone lore and knew Walter and Grace Stemme, the cemetery's next-to-last caretakers, sort of; the site's ownership claims remain challenged.

As we chatted, a Dodge pickup pulled in a gas bay. When the Ram's rattling diesel ceased, the passenger door opened and a long-legged blonde in tight jeans unwound herself from the cockpit and sauntered by and looked us over and us her. She was flaxen-haired and a bit taller than my five feet eight. She must have overheard something of our conversation as she passed, as I was still buttonholed by the adamant Missourian.

"I don't believe any of that Kentucky shit," she delicately interjected, displaying regional pride.

"What, ah, Kentucky stuff is that?" I politely answered, modifying her colorful vernacular, as a lady was now present. She frowned and shook her head, vanishing into the ZX. She reappeared with a blue-and-white case of Anheuser-Busch slung in the crook of her arm.

"I'm Shelly." Her white T-shirt boldly announced in red cursive, "Bourbon Street Mardi Gras." Shelly's cheeks were flushed and veiny, her breath was stale with hops and tobacco and her eyebrows seemed strangely black for a blonde. She was very happy.

"All that shit about Boone buried in Kentucky. I don't believe any of it. We got him. I go to his cemetery all the time. I can tell he's there. His wife too."

"How?"

"Because Kentuckians are a bunch of liars. Go ask my husband, Don—I call him my husband since my real husband cut out. He knows all about Daniel Boone."

I walked over to the driver's side of Don's high-hooded white Ram. The stout Missourian flip-flopped behind statuesque Shelly. The dark tinted window descended. Cannabis's sweet stink wafted my way. Don stuck out his head and glared.

"Who are you?"

Shelly handled my intro. "He's a history professor from Murray State University in Kentucky wanting to know about Daniel Boone."

This broke the ice for Don, a sports enthusiast. "Hey, how 'bout them Racers. Great basketball team, thirty-one and two. Hot dang!"

MSU's Racers had grabbed the nation's spotlight by smashing NCAA records to clinch the Ohio Valley Conference Tournament. ESPN featured them in prime time. The hometown crowd was pleased and the city was voted America's Friendliest Town.

Don got out of his pickup. We shook hands. Shelly handed over the Busch.

He was a big man and heavily bearded, his complexion tomato scarlet under besotted eyes. He looked like some of the burly timber fallers I'd seen in Oregon's spotted owl territory where the swill of choice is Olympia.

"I'm a Hoosier anyways, so I don't care," Don said. "Personally, I think Daniel Boone is buried in Illinois, up around Chicago, south side." He was serious.

"Chicago?"

Shelly's jaw dropped. The stout Missourian laughed and left for his car. Don reddened even redder, regained his seat and cranked his truck. He craned his neck for Shelly to get in.

I had to go. I thanked them all for their historical insights. Shelly dropped her window to pop a top and wave bye.

"Hey, call us when you figure out where Daniel Boone is," she shouted, a foaming jet of Busch spewing downward.

"Sure thing!"

GUNNING DOWN MISSOURI'S BACK roads in the wet, inky blackness an hour later en route to Hermann, I felt like Ichabod Crane casting about Sleepy Hollow. The Headless Horseman, caped and tall in the saddle, though, had yet to appear in my rear-view mirror. Cellular service was no more and houses were few.

The road—devolving from asphalt to gravel to dirt with clayey washboard draws strategically aligned to rattle jaws and axles—was bordered by craggy, old-growth oak soaring overhead in a woven tangle. Bleating does with fawns bounded from my high beams. Yellow-eyed coyotes stalked the perimeter.

A hasty turn ended at a mailbox in an earthen cul-de-sac. Dogs barked and a man yelled "Hey!" but no shots were fired. I reconnoitered—dome light on and wipers banging, scrawled directions at my nose, idling and puzzling through a rural labyrinth unrenowned for signage. Two wrong turns, a row of mailboxes, a cut left and a quarter-mile gravel driveway later, Ken Kamper greeted me at the door to help pack in my things. After giving Bernice a hug and grabbing a steaming supper plate and a glass of tea, Ken and I headed to his inner sanctum.

I'm in the Midwest's Boone Central Command, a Library of Congress worth of Dan'l data distilled into a spacious upper room fitted with blipping computers, file cabinets, a maze of book stacks, microfilm reels and reader, piles of documents, Boone bios and genealogies, wall maps and Boone newsletters from 1925 onward. Ken's desk was five flat wooden doors end to end. Blueprints furled like rabbinical scrolls topped an architectural drawing board.

We talked past midnight. From memory, Ken laid out Boone's Missouri trails with GPS precision. My eyes glazed over as my pencil faltered. Twenty years my senior he wore me past my usual fathomless Boone saturation levels. I excused myself to go downstairs where I sleepily uncased my Martin to downstroke through a D minor Django Reinhardt arpeggio (metronome blipping 63 bpm; egg timer set at ten minutes). Guitar back in the case, I face-planted on the bed and didn't move until awakened by Bernice's call to breakfast and coffee. And more coffee.

We were off to Marthasville in search of Ralph Gregory, age 105, the world's oldest Daniel Boone historian.

10

We Have His Heart and His Brain. And His Skin.

A hard rain settled the dust and the warmth had coaxed the Femme Osage into bloom. Bur oak and shortleaf pine hung heavy with pollen and humidity was up. Ken driving, between sneezes, I swilled coffee and watched the road for dead armadillos and soon counted three of the migrants, their range moving northward. Itching eyes made me glad I'd opted for glasses instead of contacts.

Ken, a member of the Friends of Daniel Boone's Burial Site in Missouri, talked about probing with metal rods to estimate interments in David Bryan's old graveyard. One headstone was "down about two feet."

"I don't think there were any slaves unless they're tied to the Bryans. There were two or three at Nathan's—you can look at tax records. He had more slaves at Ash Grove."

"What about Derry Coburn?"

"Neat guy. Everything you read about him, people loved him and his wife, Sofia, and he was given his freedom and land. He was Daniel Morgan Boone's slave. It's just not considered that Daniel Boone owned slaves in Missouri. He did in Kentucky."

Nearing Marthasville we passed muddy cow pens in bottomland and hugged the road's edge to give way to clanking armadas of farm machinery and talked about famous exhumations making the news. Zachary Taylor's remains were tested for poisoning; the results were negative. What was left of Jesse James in Kearney, Missouri, was unearthed to quell rumors that the gunslinger was in the wrong grave; Jesse was right where his tombstone said he was.

"I get it about respect and honor—whatever," Ken said. "But what motivates people to dig up other people to move them? Someone decides a person shouldn't be buried where they are and says, 'hey, let's put 'em over here.' Nowadays, it would be considered disrespectful." Then he added, "Like when Boone's sons and brother were killed—James was buried where he was killed. Israel was buried where he died. Ned was buried where he was shot. Their memory was much more important than going to a cemetery to sit for hours."

PAST A "WELCOME TO Marthasville" sign, Ken turned on South Third. Rarely does one meet a man nearly 106 who spends his days working at a historical center bearing his name and his nights writing for a newspaper. I'd clipped Ralph Gregory's articles and met him when he was a youthful eighty-two. I doubted he'd remember me.

"He will," Ken said. "He has your books."

That was no guarantee. Ralph's home library exceeded six thousand volumes.

We parked off the road paralleling Ralph's mailbox. His house's asbestos shingles needed high-pressure spraying. Blueberry and raspberry bushes crowded his yard. Ralph quit canning jam after a collapsed ladder left him dangling from a limb until neighbors rescued him. When he slipped off his roof while cleaning gutters and crashed on to a cistern, he'd given up ladders altogether. A hardworking centenarian can't be too careful.

Ken rapped on the side door by the garage. Canine spoor was plentiful. I watchfully stepped around the shady yard to the front.

"Maybe he's walking his dog," said Ken. Ralph's dented '99 Ford Escort was gone. Dented because, while idling at a stoplight, he was rear-ended "by some old guy," Ralph told the cop filing the accident report. "He was in his seventies."

Inside a hound bayed. A mewing cat wandered up to head-butt my leg, calico tail curling about my shin. A shirtless, barefooted boy across the street with a spurting garden hose gazed at us from behind the black GMC pickup he was washing.

As we'd yet to spot Marthasville's peripatetic senior historian, Ken drove us to the Washington Historical Society's Ralph Gregory Historical Library where its namesake holds court and translates French and German documents.

He'd just left, the cashier said.

As president of the Daniel Boone and Frontier Families Research Association, Ken is the dean of all things Boone here. Corralled by local buffs, he warmed to his favorite topic. Two sentences passed before he was lobbed the inevitable question: where is Boone buried?

"Everybody knows something about it," he chuckled. "Or thinks they do."

"And everyone loves a mystery," Marc Houseman laughed. Marc, the society's director, heads the Friends of the Daniel Boone Cemetery group and fields website inquiries. Kevin Wolf, a museum patron, repeated his question.

"So, is he buried in Kentucky? I read Ralph's book."

"Ralph's right," said Ken.

"Ok. So, he *is* in Kentucky then?" asked Kevin.

"No. That ain't what Ralph said," answered Ken as everyone laughed. Kevin persisted.

"Here's what I get from it: when they dug up the Boones' graves, their caskets were deteriorated. The large bones were brittle but intact. The smaller bones, if you touched them, turned to powder. They took the larger bones, and we got the rest," said Ken.

"What else is there?" I asked, keeping a low profile as a Kentucky interloper.

"Well, the small bones, muscles, veins and their clothes and two rotten coffins," Ken said, pausing. "It's pretty morbid if you really think about it." True—notions of the Boones' arms and hands, feet, ankles, short-ribs and "the rest" in Missouri and their skulls and pelvises, spines and legs in Kentucky do make for a grisly visual. None of the family aware of the facts that corresponded with historian Lyman Draper hinted of anything unusual about Daniel's burial or exhumation. All of them believed he was transferred.

"One can't discredit our side of the story and our Boone cemetery," Ken said, suggesting we visit the grave of Boone's doctor, Dr. John Jones. Derry Coburn was buried there. The husband of Minerva Callaway, a daughter of Flanders and Jemima Callaway, Jones was the state militia's surgeon and aspired to office. When rustlers and counterfeiters moved in, he ferreted out the criminals to bring them to trial. His sense of duty made him a marked man.

"The community was thrown into a state of excitement," reported the *St. Louis Globe Democrat*. "He was shot in his yard at Marthasville and the assassin never found." His death left a gap in history. Daniel had entrusted to Jones not only his health but also his legacy, relating his life to him so "that his own words might be left in the hands of a true and trusted friend." The killer stole his manuscript "penned in accord with Boone's dictation" but missed a few pages that Jones Jr. kept, later using them to light the candles lighting his home.

Ken drove to a site ringed by a low rock wall overhung with trees. John and Minerva's headstones were side by side. Other than a few markers, there wasn't much to see. "I'm sure it was larger in the 1800s. I saw it fifteen years ago when it was surrounded by brush and with the plowed area around it. The extra distance," he theorized, "was cut away by plowing." How much more had vanished due to antiquated laws, vandalism, development and negligence?

Meandering out of the drive and slowing for a school bus, we intercepted a schoolboy stooped under his backpack. He straightened to eye these trespassers from under his Cardinals ball cap. Ken's car puttered to a halt. He dropped his window.

"Your mom knows me. We're just looking at the cemetery. Did you know Daniel Boone's doctor and his granddaughter are buried up there?"

"Really?" He bent down to peer in.

Ken sensed a budding historian and gave him his card. "Tell your mom we were here. Call me if you have any questions about Daniel Boone." The boy palmed the card, nodding like he'd just had a run-in with specters from the past. We drove out to the blacktop.

Ken looked at me. "These kids need to know America's real history. Boone is a great role model and these days Americans could use some good role models. It's the only hope we have of saving what's left of these sites for future generations."

Midday found us north of Washington at the Dutzow's Deli in Missouri's oldest German community. Gottfried Duden came here in 1823, seeking land for his kinsmen wracked by poverty and Napoleon's wars. His *Report on a Journey to the Western States of North America* sparked an Old-World diaspora. Within forty years this district was home to sixty thousand Germans.

The deli's furnishings were 1950s kitsch: straight-back chairs and linoleum-topped tables. Bavarian landscapes and helmeted antique steins decorated the walls. Folks at the counter under a "Try Our New Beer Pretzel!" sign were downing steaming heaps of cabbage, ham and potatoes—in these parts, the rule denoting gluttony as one of seven deadly sins is abrogated by honoring the holy man who emptied Ireland of snakes. It was St. Patrick's Day.

Duden would like it here if he liked beer, brats and Merle Haggard's "Working Man Blues." For people-watching and the sociologically astute, the deli boasted a demographic slice of young and old, urban and rural, white collar and blue, college-bred and not, arriving via the Katy Trail, a defunct 240-mile stretch of the Missouri-Kansas-Texas Railroad turned hiking-biking lane lapping the Missouri's north bank atop a buffalo path Lewis and Clark charted.

Our table was by a louvered divider. Ken faced me and my vista was the cash register and counter. Patrons paid and picked up orders as we talked of Daniel's St. Charles clan. Ken's encyclopedic grasp of genealogy made him a sort of ambulatory Boone search engine.

"Delinda Boone Craig," he began, talking about one of Nathan's girls, "married James Craig, a Canadian, who gave the eulogy at Daniel's funeral." Her husband "was a teacher and a Hard-Shell Baptist minister in St. Charles." Hard Shells gained their moniker by embracing Calvinism's "hard" precepts and were derided for their acapella hymnody.

Boone's ecumenical sentiments were far from his eulogizer's. When his family left Pennsylvania for North Carolina, they left the Quakers who'd disfellowshipped Squire Sr. Squire and Sarah's daughter was "with child" when she married out of the faith—a double whammy of moral turpitude and apostasy. Quaker elders publicly chastised father and daughter. Daniel was fifteen. The open rebuke left an indelible mark: Daniel never officially joined another sect.

But he bore no grudge. When he visited the Olney Valley in 1781 he attended his old friends meeting. His meditative nature and lack of creedalism he forever shared with them. He read his Bible; had his children baptized; went to Flanders and Jemima's home which on Sundays became Friendship Baptist Church where John Mason Peck, James E. Welsh or James Craig preached, whichever circuit rider was available, and he "well remembered what he heard." As the congregation grew it moved out to the barn.

My thoughts passed from spiritual and otherworldly to temporal and gustatory as Ken chewed through a burger and fries and sipped on a Coke. I'd opted for a Reuben with kraut and chips.

"I've driven past this place a million times. I always thought it was a bar. This is a good place to eat," Ken said. I agreed, noshing on a kosher dill slice.

Outside a Mustang swerved off Highway 94 and into the lot and rumbled to a halt. The couple exiting pushed past the doors to stand at the register. The woman's black hair reached her capri pants cinched under a spacious chiffon blouse. Her bandy-legged pal had on a CSA tank top, camo cap,

Levi's hitched low and stub-toed boots. His shiny jet ducktail was a tad dark and the duck's back showed signs of molting. The couple was in love.

To see Ken I had to see the newest arrivals. Abelard and Heloise were a presence unto themselves. Everyone noticed them but Ken.

"Delinda Craig," intoned Ken, recalling her letters to granddaughter Olive Eadie just as, behind him, Romeo and Juliet embraced. I went blank. The couple parted for air.

"Delinda Craig," said Ken, shifting to Daniel's funeral as love train chugged on past his head. Guinevere swooned, dipping into Lancelot's arms as he braced himself. Male patrons winked and nudged, quaffing deep, satisfying draughts. Women glared, mostly at the menfolk. Ken talked about Delinda Craig.

My napkin was at my mouth, my chest and shoulders heaving as I emitted snuffling sounds ending on a high-frequency wheeze. Between clogged nasal passages and mouthfuls of kraut, mustard and horseradish I needed a respirator.

Ken's dark eyes narrowed. "I can't imagine while I'm trying to talk about something serious a guy is sitting over here across from me with a big smile on his face."

By way of an embarrassed reply, I aimed a thumb at the register kind of subtle like. Why subtle, I don't know, as Heathcliff and Catherine's bravura performance was unaffected by onlookers. Nonplussed, Ken frowned and cocked his head over his shoulder, did a double take and turned back, eyebrow arched over his horn rims.

"You know, as I've gotten older, I kind of admire things like that," he said.

The waitress brought our tab: $21.22 with tip. I paid at the table.

Back in Marthasville, Ralph's car was in his drive but still no Ralph, so we sat in Ken's car. Presently, down past a sign, came a beagle sniffing the curb, its leash held by a slightly bent man in brown pants, flannel shirt, jacket and brogans. He hobbled up grinning. Salt and pepper bristles defined a furry crescent past his Adam's apple. I stooped to pet Sandy.

"Hi, Ralph," Ken said. "You remember Ted Franklin Belue?"

Ralph blinked and leaned in, peering like Tiresias, wizened seer to Oedipus. His moist blue eyes wrinkled at the edges. We were the same height but his arms hanging at mid-thigh hinted of a once taller man. He smiled, head bobbing. Age spots marked his face. Gray swatches poked out from under his John Deere cap onto dual hearing aids. His thin, reedy voice quavered.

"I don't have your Draper book, but I read it." A pause. "Here's a thing you can answer: a man made a report in a St. Louis paper about the Boone's graves. Who wrote it?"

"I guess he recognizes you," Ken said.

Oh, my! Tiresias's opener came leveled like the Sphinx's riddle. The cryptic letter likely emanating from Frankfort was the opening salvo to Daniel and Rebecca's removal. No one knows who wrote it.

"Sorry, I'm not sure—maybe Orlando Brown," I stammered, raising my voice. Orlando edited the *Frankfort Commonwealth*, wielding his influential pen as a stealth crusader for older brother Mason's interests. Mason, a brilliant lawyer, founded the Frankfort Cemetery Company and, with a like-minded band of elites, planned the city's garden cemetery and devised the Boone exhumation scheme.

"Who's that?" Tiresias cocked his head. "I have a hunch it was someone from Kentucky, maybe Swigert. It's well written. I don't think it was someone from around here. Come on in."

I followed Ken into Ralph's kitchen past the sink. Shades were drawn and the lights were off. Like many who'd endured the Depression, Ralph was a frugal man—except when it came to book buying. Books were piled in corners, stacked on shelves and tables, scattered on the floor.

I handed him my copy of his Boone polemic to autograph. It's not often one gets to hang with a 105-year-old fellow Boone comrade-in-arms. Why did he take on Boone's burial?

"I got tired of the controversy." He'd invited scholars "to work together to solve the thing," but nobody did, so he tried to on his own. "It's sensational. Humans tenaciously hang on to so much that just doesn't make sense."

He'd measure the graveyard's part that's inside the rail enclosure: "106 feet wide at the south side, the roadside, and forty-eight feet at the north side." He probed its north end but found "no sign of slave graves." The enslaved were usually not interred in a family site's perimeter.

Ralph addressed the slave tale in his book: "If my father wanted to be buried by my mother and the bones of an unknown burial were by her remains, those bones would go!" He'd move them: "Moving bodies is not very sacred to persons." After all, didn't family members relinquish the Boones for reburial?

He talked about disinterring his aunt, who died when he was eleven, while helping relocate a cemetery. "She was buried near my great-grandparents' farm in 1921. During her funeral, I watched the wagons coming down there." Sixty years later he exhumed her. "Now here I was, digging her up." He paused, hands outstretched, blue eyes widening. "Wow!"

The coffin lid had crumpled onto her skeleton. Her clothing was frayed and discolored. "The top had come down on her bones like a butter bowl." He cupped his bony hand over his knobby knuckles and stared in the distance. "It was a sad thing."

"Kentuckians got some bones, but bones are not all that's in a grave," he said. "Material wise, what they got was less than what was left in the ground. And whatever's there now—can't be much now at either place. I've seen what happens to bodies." Bones, though, being the last part of the body to decompose, are significant throughout history as representing the bodily person at a reinternment.

Ralph had to eat and feed Sandy. His poor hearing limited our chat, which ended with his shot at the commonwealth: "Kentuckians may have got some of Daniel Boone's bones but Missouri's got something more important: We've got his heart and his brain. And his skin!"

DR. JOHN JONES'S CEMETERY, with its furrowed edges and Uncle Derry Coburn and Aunt Sofie's lost graves, caused me to ponder the true state of the Bryan cemetery when the Kentuckians came for the Boones. Supposedly thorny brambles and scrub shrouded the tiny graveyard of mostly unmarked plots.

Was this true? Was the cemetery still in use then? How identifiable were the Boones' graves? Were Daniel and Rebecca's burial places even marked?

11

I Believe Grandfather and Grandmother Are Buried Here

Fall was coming on when Grady Manus and I left the Boone Home to drive southwest on Femme Osage Creek Road along Boone's Trace to park past Tuque Creek below Daniel and Rebecca's graves. Westward, at the Bryan place, the fresh cut hay glistened from a late shower and you could smell its clean, sunny fragrance. Past the knoll steps, I grabbed some persimmons off a low limb and worked them around and spat out the flat brown seeds and leathery skin.

A tree listing over the road and shedding its fruit left an orange purplish slick mashed with tire treads. A cloud of flies hovered over a bloating opossum splayed with sweetly pungent slime, its teeth bared and maggoty entrails extruded. A flicker unleashing a staccato whir swooped to a cedar where Dylan and Chelsea had carved their names in a heart.

Before coming to Defiance Grady interpreted history at Nathan and Olive's last home 250 miles southwest in Greene County. He told how their graves were marked.

"Down in Ash Grove they were originally plain markers, like this little fieldstone here." He pointed to a stubby gray slab eight inches high, half that wide and two inches thick. Its companion toe-stone was half its size. "It was not until later that engraved markers were put up."

"Were they all about that size?"

"Pretty much. You'd have one at the head and one at the foot. Even Olive's mother's grave is unmarked. We found fieldstones but nothing like a traditional headstone."

"What about their slaves?"

"In Nathan's slave cemetery, maybe twenty yards adjacent from the family cemetery, the slaves were buried the same way." Most of the toe- and headstones were left anonymous—standard burial practice for the enslaved and poor and working-class whites.

"Were any of the slaves' graves ever given regular headstones?"

"Not until after the Civil War do you see where someone scratched a name in. But it's apparent," he paused to point to a headstone, "you have head-foot, head-foot, head-foot. It matches their plain way of life—'here's the body.' The family knew who was there."

John Mason Peck tells of Daniel enacting such a pre-burial ritual for himself. Hunting along the Osage (a three-hundred-mile northeasterly flowing oxbow of the Missouri), he grew "quite feeble" and "lay a long time in camp." Hobbling up a rise with a staff, he scratched out a grave's shape, instructing Derry Coburn "in case of his decease," writes Peck, in his first-hand narrative, "to wash and lay his body straight, wrapped up in one of the cleanest blankets. He was then to construct a kind of a shovel…and [with] the hatchet to dig a grave, exactly as he had marked it out. He was then to drag the body to the place, and put it in the grave, which he was directed to cover up, placing poles at the head and foot….So that it might be easily found by his friends."

Derry was relieved when Boone recovered and the two wended their way back to the Femme Osage, the old colonel sensing his mortality.

One might put a cedar bough at the grave's head, its evergreen foliage symbolizing eternity, its pink aromatic heartwood denoting purity. English and Scots-Irish settlers on the Blue Ridge learned it from Cherokees, says ethnographer James Mooney, confirming in his *Myths of the Cherokee* and *Sacred Formulas of the Cherokees* their reverence for *Juniperus virginiana*'s "ever-living green, its balsamic fragrance, and the beautiful color of its fine grade wood practically undecaying."

There is a nineteenth-century nameless engraving of the Boones' Missouri graves with two men sitting by Dan and Rebecca's burial mounds. They gaze at a female shrouded in mourning attire with tombstones scattered to her right. A four-sided obelisk topped by an urn rises before a spire bisecting the sky. A forest circles the vista.

Nothing in the pastorally surreal scene is accurate but the message is clear: the Boones, as strangers in a strange land, were buried as paupers. Neither premise is true. Before Daniel died, he sold his Spanish grant to Abraham Shobe for $5,000. And the Boones' original gravesites were marked from the beginning. Such is the power of myth.

Grady's blue eyes took in the horizon. "By the Victorian era, you see elaborate artwork on monument stones. Before that, back east, headstones were used. Out on the frontier, you just marked them, but a lot went unmarked."

In Murray, Kentucky's city cemetery I chanced upon on a stone chiseled "UNKNOWN SAILOR LOST AT SEA." Was he shipwrecked or washed overboard? A site overseer confirmed there was no body—a marked unknown grave with no corpse. What soul cared enough about this mother's boy to set a rock to his memory but not name him?

At Murray's St. John's Episcopal Church on the lot's north end is a meditative walk meandering past rocks, trees and shrubs, ecumenically reassuring to all but the most doctrinally obdurate. Past its Troii, the Shinto cedar post entry sundering the sacred from the profane, is a mounded repository of the church's dead, their cremains interred sans markers. More dead rest in anonymous repose along the walk. From his first days, such boneyard namelessness was part of Daniel's Quaker identity.

Travel a mile east of Stonersville, Pennsylvania, south of SR 562 on 19 Meeting House Road to the Exeter Meeting two miles from his Berks County birthplace, where he went to church his first fifteen years and saw Quaker graves devoid of human presence. The meeting is so plain that drivers in search of it still pass it by; I did twice, in spite of my wife's copiloting. Inside, Lavina and I sat on the plain high-backed pews where Dan and his kin sat to wait for a stirring to rise and speak. There are no wall hangings, no crucifix, no pulpit, no baptistery. A japanned potbellied stove warms its one austere room built on the acre that George Boone, Daniel's grandfather, gave his fellow Quakers.

Look southward—there are no markers in the Friends' cemetery adjoining the meeting. It's like a putting green until a third of the way back to a knee-high rise where deceased are stacked double. There are no stones or impressions, no mounds or plots—just grass. A plat of names and dates hints to where the dead were laid side by side, making any attempt at retrieval a forensic nightmare.

If Daniel's Tuque Creek grave was so humbly appointed, it's hard to imagine him caring. It's unlikely that he yearned to be Frankfort, Kentucky's number one tourist draw.

"I HAVE LIVED 8 years right in sight of their graves," wrote Elijah Bryan (nephew of David and father to William Bryan) to historian Lyman Draper's queries. He was twenty when Daniel died.

Elijah means the Boones. Rebecca's was the first grave, then Dan's and Flanders Callaway's, nine years later, the third. No one is sure how many are there or even the site's layout. More than half of it, say locals, lies past its rickety fence; a solitary enigmatic post may define a corner. The accessible part is about a third of an acre.

"There are head and foot stones, but not lettered. In those days there was no such thing as regular gravestones," reads Elijah's letter. "Not lettered," as in not having names and dates.

David Bryan's grandson, George Chester Bryan, born two years after the Boones' exhumation, had "knowledge of these facts." He "was born and grew to manhood on the old Bryan farm where this graveyard is located" and moved to Dawson Springs, Kentucky. On a return visit, he went to his parents', Willis and Corelia Bryan, graves, "a few feet of where Boone and his wife were buried." Of the famous pair's original makers, he said, "The old headstones and footstones that marked their burial places were still there. The headstones were simply a flat limestone slab, about 2 inches thick, 3 feet long and about 1½ feet wide, with the initials of both cut into the stone with an ordinary cold chisel. The footstones were of much smaller size."

Daniel himself commissioned them, said Eviza Coshow, a great-granddaughter. "He had Rough Stones cut by Tarleton Goe." Tarleton was a grandson by daughter Rebecca Goe, who died of tuberculosis in Kentucky at sister Levina's home fifteen years before their father passed.

Dan Morgan Boone hastened to Bourbon County to get most of his seven nieces and nephews, including Tarleton, who became a mason and worked on Boone's Lick Road near St. Charles. When Indians killed James Callaway in 1815 at Loutre Lick, Tarleton cut his stone. It is likely that he set Rebecca's two years earlier. After he cut Dan's, sixteen years passed before the Boones' graves were re-marked. Seven more bodies, in the interim, would be interred—all Bryans, except for Jemima Boone Callaway, who died August 30, 1834.

David Bryan was born in the year that New York's Fort William Henry capitulated to the French and Indians in the siege turned massacre that James Fenimore Cooper recreated in *The Last of the Mohicans*. Two years before, Daniel had barely survived Major General Edward Braddock's Pennsylvania killing field. Both men joined their era's greatest generation who clung to the Republic with the zeal of freeborn, pre-Christian Greeks battling Persia's totalitarian despots. Bryan tuned eighty in 1836.

Death's angel accosted Bryan's home that July when he buried his wife of forty-five years. Eight months later, he'd rest by Mary at Rebecca and

Top: Daniel Boone's tombstone made in 1836 by John Wyatt, is 13 inches long, tapering from $2\frac{3}{4}$ inches to $4\frac{3}{4}$ inches front to back. *Missouri Historical Society*.

Bottom: Rebecca Boone's tombstone, made in 1836 by John Wyatt, is 24 inches overall, $2\frac{1}{2}$ to 3 inches thick and 12 inches wide at top. *Missouri Historical Society*.

Daniel's feet, who succored him and his siblings. Sensing a lingering familial debt, he hired a St. Charles mason named Watson to etch the Boones' names on two new custom tombstones he'd commissioned. Arriving without his cold chisel, Watson hunted up smithy John Wyatt to forge him another one. "Watson came here on Saturday but forgot his chisel. He came to me to get me to make it rather than make the extra trip to St. Charles."

Wyatt said he'd cut and inscribe the stones "so that Watson could return home." A day or two later, in the Femme Osage, a mason (one story says "Neighbors"; another "Jonathan Bryan") quarried the limestone block to haul by oxcart to Wyatt's shop, where he spent a weekend shaping the grain, chiseling in "Daniel" and "Rebecca," guided by a rustic line-and-dot stencil, misspelling their names as "Boon" and incising the *N*s in reverse.

Daniel's stone was oblong, three inches thick and five inches by thirteen. The lower half of Rebecca's was rectangular, eleven inches by fifteen and topped with a twelve-inch disc; the halves later broke apart and a slat was affixed to the markers' back to rejoin them. In her study on cemetery statuary, art professor Dr. Maryellen H. McVicker deemed the markers "excellent examples of the earliest style of gravestone found along the Missouri River in this state."

On Monday, John Wyatt yoked his oxen to a sledge and set on it the memorials, securing them with a chain to tug over to Bryan's log home, its reinforced design and size rivaling Flanders Callaway's palatial home.

Bryan's double-hewed cabin endured until 1870, when today's manorial redbrick home was built in its place.

Greeting Wyatt was Susannah Bryan Shobe, David Bryan's widowed daughter who cared for him. Her father was ill and she'd show him to the graves. Wyatt, then, with Susie—as she was more familiarly called—in tow, nudged his team past Bryan's orchard, begun from seeds tucked in his weskit when he left Kentucky with the Boones thirty-seven years before. They ascended the rise.

Susie was in her thirties and lived in the graveyard's shadow. She knew its features and its occupants, counting among them her late husband, Archibald, and their child. It is very likely too that she went to her uncle Dan's funeral and graveside memorial a decade and a half before. Her father so trusted her that he signed his estate over to her, which included Winney and Sina, two young enslaved girls.

What was the state of Bryan's cemetery? How many markers did it have? Lawn beautification was not a developed midwestern concept but whatever the graveyard's condition, Wyatt sought out Susie's guidance to be sure that he found the Boones. By now about twelve people—Boones, Bryans and Callaways—were interred. Wyatt later told Jesse P. Crump, a Kansas City banker and Boone descendent, about that day. "For sixteen years his body [Daniel's] had laid in the old Boone cemetery about a mile from Marthasville, unmarked….It had been the Bryan cemetery for years and many unmarked mounds were in the place. After deliberating for some time Susie pointed to two graves, side by side, and said 'I believe grandfather and grandmother are buried here.'"

What did Wyatt mean, the graves were "unmarked"? Didn't Tarleton Goe, years before, set the Boones' head- and toe-stones?

Perhaps he meant the Boones' graves were not personalized until he set the tombstones. One hopes David Bryan recovered enough to see what his altruistic hands had wrought. He died the next spring and was buried beside his wife a few feet past the Boones' feet, where his marker remains today.

Susie sold her father's estate six years later to Harvey Griswold, kin to the Boones via the Shobes and Bryans, who interred Czarina H. Bryan, daughter to Willis and Corelia Bryan, in July 1844. Griswold befriended Augustus Ferdinand Grabs, a Prussian merchant and town postmaster, selling him a cabin to set up a smallgoods store and about a dozen plots in the Bryans' cemetery's northwest sector, where, in February 1844, Augustus buried his wife's mother, Margaretha Catherina Gerdes, the first German immigrant interred.

TUESDAY, APRIL 30, 1844, began like any day for Harvey Griswold, until this anonymous memo in the *St. Louis New Era* about his acre of real estate holding the Boones grabbed his eye:

> *THE GRAVE OF DANIEL BOONE*
>
> *The celebrated pioneer after a life of incredible hardship, and numerous perilous adventures…was buried about a mile from the town of Marthasville. His wife…is buried by his side.…The grave yard has grown over with a thicket of briars several feet high, and almost impenetrable. The traveler passes by the spot, and never knows that there lies buried one of the most wonderful men that has existed in our country. For many years there was not even a tombstone to mark the grave.*

The *St. Louis New Era* ran the missive with no byline. As Harvey pored over it, his jaw must have dropped as his mind churned: where did this come from? How did it get in a newspaper? He must have been perplexed. Maybe he even felt threatened—especially if he'd discovered that the dispatch also ran in Louisville and Cincinnati weeklies.

Does the nameless memo depict the true shape of the Bryan graveyard? Two months before, Postmaster Grabs, in one of his new plots therein had buried his mother-in-law near the Boones. Was his burial entourage forced to hack through an "almost impenetrable thicket of briars several feet high" to do so?

And was it true that there was not, for years, "a tombstone" on the Boones' graves? Weren't they marked with Tarleton Goe's head- and toe-stones and then, in 1836, Bryan's memorials?

As strange as this must have been for Griswold, thoughts of the dispatch would have slipped his mind had he been privy to Nathan Boone's mail. A year later an avalanche of high-toned letters from Kentucky arrived at St. Charles's post office. All of them were addressed to "Capt. Nathan Boone, U.S. Army, Missouri."

Four letters were dated April 21, but most were postmarked April 24. Fourteen trickled in by June's first week.

The crisp notes, folded to palm-size, were superlative models of literary eloquence, penned in a calligraphic aesthetic reflecting a commonwealth brain trust of five governors; judges and trustees; a U.S. attorney general; a U.S. senator; eight legislators and senators; business people; Frankfort's secretary of state, treasurer, chief justice and assistant secretary of state; a U.S. envoy to Mexico; and attorneys brandishing New England degrees whose authority stretched to the nation's seat of government.

Each concerned how Nathan's parents deserved better than a burial in a remote corner in the West and why they should be returned to "the great theater of his renown" so that honor might be paid to them at Frankfort's proposed garden necropolis. A certain Mason Brown's name appeared more than once in the letters; indeed, Brown had countersigned two of them. Senator John J. Crittenden's memorandum is representative of the lot:

Frankfort, Kenty:, April 21st, 1845

Dear Sir,

I have been shewn a letter of this date, addressed to you by Judge Brown. He appointed a committee for the purpose, requesting your assent to the removal of the remains of your Father and Mother for burial in the Cemetery at this place.

The committees, who have addressed you on the subject, are gentlemen of the highest respectability, and entitled to your entire confidence. The sentiment's that have prompted them…are common to the people of Kenty:,

The memory of your distinguished Father…belong to Kentucky—nowhere else will it be more gratefully cherished, and nowhere will his remains be better assured of an honored & revered resting place—

I hope, Sir, that it may accord with your feelings to grant the request…that the field of his fame may become the burying-place of Daniel Boone.

Very respectfully,
Yr's &c,
J.J. Crittenden

There was a problem. Eight years before, Nathan moved 250 miles southwest to campaign in Kansas and Nebraska. There's no tangible sense of when he saw the letters about his father and mother that read about the same, varying in length, detail and verbosity and having the same bent as the mysterious *St. Louis New Era*'s unnamed notice published a year before.

It was quite a coincidence, really.

Or was it?

Part II

Kentucky, 1842–2020

12

Our City Is Without Burying Grounds

The plan to move Daniel and Rebecca Boone from Missouri to Kentucky had its origin in a memo dated Tuesday, April 12, 1842, to Orlando Brown's weekly, which ended with the line: "Our city is without burying grounds."

Colonel Ambrose W. Dudley's letter to the *Commonwealth* was that of a town father trying to do right. As president of Kentucky's Branch Bank and Frankfort's quarter master general, any indelicacy in handling this thorny issue might threaten his reputation. "It is requested that no additional applications should be made for the privilege of interring the dead at Bellevue. It is very painful to be compelled to refuse; but there must be a stopping point."

That Kentucky's capital, on the cusp of a dramatic burst of prosperity, had no city graveyard was, as Dudley put it, "unpleasant." Certainly it was ironic.

Aurora Borealis's freak arrival two years before, which veiled Kentucky's skies in blues, pinks and violets, seemed to herald Frankfort's lurch toward modernity and a yearning for culture. Many American cities were undergoing similar transitions. Much of the change southward was coming in on the sweaty backs of slaves.

In Frankfort's bustling manufacturing center, chattel revenues outstripped sales of horses and land, hemp and bourbon. By 1840 the capital city had 2,846 enslaved. By 1850 there were nearly 3,500.

Turnpikes, ferries and bridges linking Franklin County beyond the Bluegrass helped grow its citizen population to 12,462. There were schools, Reverend Philip Slater Fall's Female Eclectic Institute and drama clubs—even public waterworks.

Sundays blended rituals sacred and profane. Congregants flocked to Methodist, Presbyterian and Baptist services. Episcopalians and Roman Catholics offered the eucharist. Opposing them in public debates and claiming to "speak where the Bible speaks" was evangelist Alexander Campbell, whom John Moore lodged in his Georgian home on Montgomery Street (now 326 West Main), along with Senator Henry Clay when he served in the state legislature.

Congregants of another sort flocked north of town to a green near the Elkhorn's Forks to race horses, fight gamecocks and hold turkey shoots. These freewheeling, bourbon-fueled sprees often ended in brawls replete with stabbings, eye-gougings and duels, as police jailed the disorderly and tried to shut down the public nuisance.

Strolling the streets at night meant toting a lantern. Any hint of a walkway was sunken or upended, mire-caked or dunged from the hundreds of cows, horses and pigs. Stumps, roots and potholes hampered coaches. The stage departing for Louisville at 8:00 a.m. arrived at 5:00 p.m.—if all went well, and usually it didn't. One Brit slogged "a mile through mud and water" to get to a barbeque but John Loudon McAdam's crushed stone roads were making life better.

Riding to Lexington thirty miles on the inelegant carriages—huge, black, high-seated cubes jouncing on leather springs—the plodding draft teams tugged along three-inch iron rails took two and a half hours. The Lexington and Ohio's *Daniel Boone* replacing them made twelve miles an hour, halving travel time. Steam- and coal-powered locomotives brought accidents as wheels dislodged haphazardly spiked ties, the thunderous reverberations ricocheting rails through floorboards, impaling travelers and hurling trains over embankments.

Soot-belching, multitiered steamboats, like the *Argo*, *Clinton*, *Eagle* and *Plough Boy*, churned the Kentucky and Ohio to deliver glassware, lumber, cotton, hemp and tobacco. Wharfs were piled high with hemp and bourbon barrels. Factories abounded. The fortified penitentiary north of town was near the armory.

Aaron Burr, Zachary Taylor, Daniel Webster, Louis Philippe (before he was France's King) and the Marquis de Lafayette paced Frankfort's square, Kentucky's epicenter bounded by the homes of a tightknit cadre of lawyers, military men and politicos like Senator John Brown (died 1837), the last continental congressman. His redbrick manor, Liberty Hall, on Wilkinson Street—named for General James Wilkinson, who founded the city in 1786 and lived nearby in his huge two-story log house—remains an archetype of aristocratic sophistication.

Liberty Hall, built circa 1796, designed by John Brown, the last surviving member of the Continental Congress and one of Kentucky's first senators. *Willie MacLean, BirdsEyeFoto.com.*

The modern world's beginnings seen in Frankfort's generational differences startled urbane visitors. Aging Revolutionary War and War of 1812 veterans, slaves, paupers, drunks, salacious sporting ladies from bawdy houses, coarse rivermen and buckskinned woodsmen—accoutered with 'hawks and knives, shot bags and powder horns, long rifles shouldered and ponies furry with wolf scalps for bounties—shambled alongside doctors, ministers, lawyers, governors, sharp-dressed women and a thriving bourgeoisie.

Everyone, somehow, in this motley parade of humanity fit in—except for the dead. Dying in colonial America was a stoic affair of austere graveyards stabbed with decrepit leaning crosses and grim eulogies of life's brevity, reminding parishioners of mortality and of the judgement to come, when the sheep shall be parted from the goats. Burial grounds were neglected. Downpours and floods exposed skeletons. Dogs gnawed unearthed corpses.

Frankfort's untended private graveyards were in no different a shape.

"I don't think Dudley's quote—the 'city had no cemetery and so we had to create one'—is valid," Russ Hatter told me, sitting at his desk in his second-floor office of the Capital City Museum at the corner of Ann (named for James Wilkinson's wife, though he called her Nancy) and Broadway, across the railroad tracks sundering the street from Thomas D. Clark Center for Kentucky History.

"Earlier cemeteries had reached capacity. Writings about Frankfort's early graveyards are murky and confusing." He paused, tilting his head to run a hand over his thinning hair.

Russ is my height, older and certainly wiser, labors under greater baltitude (arguable) and seems to always be smiling. Anything that's occurred in Frankfort since its founding he can likely deliver by rote and in glorious detail. Partly because for years he's given walking tours of its square—his ghoulish nighttime Murder and Mayhem Tour always sells out—but mostly because he is a virtuosic son of the South skilled in the world's true oldest profession: storytelling.

"I've tried to bring resolution to the graveyard mysteries but have never been satisfied. Take Bellevue that Dudley is talking about, as it filled and space around it was filling up with dwellings, the powers that be created the beautiful Frankfort city cemetery."

What's left of the derelict burial site might be at Fifth and Swigert at Thorn Hill—a fenced acre or two that a neighbor described as a "clump of old ivy-strung trees" and a city official called "a good location for immorality" for teenagers. But some say Bellevue was between Thornhill and Wilkinson. Others confuse Bellevue with Bellfont, another tiny but abandoned graveyard nearby. Russ dissents, sort of.

"Bellevue might have been what's called 'the Forgotten Cemetery' at the foot of Fort Hill at the end of Ann," he said, before reeling it back. "We just don't know for certain. I'm still perplexed."

Governors buried in Bellevue (and elsewhere) were later reinterred in the big "garden cemetery"; sixty or so of the eighty-six Kentuckians slain in the Battle of Raisin River may rest therein awaiting reburial. Orlando Brown, says Nettie Henry Glenn, transferred his parents, John and Margaretta, to the new city necropolis.

"We know of one of the Liberty Hall Browns whose tombstone is still there," Russ said. Often these removals and reburials were costly affairs, "since many of the old monuments were massive and some of the coffins were made of iron."

One of Frankfort's strangest tales is the finding of the Forgotten Cemetery at the end of Ann Street north of Mero. On March 11, 2002, workers bulldozing a foundation for the Transportation Cabinet Office north of the Old Capitol were startled by skeletonized fragments in the rubble's backfill, triggering frantic calls to officials.

Researchers checked maps and pored over history books and deeds all the way back to Hancock Lee, a Virginia surveyor. Virginia governor Patrick

Henry signed Humphrey Marshall's note to the tract. Marshall, a lawyer and historian, sold it to James Wilkinson, its title's fate unknown as the site became an integrated potter's field for paupers, slaves, convicts and homeless.

In the 1870s Sig Luscher developed a nearby brewery and expanded it over the graveyard's center into the Capital Brewery complex, his workers pickaxing through femurs, skulls, spines and ribs and spading up beads, shroud and ribbon, nails and glass. Much of the area was later demolished and asphalted over for parking lots and the Capital City Tower.

It was there the remains of some 250 people were discovered, exhumed and written about—a few were facially reconstructed in clay to preserve some hint of them—and reburied atop Fort Hill in Leslie Morris Park. Seventeen years after their discovery, Sig's great-great-great-grandson reopened Grandpa Luscher's brewery near its original site—an ironic coda to the story.

"The town fathers knew they had to consolidate the graves into a better place," said Russ. "Like what they did with Mount Auburn Cemetery in Boston, Mason Brown's model for Frankfort's 'garden cemetery' that got us Rebecca and Daniel Boone."

"What was gained by bringing the Boones here?" I asked.

"A beautiful cemetery. Everything was about money. Brown had been in Boston. He saw a beautiful cemetery. Dudley says, 'We aren't accepting anymore graves—you're going to have to come up with something.' They came up with a rural cemetery like the one Brown saw."

Mason Brown was a cosmopolitan man of the Second Great Awakening, culturally akin to his northeastern colleagues infusing their progressive world with Romantic literature, transcendentalist thought and Hosea Ballou's Universalism. They extended charity to the living and the dead, embracing the concept of interring their deceased in well-tended "cemeteries"—a derivative Greek term implying "to place to sleep." No line was drawn between those living in this world and those alive in another. Couples courted among the dead. Picnickers communed and fellowshipped with them.

Napoleon's Pere Lachaise was the world's first garden cemetery. It filled slowly until France's famous seventeenth-century writers Moliere and Jean de La Fontaine were trucked in, inspiring arriving poets to recite verses and reserve their own lots. When the marketing wags transferred over the bony rubble of legendary consorts Pierre Abelard and Heloise d'Argenteuil, the thousands flocking there to see their graves longed to be buried near the seven-hundred-year-old lovers eternally pursuing their amours in the hadean realm. (The church, frankly, was relieved to get the pair off its turf and under more secular sod.)

Cambridge's Mount Auburn, America's first rural cemetery, was begun by Dr. Joseph Bigelow who was trying to end epidemics and said that corpses spread diseases and should be interred far from homes, but in areas aesthetically pleasing. Alexander Wadsworth (cousin to Henry Longfellow, who is interred there) turned 174 acres into ten miles of roads, paths, clearings, hills, ponds and forests, filling it with the graves of the rich and famous, pious and literary.

Visitors marveled—seventy thousand came annually, rivaling Niagara Falls' and Mount Vernon's crowds. Even Emily Dickinson, at sixteen already a recluse, left Amherst to walk among its verdant gardens. "It seems as if Nature had formed the spot with a distinct idea in view of its being a resting place for her children." Death tourism bankrolled the town, inspiring Fred Olmstead's Central Park and forested cemeteries in New York, Pennsylvania, Maine, Rhode Island, Ohio and Maryland—and in Frankfort, Kentucky, the catalyst was Mason Brown, who visited in 1832.

"Mason helped create the Frankfort Cemetery Company and had the idea if we can have someone famous, then we could get governors," Russ said. They'd proceed to get big-name people—war heroes like Richard Mentor Johnson, frontiersmen like Bland Ballard, poets like the pallid bard of morbidity Theodore O'Hara—who were famous then. Russ went on, "Boone was the stimulus. If you can get Boone, you can get the other guys. This will be a place folks will want to be buried in with heroic monuments. It will be a big draw for Frankfort."

Until ravaged by the Civil War, Frankfort was as influential as a political and cultural dynamo as the states along the eastern seaboard. The Crittendens, the Blair family, Amos Kendall—these people who were so influential in Washington, D.C., had their start in Frankfort.

DANIEL BOONE WAS NOT the city's founder, but he was Franklin County's, and Kentucky's, native son. Seventy-three years before Ambrose Dudley's letter appeared in Orlando Brown's newspaper, Boone roamed this hunter's paradise. In John Filson's Boone "autobiography," he put on the map, literally, the first Far West, *Kenta-Ke*.

The Algonquian word denoted a great meadowland—a ripening Eden, unbroken by plow, unmarred by axe, untamed by gun. Others said *Kenta-Ke* implied a "Dark and Bloody Ground." It was—Indians shot Stephen Frank in 1780 at a shallow on the Kentucky's north bank near Leestown, an outpost that Hancock and Willis Lee founded. Indians killed Willis near the crossing dubbed Frank's Ford. Its rippling shoals are still visible at low water.

Boone stalked its sprawling saltlicks, hid in its dense brakes and gazed at its flowery, virginal pastures, tall timber, wide rivers and seas of fertile land loose as an ash bank. Street-wide, hoof-beaten buffalo paths, his day's turnpikes, sundered Eden from the Ohio to the yawning gaps at Cumberland Mountain and Pine Mountain. Shawanoes and Cherokees warred along the treacherous Path of the Armed Ones, *Athiamiowee*, and along its rocky, meandering offshoots cutting through dense laurel thickets and canebrakes, spiraling northwest to the Falls of the Ohio—now Louisville.

This was a dangerous place for a lone white hunter trespassing in Indian land and firing a flintlock rifle, dressing and stockpiling deerskins, stretching beaver pelts on willow hoops, kindling fire, exploring and trapping, evading Algonquians. Yet deep in this heart of darkness, *Kenta-Ke* nurtured Daniel Boone. Alone for much of two years, a melancholia induced by "a thousand dreadful apprehensions" wilted at the bounty before him.

"I undertook a tour through the country, and the diversity and beauties of nature I met in this charming season expelled every gloomy and vexatious thought," the hunter told his first biographer, John Filson. Through Boone's eyes we glimpse a Long Hunter's Elysium. "The buffaloes were more frequent than I have seen cattle in the settlements, browsing on the leaves of the cane… fearless because ignorant, of the violence of man. Sometimes we saw hundreds in a drove, and the numbers about the salt springs were amazing."

Nearing what is now Frankfort, he felt he'd reached Canaan. "Soon after, I returned to my family, with a determination to bring them as soon as possible to live in Kentucky, which I esteemed a second paradise, at the risk of my life and fortune." He'd pay dearly—two sons and a brother slain, horses and furs stolen, captivity, a siege—and endure hardships unimaginable today. He'd blaze the trails that made *Kenta-Ke* part of America, as he'd do in Spanish Missouri.

In his wake came the young Brit, Nicholas Cresswell, whose diary waxes eloquently about the bluegrass's crown gem. The McAfee boys and Abraham Haptonstall, James Strother and Hancock Taylor surveyed it until Shawnees shot Haptonstall and Taylor, who spent his last day signing deeds as blood seeped from him. More hunters and surveyors came—Virginians and Carolinians, mostly. Then settlers.

After Virginia's legislature created Kentucky County, its divisions, Jefferson, Fayette and Lincoln, touched at Frank's Ford, morphing into Frankfort. Its resources and centralized locale, bisected by rivers and pathways, gave it accessibility to become the commonwealth's capital after statehood in 1792. Seven years later the perennially restless Daniel Boone hied to Missouri and died there.

BOONE DIED THE YEAR Mason Brown graduated from Yale and his younger brother Orlando from Princeton. Mason served on Kentucky's circuit bench. Orlando set up a law office in Alabama.

Their father divided his ten-acre lot between them and commissioned architect Gideon Shyrock, who designed the Old Capitol, to build Orlando's home. Finished in 1835 for $5,000, its Greek Revivalist lines are a bold statement about the Enlightenment ideals the Browns, slaveholders all, selectively hewed to. Mason inherited his father's law practice and the family estate, Liberty Hall—bordered northerly by the Kentucky, westerly by Wapping Street ribboning past the wonderfully named Love Tavern and easterly by Montgomery. Wilkinson Street fronted his five acres.

Past the slave cabin behind his home and down the riverbank—father and sons held more than thirty enslaved here and elsewhere—his wharf on the Kentucky jutted into waters so fordable that during droughts one could walk to shore. His home's window glass was Philadelphia-made, mule-trained to the Monongahela and boated down the Ohio to his dock. Two ferries crossed nearby—one bisecting northwest past the ford; one cutting northeasterly near Fishtrap Island's grain and sawmill.

Mason's intellectual bent showed itself early. "It really is a pity that so promising a scholar should be checked in his literary progress for the want of books," John wrote to Margaretta about their gifted three-year-old. Their second-floor library grew as Mason hardened into a stern-looking man with onyx eyes, a sharp nose and a soft, rounded chin that belied a grit not unlike the scaly catalpa that today still grows just out his front door—a firmness needed as secretary of state under Governor Charles S. Morehead, his coauthor on *A Digest of the Statute Laws of Kentucky*.

Orlando's heart was not in lawyering. "The family darling" missed his heroic social tippling and "slippered talk with friends." He returned home. Rakishly handsome and pale, he's in a black cape in one portrait, clutching a red bejeweled fob to his bosom—the effect less Byronic and more emotive Emo embalmer in full goth with high tousled black hair, pouty lips and rouge-tinted nose. He's perfectly posh and fashionable in another stylish rendering, seated on his luxurious armchair.

His calling came in editing the *Commonwealth*, which he cofounded with Albert Gallatin Hodges. He crusaded for Mason's interests and would during

Top: Mason Brown, by Chester Harding. *Bob Lanham; Liberty Hall Historic Site Collections.*

Bottom: Orlando Brown Sr., by Louis Morgan. *Bob Lanham; Liberty Hall Historic Site Collections.*

the Civil War hurrah the Northern cause (while renting out Alexander Sanders, one of his seventeen slaves, to Company A's 116th U.S. Colored Infantry). A lyrical yet undisciplined writer, he began a governor's compendium that he never finished, in his editorializing and authorship completing only a ten-page pamphlet. "His legacy to the historical bibliography of Kentucky was not extensive in quantity," read a postmortem tribute.

The brother's siblings died young. After Euphemia overdosed on calomel, the day's addictive mercury- and opium-laced tonic, her great-aunt arrived to console her niece, and then, eerily, auntie died too. No one knows where they buried her—maybe near Margaretta's garden or closer to the river. Passersby on moonlit nights still report seeing the "gray lady" in a long black veil peering from Liberty Hall's palladium window.

THREE YEARS HAD PASSED since Colonel Dudley published his memo to close Bellevue's graveyard.

Mason Brown moved fast to avert Missouri's efforts in the works to honor the Boones, telling Nathan Boone, "We have seen…that the Legislature of Missouri have appropriated $500—to erect a monument over the grave of your honored father," referring to Ben Emmons's motion approved during St. Louis's constitutional convention. Kentucky, Brown said, had reserved a more fitting scenic spot upon which "$10,000 will be expended."

In April 1845 Kentucky's legislature passed an act "incorporating the Frankfort Cemetery Company," authorizing the making of a beautiful cemetery, with Daniel and Rebecca Boone's interment "as the first to be deposited within its walls." For $3,801 the FCC bought from Dudley a picturesque thirty-two-acre tract, Hunter's Garden, on a scenic rise east of town overlooking the Kentucky River. Securing another $5,000 for "embellishment," they solicited bids for lumber and other supplies and hired Robert Carmichael, "a scientific florist from Scotland," for $500 a year to commence laying out Frankfort's necropolis.

Captain William Harris, a thirty-year veteran of the U.S. Navy, and Orlando Brown formed a committee "to secure the consent of the Boone's descendants and bring the remains to Kentucky," assisted by Thomas Crittenden, William Boon and Philip Swigert. The steamer chosen for this auspicious mission was a wooden-hull, 169-ton packet piloted by Captain Grafton Molen, who'd christened his new side-wheeler with the perfect name: the *Daniel Boone.*

13

The Gentlemen from Kentucky Finally Carried Their Point

Up in the pilothouse Master Grafton Melon was at the *Daniel Boone*'s helm, guiding his wheezing steamer along. For years, he'd put in six-day workweeks, leaving Cincinnati at 10:00 a.m. on Tuesday, Thursday and Saturday and departing Maysville at 9:00 a.m. on alternate days. He contracted this Missouri trip with the Frankfort Cemetery Company, leaving William McClain in charge.

Cincinnati (mile marker 546) to Carrollton (mile marker 471) was seventy-five miles downstream to gain the Kentucky and on to Frankfort for fares. Riverboat pilot and Daniel Boone Home lead interpreter William Ray gives us a glimpse of the next leg of Captain Melon's voyage, from Frankfort to Marthasville:

> *The trip started by backing the* Daniel Boone *out the Kentucky's bank at Frankfort. Easing past Benson Creek, he'd work northward 63 miles to Carrollton, having gone through four locks, to ease into the slow-moving Ohio. He'd float La Belle Riviere for 546 miles, past the Falls at Louisville, through hills and oxbows, the river flattening as it neared the Mississippi's confluence at Cairo. Rounding the point, the boat climbed past Cape Girardeau, St. Genevieve, and St. Louis until reaching the Missouri—195 miles upstream. Upon entering the Big Muddy his last 73 miles would be the hardest, bucking a current that began in Montana. Nearing Marthasville he would have stepped on the whistle treadle blowing long and short blasts particular to the* Daniel Boone *to announce his*

> *arrival. After nosing her into the bank and getting a few lines out, he could then take his ease.*

The *Daniel Boone* was of medium tonnage and sturdy as a mule—able to push up the fickle Mississippi and the lashing, sawyer-ridden Big Muddy that Mark Twain deemed "too thin to plow, too thick to drink" and Captain William Clark blamed for his Corps of Discovery's "Deassentary," its turbid waters consisting of "a Comm Wine Glass of ooze to every pint."

Aboard were the FCC's smartly dressed envoys Philip Swigert and Thomas Crittenden and, maybe, William Boon. They represented three generations of Kentucky political clout, wealth and pedigree.

Back at the Capital City Museum, my pard Russ Hatter, his brownbag lunch sumptuously spread before him on his book-heavy desk, filled me in on the influential Swigert brothers.

"Philip and Jacob Swigert were lawyers. Jacob was a judge. Philip was Frankfort's first mayor. They were your movers and shakers of the city. If there was a dollar to be made, they were there."

Phillip, fifty-two, also stayed busy as bank president, U.S. deputy marshal and state senator. The brothers invested in the Frankfort Water Company, stagecoaches and railroads—things people needed. Philip owned twenty-two slaves—a sizable number. His residential property, the Terraces, took up a block of high-end real estate. As grand master of Kentucky's Masons, he was "pope" of the "Frankfort Clique"; at his word, careers were ruined or created.

When Russ got off the phone, I asked about the Terraces—what happened to it?

"Sad story. Fine mansion, built in the 1840s by slave and prison labor over on 319 Wapping Street." He paused and, letting out a sigh, went on. "In the 1950s, the city of Frankfort bought the Terraces to refurbish into City Hall—beautiful old building. But they changed their minds and tore it down and made a parking lot out of it." Russ shook his head.

Swigert's fellow Frankfort Cemetery Company stowaway aboard the *Daniel Boone*, Thomas Leonidas Crittenden, the son of U.S. senator John J. Crittenden, was the state's commonwealth attorney.

"Thomas came from good stock," Russ said. "His father was a driving force here. The most honest politician America ever had."

"These days the bar on that one is mighty low," I said. "Enter political life elected as one of the people, exit as a Russian uranium peddler."

"Not him. When he died, he died poor," Russ said. "He wasn't a millionaire."

Like his father, Thomas would show his grit in war, first as General Zachary Taylor's aide at Buena Vista and as Union brigadier-general fighting the rebel "secesh." He'd lose his only son, J.J. Crittenden III, at the Little Big Horn with General George Custer.

William Boon, Daniel's last nephew, voyaged home with Swigert and Crittenden. Prior to the trip's first leg, he may have already left for Missouri to get consent signatures from Boone kin to exhume Daniel and Rebecca; the record isn't clear. His letters in May and June show him traveling between Jefferson City and St. Louis.

In his May 14 note to Nathan Boone he asked him to reply care of his son "Hampton L. Boon or Hiram N. Baber, in Jefferson City." And "Cols. Harris & Brown upon being advised of the contemplated removal of your parents…will meet me in St. Louis." He told Lilburn W. Boggs to send referrals "for the next 15 days" at Jefferson City.

With five FCC members traversing Missouri, Hiram Martin Chittenden, in *History of Early Steamboat Navigation on the Missouri River*, credits Joe La Barge using the *Kansas* to assist them. But the *Kansas* he speaks of, renamed *Daniel Boone*—and west of the Mississippi there were four *Daniel Boones*—was built two years after Dan and Rebecca were reburied. Since La Barge later declined an FCC invitation to a Frankfort banquet once they got the Boones' home, he must have been involved.

Maybe La Barge, working out of St. Louis, transported Boon back to Marthasville or conveyed Orlando Brown and William Harris, who were in Missouri facilitating the pending exhumation's fragile politics, on ahead to St. Louis's constitutional convention amid plans to converge with Boon, possibly en route from Jeff City.

The FCC's role for Daniel's nephew, who dropped the *e* from his surname, is puzzling—certainly, his surname and family ties gave the FCC access. In 1799, George Boone's third-born son flat-boated with Nathan and Olive to Missouri to rendezvous with Uncle Dan in St. Louis. Unable to secure land William left the territory to join the Illinois Rangers. He and wife, Nancy, moved to Montgomery City nine years later. Sometime after Nancy died in 1835, he returned to Shelby County, Kentucky, and remarried.

When Nathan moved to Ash Grove in 1837, Boon may have still been in Missouri socializing with Lilburn W. Boggs, who served as a state senator and governor, and Hiram H. Baber, state auditor. Boggs and Baber were brothers-in-law, married to the daughters of Daniel's son Jesse (Harriet and

Panthea). Baber's hand in Nathan's financial woes in the Femme Osage had forced his foreclosure, inciting his move west and hushed talk among the clannish Boones.

How could Boon, living 150 miles north of Nathan before his Kentucky return, not have known the vicinity of Nathan and Olive's Ash Grove homeplace? If Nathan was campaigning in Kansas or Nebraska with his dragoons and Boon was looking for him in western Missouri, why was Nathan's mail—Frankfort's urgent dispatches from Senator Crittenden, Mason Brown and the rest—shunted 250 miles eastward to the Feme Osage in St. Charles?

There's no proof Nathan knew about his parent's reburial before it happened, despite the *Commonwealth*, on July 29, 1845, marking the arrival in Frankfort of the Boones' body parts, declaring how "Captain Nathan Boone of the U.S. Rangers" approved of it. Did he? Were his consent letters lost in the FCC's devastating fire of 1853 that torched all of their records? Maybe.

Nathan Boone died October 16, 1856, at seventy-six. The Kentucky Historical Society bought many of his papers, which included the FCC's letters. Their tinge of wood smoke and maple sugar cure animated a nearly zen sensory state as I pored over them, marveling at their chirographic beauty and gracious aesthetic. There was also a copy of the *Commonwealth*'s detailed program of his parents' impending reburial processional.

Apparently, by the time he learned of the transfer of his parents and heard that his relatives had consented, then, tacitly at least, he must have been good with it too. The topic, amazingly, didn't even come up when Lyman Draper interviewed Nathan and Olive in 1851. There was *never* any doubt among this generation of Boones or their kith and kin that Daniel and Rebecca Boone's remains had been relocated to Kentucky.

THURSDAY, NEARING 10:00 A.M. on July 17, 1845, William Boon, who had rejoined his FCC kinsmen at Marthasville's landing, accompanied Thomas Crittenden toward Main Street.

This postage stamp of a world they entered was as far from the bustling hub they had left as east is from west. La Charette's frontier ambience had yielded to Marthasville's township grids, clapboarded houses and a "Publick Ground." Postmaster Augustus Grabs's smallgoods store on Main was prospering. Dirt roads crisscrossing Warren County passed inns and taverns, Protestant and Roman Catholic worship houses, vineyards, farms and the Masonic Lodge founded by one of Warren County's wealthiest citizens, Harvey Griswold.

At thirty-nine and the town's premier property holder, Griswold owned David Bryan's homeplace and its adjoining graveyard. Ensconced in his new home, Harvey had reason to pace. If the FCC was successful removing the Boones, he would lose money. He could not let this happen.

The negotiations were even more critical to the FCC delegation. Missing, perhaps at first, was the legal mind of Philip Swigert. Was he was out rounding up the Bryans, Hays, Lammes, Howells, Callaways, Shobes, Coshows, Joneses and others for this theatrical presentation's climactic end? Or was he with Boon and Crittenden?

Their carriage jostled along Main—no macadamized roads here—and cut right, rising to a grand abode "on the best hill in the Warren County." Griswold's federal redbrick three-story home spoke as eloquently about his family's rung in this insular society as stately Liberty Hall declared about the Browns' in Frankfort's cosmopolitan world.

Past the shaggy cedars and the door's wide threshold, the Kentuckians faced an oaken and walnut classical center corridor that gave echo to their steps as they paced into one of the four spacious parlor rooms flanking the hall. Harvey appeared, maybe with his wife, Mahala Shobe, a Boone relative. Greetings were perfunctory as the rival factions in this strangely choreographed ballet over skeletonized parts postured, like dueling fencers with rapiers aloft, icily eying one another.

It would have been proper for Mahala, in a show of hospitality, to ease the encounter's fragility by setting a light repast for her refined guests with tea or coffee (or spirits) and then to depart as the men got down to the business. She would bear sixteen children. Six reached adulthood. Twelve rest with their parents in the Harvey Griswold Cemetery.

Crittenden, as attorney, likely spoke first. Lean and sharp-featured, with a stylish goatee and attired as the spit-and-polish soldier seen in his Mexican War daguerreotype, his manly vigor evoked a martial aspect. One man, twenty years later, framed him as "tall, slender, with a full black beard and hair down to his shoulders," as a Civil War brigadier general for the Union.

Boon, twice Griswold's age, bearing a hawkeyed visage crowned with gray hair brushed back—in his portrait he's attired in a white linen shirt shut at the collar with a dark crevette to match his coat and vest—would act as the elder statesman, whose military service with Dan hearkened to a bygone era, and the last nephew of a famous dead uncle and aunt trying to get their venerated remains moved.

Crittenden—as recalled in Earl Griswold's notes passed down from his grandfather—asked "for permission to disinter the said remains...to have a secure, permanent and beautiful spot in which to deposit the remains of their dead, and this spot may become the final resting place of Kentucky's illustrious sons." That lovely spot was secured and waiting—Hunter's Garden, nestled high atop Frankfort's most sublime vista.

He condensed the FCC's case into three main points: 1) "That the capitol of Kentucky should be the final resting place of Daniel Boone and wife." The cemetery's most beautiful part would be reserved for the Boones; 2) "That the Company pledge themselves...a monument every way worthy...[of] this pure, noble and fearless pioneer"; and 3) That the FCC had taken "immediate steps to obtain the Consent of the relatives of the deceased that his remains and those of his deceased wife may be removed to Kentucky."

Griswold objected, as was expected. He parried his objection with his own rebuttals: Daniel yearned to be in Missouri where he lived the longest. He had picked out his grave by his wife, where he'd rested now some twenty-five years; his sacred last wishes must be honored.

The Boones, he said, "should not be placed where their friends and family could not control them" or where Missouri couldn't memorialize them as promised. The state had put up the munificent sum of $500 to honor "the memory and remains of this illustrious pioneer of the West." (The ever-polite Kentuckians surely smiled on hearing this.)

And there was the matter of his personal finances. He'd "paid an extravagant price for the farm on which said remains were interred... removal of them would greatly lessen the value of the property." He stood to lose a lot of money should the FCC have their way.

At this, the Kentuckians withdrew from their satchels "satisfactory evidence that the immediate relations of Col. Boone had been consulted." Included were letters signed by Boone descendants; official missives from governors, attorneys and senators; maybe Lilburn Boggs's and Hiram Baber's communiques on Missouri state letterhead; embossed FCC memos; and Frankfort surety bank guarantees of $10,000 for a Boone's monument to permit them to "have those sacred relics."

Boon—as hangdog earnest as any Philadelphian lawyer—maybe read the June 3 letter he'd sent to Boggs about how he'd met with "Nearly all the relatives...all of whom cordially concur in the removal of their remains...& entertain no doubt that the consent of Nathan Boone would be cheerfully & unhesitatingly given."

Harvey knew he didn't have a snowball's chance. Flailing at the sudden tidal shift, he pronounced a Herculean stipulation: most of local Boone's kin nearby knew nothing of this. Before he'd give consent for the Boones' removal, the FCC needed to get theirs as well.

How might one logistically pull this off in a thinly populated rural setting in 1845? Did the FCC agents foresee this gambit and have a plan in the works?

While Philip Swigert's friends were busy deflecting, had he been circling the town and countryside rounding up Boone's kin? How this went down is not said, only that "the committee then caused those relatives of Boone to be assembled," and after hearing "the object of their removal of said remains…unanimous consent was given."

An alternate, credible account from the *St. Louis Globe Democrat* paints, at this fork in the art of the raw deal, a less fulsome image: "Strong protests were made by the Warren County folks. Griswold opposed the proposition with all his might. Kentuckians argued and coaxed."

In this rendering, the Kentuckians reminded Missourians that the Boones were buried on "private property"—there was no assurance that the site could be protected. Two: Missouri's $500 allotment for a memorial showed how little "the mossbacks of that day" cared about Rebecca and Dan. Three: the FCC renewed its vow "on Kentucky's great intentions"—not a cent less than the promised $10,000 would be spent making immortal the Boone's sacred remains. Twenty times what Missourians had proposed!

And thus, "a reluctant consent was obtained."

But there was still the issue of Harvey's financial loss if the Boones were taken.

The Kentuckians swore a solemn oath to Griswold, witnessed by all those present: "We faithfully pledge ourselves that the company for which we were acting would fully indemnify him for any injury to the value of his property occasioned by the disinterment and removal of said remains, and we hereby bind ourselves to make such a pledge good and to comply with it." Undoubtedly it was all very fine.

So it was that the FCC carried the day before a host of Bryans, Lammes, Coshows, Howells, Callaways and Hays. All were invited to gather "at the graves of Mr. and Mrs. Boone to witness the resurrection of their remains" at 5:00 p.m. on this very Thursday, July 17, 1845.

There was sure to be a crowd.

14

Desecrated to Gratify a Spasm of Kentucky Pride

Nearing 5:00 p.m., July, 17, 1845, the sun over the Bryan graveyard was in its western descent.

Marion McKinney of Warren County helped get the Kentucky commissioners—Thomas Crittenden, Philip Swigert and William Boon—from Griswold's home and over to the grassy knoll to the Boones' graves while a "large concourse of ladies and gentleman, consisting of family relations," began to filter in. The daylight was good. The waxing moon, visible in the east since noon, would give illumination enough after dark for the gravediggers to not depend fully on their candle lanterns.

The cherrywood cists lay eighteen to thirty inches below the feet of Jefferson Callaway, Henry Angbert and King Bryan; burying folks "six feet under" is a myth from medieval Europe's Black Death days. As their spades clomped and sliced downward, the men paused to put aside the markers David Bryan had ordered nine years before. Fifty years thence, McKinney, at seventy-five, would identify these same gravestones for the Stephens Museum at Central Methodist University in Fayette.

Jeff Callaway, thirty-eight, headed up the Black digging crew. He was a free man, had toiled for his liberty by the sweat of his brow and well liked in the community. David Bryan often hired him to work on his farm and he'd get paid for this job too. His young son, Alonzo, sat watching. Three hardened field hands scooping out shovel bites of dry soil would have made short work of this, even if they were axing out roots or spelling each other off.

In under an hour or so their tools grazed the coffins, crumbling their decayed tops; it being now dusk, with care they spaded dirt from the slim parallel sides showing with each toss. The crowd ringing them inched closer, peering downward, as splinters and rotted cherrywood shards surfaced in the backfill. They saw the gray bones and the stained linen.

The *St. Louis New Era* days later ran the one anonymous eyewitness report of the unearthing: "The large bones were found to be perfect in size and shape but of a very dark color, and so far decomposed in substances to have lost their strength and weight....A number of the smaller bones were rotten and could not be raised in form; the coffins were entirely rotten and gone, except the bottom plank which remained in a very imperfect state."

Once they exposed the Boones, someone—a Kentuckian or a gravedigger or a family member—eased down into the gaping troughs, likely with a lantern in hand, to begin retrieving their skeletons.

Were their skulls lofted for all to see? Dirt was brushed from femurs and arm bones, and detritus was flicked from pelvises and spines. There were long bones, ribs, tattered linen, teeth. Griswold, tradition says, got Dan's jawbone; his signet cufflinks went to great-granddaughter Eviza Coshow, who was now twenty-six. Bone and wood shards and shroud mingled in the reddish soil. The men set the largest tannin-darkened bones in compact pine boxes. Souvenir hunters scarfed up the fragments.

Thomas Crittenden, lifting his voice above the din, explained to the crowd "the object of their removal," thanking everyone "for the liberal surrender which they had made of what to them must be dear, and to the society...a treasure, and—to Kentucky a prize of inestimable value," promising to do honor to the pair "creditable to the state to which they were to go, and gratifying to the friends who had surrendered them."

Back in Frankfort, his graveyard speech would be called "neat, appropriate, and well-delivered," as reported in the *Commonwealth*: "Our talented young townsman, Mr. Tho. L. Crittenden acquitted himself handsomely in the eloquent address he delivered on the interesting occasion of exhuming the bones."

After he finished, Joseph B. Wells recounted some of Boone's acts and told of the man himself—how his "peculiar boldness and love of freedom" pulsed with uniquely American rhythms that sought new vistas, confronted hardship with courage and embodied the restless spirit of a bustling young nation. He was the pathfinder, "leading...emigration and empire westward." Missouri should have done more. It was left to Kentucky to "faithfully carry out their object by doing suitable honors to the remains of their faithful ancestor."

The deed was done.

Hours later a gibbous moon swelling from the clouds cast on the ravaged graves and smashed coffins its luminescent pall of ambiance.

NEARING 5:00 P.M., JULY, 17, 2020, the sun over the Bryan graveyard was in its western descent.

I parked my Dakota near Tuque Creek Bridge to cross Boone Monument Road and jogged the stairs past the retention beams to get to the oblong pinkish gravestone. The Boones' graves were under a mat of vinca festooned with tiny U.S. flags and red, white and blue plastic flowers.

Easing against a cedar away from poison ivy, I sketched this one-third acre. It was in the eighties, humidity tolerable. A westerly breeze rustled the oaks and walnuts and hackberry. A sinking sun ray landed on a pinkish furry blob on a persimmon—a huge imperial moth, its wing lobe torn in a crescent, colors fading. I swatted sweat bees and flailed at a kamikaze horsefly that left a welt. Cicadas let go of their stark, raspy laments as I mused over who might be under my knee.

The big arrow in Daniel-is-still-here apologists' quiver is that in 1845 the FCC envoys opened the wrong grave—an abandoned slave grave. Daniel was actually buried below Rebecca's feet or maybe above her head, the mystics contend—not beside her.

In the esoteric afterworld of mortuary protocol, wives are usually laid to rest on the husband's left. Of course, a walk in any cemetery shows this is not always true. And some husbands' graves have spouses on both sides. Kentucky governor John J. Crittenden's has three.

Consider, delicately put, would Nathan Boone or his kin knowingly bury Rebecca beside human chattel? Slaves were rarely buried inside of Anglo cemeteries. Even if, upon burying Dan, they opened an old slave grave, why wouldn't they move the bones? Celebrating diversity was not a conspicuous nineteenth-century slaveholder virtue.

"The remains were buried besides those of his wife," Nathan told Lyman Draper. His father was buried like any husband: beside his wife—nothing complicated. The family in that day, immediate and extended, always thought the Boones had been transferred.

Were slaves ever interred at Bryan's cemetery? Its active burial dates span from 1813 to 1873.

In 1926 Mary Johnson McIlhiney collated available on-site data, counting Dan and wife as present. Jemima Callaway and Flanders's plots adjoined her parents'. The others here—another fifteen or so—are mostly Bryans by birth or marriage, and there are some Germans—Abraham Grabs's kin are buried at the north end. There were no slaves. Several years later Boone genealogist Lilian Hays Oliver compiled another such list. No slaves.

There are still a few headstones and illegible markers. The Boones' 1836 markers are in Central Methodist University's Stephens Museum. Markers for Corelia Bryan (died 1873), Czarina Bryan (died 1844), John "Long John" Bryan (died 1836) and Willis Bryan (died 1867) remain but are weathered. The DAR recently re-marked Flanders and Jemima Boone Callaway's graves with flat marble headstones.

In 2012 Missouri University of Science and Technology students with ground penetrating radar tallied twenty-three marked and unmarked graves inside the fenced space of "108 ft by 86 ft." There were anomalies, of course; the soil had been disturbed near the Boones' grave—slipshod twin disinterments by shovel and maybe pickax do tend to leave a mark, as do centuries-old tree roots. The mystics cling to this furtive data, hoping that there is some slave DNA in there somewhere, along with Dan's—just maybe.

A knotty old cedar post past the fence's northeastern corner is said to be the cemetery's border. The GPR crew did not test there; the legal and ethical implications of possibly sensing unidentified human remains on farmland seasonally tilled and planted can get complicated quickly.

A car pulling in below the bluff interrupted my reverie. A mother with two boys soon appeared at my tombstone redoubt, puzzled at the unexpected grinning cemetery greeter in Ray-Bans, Sinatra fedora, blue T-shirt and jeans. Someone needed to break the ice.

"Howdy, Ma'am. Y'all from around here?"

"No."

"Y'all like Daniel Boone?"

"The Alamo guy?"

"That was Davy Crockett. Did you know that right here, 175 years ago today, Daniel Boone and his wife's remains were dug up and taken back to Kentucky?"

"What?" She turned away. Her sons, poking around where some Germans rest eternally, drew nearer to her. She backed off a few yards.

"Sorry. I thought maybe you were here for that. I am."

"We were driving past." She crossed her arms. "My boys wanted to see what's up here." She eyed my sprawl of roving authorial flotsam and jetsam—camera, pencils, folders, recorder, legal pad, Stanley thermos, Hershey wrappers—and departed.

The sky darkened. Purple martins swirling from gourd aeries high atop poles at Bryan's farm cartwheeled across the fading skyline. My left temple transfused mosquitoes. Mothra hadn't budged.

A second car rolled in. The tall man exiting resembled a venerable Clark Kent body double. Ken Kamper was soon beside me talking about the events here long ago.

"What do you think about William Boon?" I asked. Boon had the Frankfort Cemetery Company's kinship angle covered and had the Missouri contacts. "Was he a bit of an outlier?"

"He was an opportunist," Ken said. "There's no way he didn't know Nathan wasn't in the Femme Osage when they mailed the letters to St. Charles. That was intentional—a way to ensure Nathan wouldn't see them until after it was done."

"Boon's role was to collect a bunch of Boone family signatures consenting to the removal, right?"

"It was. But I doubt he got any Boones," Ken said. "There were none around here then. There were no Boones at the graves to meet with the FCC guys. Lots of Bryans and Callaways, Lammes—what have you. No Boones. They weren't around."

"And it wasn't 100 percent they were in favor of it," I said. "There were dissenting voices against digging the Boones up and moving them to Kentucky."

"Eviza Coshow told Lyman Draper the Bryans were against it. Some on the Jones's side didn't like it. And there were some others."

Mrs. Coshow did not mince words about the removal: "My father and mother were sadly out of fix when they thought he had been so badly treated about his land titles to come and dig his old bones up after Picking out the Place for his wife and telling them all to lay him by her side. Carrying them to Kentucky—laying some Old Stumps around their graves."

James Boone likewise criticized the reinterment. Daniel left Kentucky vowing to never return due to "mistreatment he had Received—in consequence of that promise I objected to his Remains being Removed to Kentucky," he told Draper ten years after his grandfather's reburial.

"Griswold didn't know what he was up against," I said. "The FCC guys were master politicians and attorneys. He caved to pressure. I think he was trying to do the right thing."

"Either that or somebody paid him off. Or he was taken in too. Plus, Crittenden promised they'd reimburse him, which of course, they didn't do." (The FCC also refused to pay the $3,801 owed Colonel Ambrose W. Dudley for Hunter's Garden until he threatened to sue them.)

Ken theorized that the trio overwhelmed the naive locals with bombast, maybe passing a jug to seal the deal. Perhaps the townsfolk, impressed by these courtly Kentuckians so refined in speech and generous in largess, laid a feast before their well-attired mannerly visitors. Or, maybe it was the other way around—the Kentuckians footing the bill.

"The relatives, mainly Bryan's, couldn't have cared less. If they were there, it was probably because of the free food and drinks and the feeling of self-importance." Ken paused. "My guess is that they never kept the cemetery up."

He left me on my lonely hillside vigil to go help Bernice tend to the grandkids.

Was he right? It was hard to imagine three Kentuckians and a riverboat crew—groups unrenowned for sobriety—not stowing aboard the *Daniel Boone* some distilled commodity that made Bourbon County famous. Corn liquor was standard fare for cutting deals and toasting and warding off chills on river voyages. It was good for whatever ails you. We'll never know.

I tried to conjure Griswold's gloom as darkness veiled the FCC men's coaches with their boxes exiting easterly down the draw, voices dimming, squeaking wheels and clomping hooves growing faint, the crowd thinning, with ghoulish moonlight on sullied graves, dirt mounds, smashed coffins, splintered bones, soiled linen, tombstones cast aside, musty funk hanging in the air.

If Nathan had happened by—his FCC's letters lost in transit—how might he have reacted?

Foreground reveals ground impressions of Daniel and Rebecca Boone's exhumed graves and possibly discarded headstones in David Bryan's cemetery, circa 1880. *State Historical Society of Missouri.*

It would have been a long night for Harvey with Dan's dirty jawbone for solace; maybe the Kentuckians left him a horn or two of some Elijah Craig. Harv never backfilled the Boones' graves and their markers—the inscribed pair commissioned by David Bryan—were still by the yawning pits when he died a bitter man ten years later. His anger grew in his son, Dr. Sylvanus Griswold, who passed on to his son Earl the acrimony embodied in Sylvanus's words in the *Missouri Historical Review*: "Not one cent has ever been paid."

BOONE

PROCESSION ORDER.

It is requested that all business be suspended, and that all persons unite, and strictly observe the following ***Order of Procession***, for the re-interment of the remains of the great Pioneers of the West,

DANIEL BOONE AND WIFE,

in the Frankfort Cemetery Grounds, on Saturday, the 13th instant.

PROGRAMME.

MARSHAL—GEN. JOHN T. PRATT.

No. 1. Military.

Music.

Pall Bearers. HEARSE. Pall Bearers.

No. 2. Relatives and Companions of Daniel Boone and Wife.

Marshal---Gen. Leslie Combs.

No. 3. Officers and Soldiers of the Late War.

L. HORD & JOHN WATSON, ASSISTANT MARSHALS.

No. 4. Committee of Arrangements.

Orator of the Day and Officiating Clergy.

No. 5. President and Members of the Frankfort Cemetery Company.

No. 6. Governor, Suite, and Officers of the State, and United States Departments.

No. 7. Judges of Superior and Inferior Courts, and Officers.

No. 8. Members of Congress and Legislature.

No. 9. Trustees and Officers of the City.

J. SWIGERT & COL. E. H. TAYLOR, ASSISTANT MARSHALS.

No. 10. The Rev. Clergy and Members of the Methodist Episcopal Conference.

DOCTOR E. H. WATSON, ASSISTANT MARSHAL.

No. 11. Masonic Order.

No. 12. Independent Order of Odd Fellows.

No. 13. City Fire Companies.

WM. M. TODD, ASSISTANT MARSHAL.

No. 14. Male and Female Sunday Schools and Teachers.

SAMUEL HARRIS, ASSISTANT MARSHAL.

No. 15. Day Schools and Teachers.

MARSHAL—GEN. L. DESHA.

No. 16. Officers of the Militia in Uniform.

No. 17. Military.

Music.

R. H. CRITTENDEN, ASSISTANT MARSHAL.

No. 18. Ladies and Gentlemen on Foot.

No. 19. Gentlemen on Foot.

MARSHAL—MAJ. E. H. FIELD.

No. 20. Strangers and Citizens in Carriages.

No. 21. Strangers and Citizens on Horseback.

R. KNOTT, ASSISTANT MARSHAL.

A guard will be stationed at the Cemetery Gate, to prevent the entrance of any one, until the Procession have passed.

At 10 o'clock, the 1st Gun---Divisions will form.

At 10½ o'clock, the 2nd Gun---Procession will move off.

Each Division taking its position in line per marginal numbers, on the march: and pass down Wapping, thence Washington to Main and out Main to the place of interment.

The Procession will return in reversed order of Divisions, the body of Military on the right.

No horseman admitted into the Cemetery Gate.

No carriage permitted to leave the Cemetery Avenues except under permit of a Marshal.

A. W. DUDLEY,
Chief Marshal.

Frankfort, Sept. 12, 1845.

NOTE—Nos. 1 to 9, will form in Wapping street. No. 10, near the Presbyterian Church, or any point chosen by them. Nos. 11, 12 and 13, on Wapping foot ways. Nos. 14 and 15, on Wapping foot ways below Washington. Nos. 16 and 17, on St. Clair street. Nos. 18 and 19, on Washington foot ways. Nos. 20 and 21, on adjoining entry streets. All Flags, Banners, &c., will be brought out by the Divisions having them. A sash

1845 Boone funeral processional program. *Kentucky Historical Society.*

Earl met Marthasville's senior historian Ralph Gregory at a far earlier date than when I met the always insightful Mr. Gregory (who knew Sam Clemens's daughter, Clara). "Earl seemed to me as angry as his father, Sylvanus, had [been] at the unfulfilled promise and obligation of the men who took the remains of Daniel Boone and wife to Kentucky," Ralph recalled.

Past 9:00 p.m., I hiked down the knoll. David Bryan's windows were lit with electric candles. The twilight shrouded by ominous thunderheads was slashed by heat lightning.

MEANWHILE, BACK IN FRANKFORT, on Tuesday, July 29, 1845, the *Commonwealth* heralded long-awaited news: Daniel and Rebecca were home at last. "The remains of these noble Pioneers will finally be deposited with the respect and ceremony, in Boone's Grove, a beautiful spot…devoted to the early Pioneers of the West."

The details came later, along with a processional program. "On Saturday, the thirteenth day of September, their mortal remains will be finally committed to the soil of Kentucky." Attending in full regalia would be military companies, dignitaries, Masons, Odd Fellows, heads of state, marching bands, the Boones' kinsmen, war heroes, governors, state and national senators, congressmen, multitudinous preachers, bishops, pastors and many more—including Sunday school teachers—of the masses who revere Kentucky's cherished past.

"We cordially invite all to join us in the pious duty of interring their honored remains."

15

The Skull of Boone Was Handled by the People Present

Mason Brown's presence at the *Daniel Boone*'s arrival at Frankfort's wharf would have been no surprise. Thomas Crittenden, William Boon and Philip Swigert would soon find themselves at Liberty Hall detailing their river trip.

The same morning 173 years later I met Russ Hatter in front of Mary and Mason's home. A policeman slowed as I leaned on my Ram's tailgate slurping coffee from my thermos cap and watching a pickup swerve past a cat chasing a squirrel by the fence in front of a catalpa planted before Mason's dad built Liberty Hall.

"Here comes that cop again checking us out," Russ grinned, waving at the white sedan.

"Next time let's jump Mason's fence and take off," I said, gazing at Crittenden's three-story earth-toned home next door to Liberty Hall. It looked impregnable.

"It's a fortress," Russ said. "Built of rock, brick, logs and clapboarded over." A military home for a military man. Thomas often rounded the corner to Montgomery (now Main) to visit his senatorial father at his sprawling two-story Federal estate built on Aaron Burr's lot.

We cut over westward along Wapping—past U.S. Supreme Court justice Thomas Todd's house (1818), past the Vest-Lindsey home (1798) and past the Rodman-Hewitt house (1817) which borders the Kentucky bending rightwards to the lee of the Browns' estates, bisecting the city in a long, slowly churning *S* curve. Most houses here were once self-contained units, with livery stables, gardens, slave quarters, burial plots.

"These old homes get added on to through the ages," Russ said.

"This was Kentucky's power base. These powerful politicians and attorneys were neighbors walking across the street to talk to each other and eating together," I said.

Englishman John Instone named the street for George III's wharf, Wapping Old Stair—London's fairest walk and a popular pirate hanging-gibbetting venue, offering morality lessons and aromatic insights into tarred-body decomposition. The king's influence has waned and 1936 marked the state's last hanging (and the United States' last public execution), but the city's earliest wharf, Russ thought, was past Wapping and St. Clair's, conjoining near the river.

"Back in the day, you would have gotten off the boat—there was a long road, with huge wide places to land steamboats to load and for passengers," he said. Wagons or carriages lined up for fares, waiting to whisk travelers along crushed stone streets into Frankfort's heart. "Like taxis. After unloading Daniel and Rebecca, they would have come up that way too."

"The way we're going now?" Alerted by a historically induced shiver I moved in closer.

"Swigert, Boon and Crittenden may have brought them the way we're going, up St. Clair and then to the Old Capitol, supposedly." He raised an eyebrow and shrugged.

"Supposedly" is right. Here the trail gets fuzzy as details blur. Tradition says the Boones "lay in state" in the capitol until their funeral on September 13. Lying in state connotes dignity and ceremony—reverential crowds paying respect and filing past looping velvety ropes. President Ronald Reagan lay in state. Senator John McCain lay in state. Premier Margaret Thatcher lay in state. Pope John Paul II lay in state.

Was this the scene in the state house leading to the Boone's reinterment?

John Mason Brown, Mason's son and the one witness to write about it, says the Boones' body parts were kept in the crates they arrived in from Missouri—pine boxes long enough for femurs, wide enough for pelvises and high enough for skulls—until Friday night, September 12, when their bones were uncrated and set in coffins. One doubts that before their burial the two pine boxes were publicly exhibited.

"I still have a most vivid and accurate remembrance of all that occurred," John Mason said. "The bones of Boone were taken from the box and placed in a handsome coffin provided for the reinterment—I was present when it was done." (A graveside witness called the coffins "plain and simple.") Philip Slater Fall, a skull caster, told his grandson the remains "were laid in the Old Capitol...prior to their interment." His words might be taken several ways.

We turned left on St. Clair—named for Arthur St. Clair, responsible for the United States' greatest loss against American Indians—to cross Main (then called Montgomery for Continental army officer Richard Montgomery, martyred by cannon fire at Quebec). Most buildings here were post-1850.

A block later was Broadway, bisected by train tracks. A few steps more led to the Old Capitol's columned portico. Broadway in Mason Brown's day was Market, for Market House—a sizable structure that sat in its middle, hence the street's obvious width. The railroad that's here now came later. Retracing our steps it was plain that Wapping's wharf could empty thousands of visitors from the steamer flotillas jammed at the docks to walking distance of the funeral route. From there it was about two miles to the cemetery up the hill.

GETTING TO FRANKFORT'S HEART by train from the city's east end was complicated and potentially hazardous. Passengers stepped off at the depot on the top of the hill (where Kentucky State University is today) to be shuttled in near the capitol by way of a manually powered system of lifts and transports.

Kentucky had one of the earliest railroads west of the Blue Ridge; the *Daniel Boone*, built 1835, was Lexington's first locomotive. Trains didn't enter Frankfort proper, as the city's challenging topography thwarted their limited horsepower. For the Boones' funeral, hundreds of visitors—maybe more; crowd size was estimated to be up to twenty thousand—came by rail, the stodgy boxcars chugging in and stopping just short of the town's eastern edge.

"You'd get off the train or stagecoach and take a wagon to the incline," Russ said. "The incline would lower you down into the valley, where you'd get another wagon into town."

"Wow. What powered the incline?"

"Pulleys."

"What powered the pulleys?"

"They had slaves and oxen. They had mechanisms they'd devised. Sometimes it would get away from them, and you'd have bad accidents. Abraham Lincoln visited here three times, arriving by train or by steamboat."

This coordinated effort of man and mule power kept dollars churning in Frankfort's economy. Muleskinners and lift operators were tipped.

Concessionaires offered food and drink—a horn of rye bourbon, a refreshing julip, a nip of peach brandy. As the lifts emptied and visitors awaited their turn, way stations allowed one to sit a spell to chat, enjoy a light repast and heed nature's insistent imploring.

"So, is it possible to walk the Boones' processional route?" I asked Russ in his Capitol City Museum office. "You can only replicate parts of it?"

"Yes and no," said Russ. "Maybe to Main and on to the top. Some of it is guesswork."

The nearly twenty thousand attendees trudged almost two miles uphill in stylishly gothic linen and wool mourning attire behind a mile-long, slow-moving entourage. Such a spectacle was rarely seen even for presidents, heads of states or royalty, much less for a trailblazing deer-slayer. Assembling such a cavalcade would have been challenging logistically.

Crowd concerns were enlarged by the Methodist Episcopal Conference in progress downtown. "Downtown" is used here warily, as much of Frankfort's downtown didn't exist then. Finding lodging, unless one had mailed in a reservation—and pulling that off seems incomprehensible—would not have been easy. And finding a public bathroom, sanitary or otherwise? Forget it.

"These two events," as one of the city's earliest historians, Lewis Johnson, makes clear, "filled every house in the city, both public and private.…All the boats which were in the Kentucky River trade were crowded to their utmost limit, and…the railroads and stage coaches from the interior brought thousands of people to the city." It must have been quite a weekend.

"So, how they'd get…" I went blank, completely baffled.

"See, the parade is going to have a bunch of people involved," Russ cut in. "It's staged, timed. They've got the people up Wapping, down Washington and St. Clair, crammed in every nook and cranny. And military bands. Old guys in coaches. Preachers and teachers."

"Right. Thousands packed the streets—hard to believe. Where do you put all these people?"

"Anywhere, everywhere—side streets, alcoves, corridors, alleys."

"The parade masters staggered how groups fell in behind the processional. You pass a street—this group falls in. Another street, that group falls in."

Saturday morning's directions from Wapping to the burial ground on the hill, published in the *Commonwealth* and maybe in some of the city's other three or four newspapers, seemed straightforward. Likely, it worked better on paper.

At 10 o'clock the 1st Gun-Divisions will form.
At 10½ o'clock, the 2nd Gun-Procession will move off.
Each Division taking its position in line per marginal numbers, on the march: and pass down Wapping, thence Washington to Main and out Main to the place of internment.

FRIDAY NIGHT, SEPTEMBER 12, 1845.

The night before the funeral the Boones' boxes were in the capitol built fifteen years before. Designed by Gideon Shyrock for $85,000, its Neo-Grecian architecture elevated classical sublimity in state houses nationwide. A landmark since the current capitol's opening in 1910, the Old State House was absorbed by the Kentucky Historical Society, which curates the Thomas D. Clark Center for Kentucky History and Kentucky's Military History Museum.

Seven men and an eight-year-old boy gathered near two empty coffins layered with shavings. Dr. Lewis Sneed unboxed the brown bones, arranging them in the cists from the skulls downward. "It was my first sight of a skeleton," John Mason Brown told Lyman C. Draper.

His father passed Dan's skull to William Boon, Philip Swigert, A.G. Carrack and Robert Carmichael. After "its peculiarities were commented on," the judge put the cranium in little John's hands so that he could say he "had lifted it" before duplicates were made.

Molding Boone's skull made sense considering phrenology's popularity—the fad sparked interest in the heads of the rich, famous and infamous. Skull bumps supposedly gave clues into aptitude and behavior, emotions and reasoning capability. Intellectuals like Horace Greely and Reverend Henry Ward Beecher embraced the faux science, as did Queen Victoria and, apparently, Mason Brown and those assembled.

Two skilled casters—Henry C. Davis and Philip Slater Fall, an English ex-Baptist preacher turned Alexander Campbell acolyte—set about duplicating Boone's cranial pate in plaster of Paris, his lower jaw residing in Missouri with Harvey Griswold. Fall, at the behest of Mason Brown, molded two or three skulls for him and kept one for himself.

Dr. Robert Peter, an English-born doctor at Transylvania College, had "sent Mr. Henry Davis…to obtain the mold." Davis was an understudy of Kentucky's famous sculptor Joel T. Hart—then in Florence, Italy, where he died (and exhumed for reburial in Frankfort's necropolis). Brown the younger, having a "distinct memory of the taking of the casts," watched Davis "pour wax until a mold was formed and then made two plaster casts therefrom."

Peter, on receiving his plaster head that Mason Brown "certified as to its correctness," cast from it another one or two Boone skulls, sending one to Philadelphia to famed phrenologists the Fowler brothers, who, after "reading the character" of the skull, "published it in *Phrenological Journal*." Near the end of his productive life, Dr. Peter's other skull cast went to author and historian George W. Ranck, who donated it to Louisville's Filson Historical Society.

John Mason Brown, son of Mason Brown. *Bob Lanham; Liberty Hall Historic Site Collections.*

Mason Brown, who likewise had another Boone plaster skull or two duplicated from Fall's replica, loaned phrenologist John G. Tompkins a skull of Dan's for analysis. Ten years later he mailed another to the Smithsonian, where it burned up in a fire. Another one stayed with his son, John Mason Brown, who had an additional "three or four copies cast," mailing one to Draper at Wisconsin's State Historical Society, who could "rely upon it that it is perfectly genuine." Draper's cast crumbled and was discarded. Like Dr. Robert Peter, young Brown mailed yet another Boone skull cast to the Fowlers' phrenological services.

Philip Slater Fall donated his Boone head to the Kentucky Historical Society in about 1880—its provenance assured by his grandson Philip Fall Taylor's memo published September 1907 in the society's *Register*, that "these facts were stated to me by Rev. Mr. Fall, who was my grandfather…to verify the authenticity of the plaster cast now in the Historical collection."

And of John G. Tompkins "reading" of Mason Brown's Boone plaster skull cast?

Tompkins, back in his lab, scrutinized the mortar pate, his fingers trailing from the nape to the occipital bun to the brow. He felt of its bumps and dents. He rubbed the swelled mastoid behind the ear, feeling its superior and posterior borders. He examined its sutures, fitting calipers on the cranium fore and aft, side to side, likely gazing at a mail-order human head chart and consulting Lorenzo Fowler's *Illustrated Self-Instructor in Phrenology and Physiology*.

On February 9, 1846, the *Frankfort Constitution* published his report in a sellout edition. "Boone was a man of great physical powers…untiring in his energies. He could jump farther and higher, and run faster than almost anyone else." He was "always alert, was never to be taken by surprise." If asleep, "the faintest of sounds 'would instantly arouse him.' His instincts predisposed him to be 'fond of traveling. He could not be lost in the woods.'"

Tompkins's studied conclusions did not disappoint: "Such is the character which I deduce from his head. Was it his real character!"

Frankfort's town drunk might have guessed as much, but no matter, the following day, September 13, 1845, would mark the city's memorializing of Daniel and Rebecca Boone and the inauguration of the city's garden cemetery, brainchild of Mason Brown. Events began early in the capital city, which was already congested by the huge crowd.

And still they came.

16

The Most August Funeral Solemnity Ever Observed in Kentucky

Saturday, September 13, 1845: First light portending of bad weather.

And so they came by water, by land, by horse, by iron horse and on foot without shoes, like the pauper Ellison Williamson, Daniel Boone's seventy-eight-year-old Kentucky huckleberry who fought Simon Girty at Bryan's Station—now so impoverished that he walked barefoot the sixty miles from Bank Lick in Kenton County to Frankfort.

Nearly every state in the Union was represented and every county in the Commonwealth. A bustling human sea nearly twenty thousand strong flooded Frankfort, filling inns, homes and taverns.

Side-wheelers plowing the Kentucky marked twain amidst the shipman's calls: "Stop the starboard! Stop the lapboard!" Paddleboat captains hitched their wheezing leviathans to the cleats and heaved gangplanks for somberly dressed men and women to stroll to the waiting hacks and carriages. Porters stowed their small hide-bound wooden chests and the faddish carpetbags that train and steamboat travel brought into being and old, well-oiled leather portmanteaus with patinaed brass buckles.

It was no different east of the city on the hill. Locals stared at the ever-arriving hordes disembarking from stagecoaches along the Lexington-Frankfort turnpike swelling with visitors from the interior and the hundreds spilling from the chugging, soot-belching locomotives.

And so the multitude came. Never again would any event be so replicated in the commonwealth's capital city. Businesses remained closed.

The first signal gun sounded at ten o'clock southwest of the capitol.

Luminaires of group numbers 1 to 9 fell in sequentially, as in the Boone procession order in the *Commonwealth* and the *Kentucky Yeoman*, cramming along Wapping and Buffalo Alley ahead of number 10's clergy and Methodist Episcopal Conference members at the Presbyterian church. Numbers 11 through 15, richly attired Masons and Independent Order of Odd Fellows, fire officials, Sunday school marms and teachers packed into Pettycoat Alley and Catfish Alley. Numbers 16 and 17—spit-and-polish militias—backed into St. Clair near the Ladies and Gentlemen on Foot (numbers 18 and 19) in Washington's egresses. Numbers 20 and 21, "Strangers and Citizens in Carriages" and "Strangers and Citizens on Horseback," somehow found room "on adjoining side streets."

Remarkably, riding with the pioneers of Boonesborough and Harrods's Town were two elderly Black gentlemen—"the first whoever trod the soil of Kentucky, and his steps were sustained another, also of African descent." One of them was Jack Hart, who helped build Boonesborough, survived its siege and fought at the Battle of Blue Licks. Hart's wife was with him. The other Black men may have been Monk Estill's kin from Montgomery County.

Thirty minutes later the second signal gun fired.

Marshal A.W. Dudley shouted to his marshals guiding the twenty-one ranks amid clattering horses, transports and spectators and under the bright flags and banners snapping in the quickening wind. Scott County processional marshal general John T. Pratt fixed his sash and badge and took the van. The band behind him readied for the stately "Dead March."

Four white horses, wreathed in hemlock, cedar boughs and wildflowers, tugged at the hearse's traces. Before the Boones' coffins marched eight militia corps, resplendent in blues, reds and creams with firelocks shouldered, boots incessantly thudding and hat plumes nodding. The thirteen pallbearers in the open carriages wheeling alongside the hearse were a venerable lot of aged veterans of the British and Indians wars and settlers and hunters.

Shelby Countian woodsman Bland Ballard's coach was part of contingent "No. 1." Other 1812 vets included Robert McAfee, who served in the legislature like Ballard. Everyone recognized William Linville Boon, who'd done so much for the Frankfort Cemetery Company to help make this grand event happen.

Beside him rode Richard Mentor Johnson, whose pedigree was no less distinguished. His parents survived Bryan Station's siege. He had served in the U.S. House of Representatives and was wounded at the Thames but

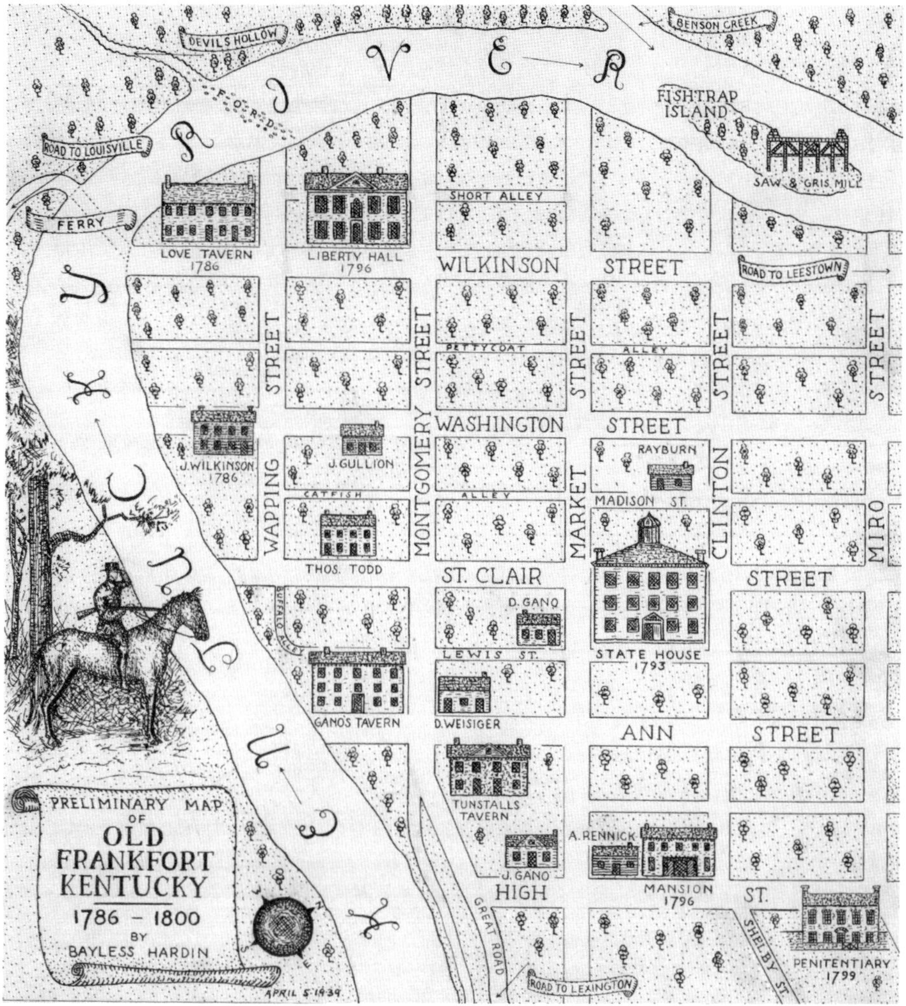

Bayless Hardin Map of Old Frankfort. *Kentucky Historical Society*.

survived—barely. His boast that he slew Tecumseh, the great Shawnee leader, ushered this son of Fayette County in as vice president to Martin Van Buren.

A year older, his nephew Cave represented Boone County. He arrived at Boonesborough in 1779 to join his brother Robert at Bryan's, their selfless valor aiding Colonel Benjamin Logan's service with George Rogers Clark's forces in Illinois against George III's redcoats. "I have all my life been a farmer.…I have served my day and generation," he said, modestly leaving out his roles as militia colonel, justice of the peace and sheriff.

Revolutionary War hero Harry Lee rode for Mason County—he of the lineage of "Lighthorse" Lee and kin to the famous brothers Willis and Hancock, who founded Leestown. Patrick Henry appointed Lee militia captain; by statehood Governor Isaac Shelby commissioned him lieutenant-colonel and then brigadier general. A surveyor and judge, and Northwest Territory soldier, General Lee owned more than one thousand acres of rolling bluegrass.

Colonel Humphrey Jones, from Madison County, also secured wide, fertile veldts of bluegrass, bequeathing his acreage to three of his sons but giving none to his fourth, Robert, who was a fervent abolitionist disciple of Reverent Josiah Gregg Fee. Fee's sermons of racial equality and interracial communities provoked riots and gunshots.

So many names, so many faces—the immense crowd aligning the designated routes, now splitting down the other avenues and opening from Washington to Main, could scarce take them in. "It seemed as if the valley of Frankfort," reported one who was there, "could scarcely afford the space to form them into line, and indeed this was only effected by the commencing at the extreme edge verge of the city, throwing and doubling the files into close order...occupying several streets in the march."

Then there were the statesmen, Governor William Owsley ushering in his political peers, friends and foes alike; all party hatchets were laid aside on this momentous day. In his overcoat draped over his vest, its buttons straining, came Charles Slaughter Morehead, a bull walrus of a man; his girth was as impressive as his legal prowess and brilliance before the bar. Destined to be a pro-South governor and House speaker, he brooked no fools in the political arena.

Assistant Secretary of State Colonel Preston Samuel Loughborough's inclination toward corpulence did not lessen his thoughtful eyes, high cheekbones and Roman nose; his ruffled hair accentuated his good looks. Walking along, he and his wife, Nancy, celebrated their anniversary, not knowing that next year he'd walk Nancy's death route and then take his own life.

Leslie Combs was dapper and handsome, slender in build, and his straight hair defined with a left part. Reserved but approachable despite his Unionist stance, he was as civil to the Southern stalwart Morehead as he was in 1812 to the Brits who wounded him and took him hostage, circumstances inuring him to the roiling politics he faced as House speaker.

The craggy-faced brick mason Thomas Metcalf radiated his nickname, "Stone Hammer." A captain in the 1812 War, his gray, mohawk-like

Frankfort Main Street, circa 1880, by Paul Sawyier. *Gene Burch; Capital City Museum.*

comb was heightened by his eagle glare and black cravat, weskit, coat and stiff white shirt, with his gold-topped ebony cane clutched near. In stern looks, subsistence stature and spare policies he resembled Andrew Jackson, down for the common man's struggle in opposing slavery restraints and banks, yet he backed the Whigs as a U.S. senator after serving as Kentucky's governor.

Behind Mason and Orlando Brown and the Swigerts, Thomas Crittenden and the rest of the Frankfort Cemetery Company, representatives of the town's clergy followed the entourage to Main as the avenue broadened near John Hampton's tavern where the street rose. The darkening sky's droplets, spurred by thunder and a quickening wind, shrouded the trek in apt melancholy ambience that heightened the silence laced by the "Dead March" as "the grand procession moved solemnly toward the cemetery."

Looking back from here on "the grand procession," I told Russ Hatter, the view would have been awe-inspiring—a veritable who's who of Kentuckians.

Russ nodded, his eyes on the traffic. "This town was loaded with influential people who were very strong in the early Kentucky days. After the Civil War, it's over. Bye, bye."

Past Main and High (which General James Wilkinson spelled "Heighe" for his mother's maiden name) across from the Hampton House, the cortege stepping behind the whipping banners, a sash-girded marshal in each segment's van, ascended in grandeur under the charcoal sky. On they came.

So, too, did we, though lacking in grandeur passing the old arsenal, dodging noon's rush and panhandlers, bikers and dog walkers along Highway 60. Were we still on the route?

Sort of, Russ said, pretty close to it.

Reverend William B. Landrum, a Methodist Episcopal Conference envoy, said any "description would only mar the beauty of this array." Deflating its splendor "midway up the pike" on the prison rooftops were uniformed emaciated inmates—gaunt from the state's brutal leasing system and malnourished and ravaged by scurvy and pneumonia—"looking in awful silence upon the moving masses; the sorrowful exclamation of everyone was, 'The contrast!, Oh, the awful contrast!'"

The elongated phalanx's vanguard coiled right, compressing between the cemetery's gates toward Hunter's Garden—renamed Boone's Grove—to widen on its egress. Guards kept riders out, checked carriage permits, shooed folks off the plantings and warned everyone, as a light rain began to fall, to stay on the site's three roads. Then there were the first peals of thunder.

"Was the cemetery's entrance the same?" I asked. Our day was bright and sunny and hot. My allergies kicked in as I dripped sweat and hacked phlegm.

"No. The entrance was not at Glenn Creek like today," Russ said. "You'd go a short distance up the hill and turn right and go through the woods and trees to Hunter's Garden to the Boones' graves. Back then it was like a little forest. That was part of the cemetery's beauty."

"There was a back road at the base of the hill near the river," I said.

"It's long gone now. You can kind of see a few remnants of it."

One writer beholding the glen they'd entered, dotted by soaring hickories and oaks, likened the experience to William Cullen Bryant's evocative ode *A Forest Hymn*. The paean's opening line reads, "The groves were God's first temple."

Strong winds buffeted the murky sky over the river. Thunder boomed off the clifftop by the open graves, the cists still on the hearse as the horses stamped anxiously. The late morning cooled. Prayers beseeched the heavens to hold back the rains, portending worse with each gust parting the leaves above thousands ascending the sylvan corridor.

Near the top, leftwards, the tight, long mass loosened to spread into a natural amphitheater "hollowed out as a bowl by the hand of nature," its pastoral sublimity enhanced by horticulturalist Robert Carmichael's plantings. Somehow, it all fit—even the gloomy weather, its somber rumblings challenged and tamed by the "soul-solemnizing of the music" as the five speakers took their places "for the last religious service to the memory of Boone."

Abner Goodell, pastor of Frankfort's Baptist church, was first. The forty-year-old Vermonter's rhetoric was "clear, practical, and pungent," and he was a virtuoso of hymnody—his original acapella spirituals taught by "lining." So it was done here, Goodell "lining" the hymn he'd composed just for this day which no one thought to record.

A chorus no less than ten thousand strong lined in time to his modal call-and-response dirge, with him half-singing, half-chanting his lyric's first line—as in "amazing grace how sweet the sound," the mighty choir echoing "amazing grace how sweet the sound," then the second line, the third and on and on until the last swelling wall-of-sound refrain filled the glen.

Such a Jericho-esque shout of human voices was bone-chillingly powerful. Men wept.

Bishop Joshua Soule, sixty-four, rose to pray. Tall, robustly handsome and garbed in collared clerical raiment, Maine's gracefully aged "Boy Preacher" and presider over the Methodist Episcopal Convention led "one of the most appropriate and able prayers ever uttered by man," said Reverend William Landrum, who wished it "stereotyped in every heart."

The honorable U.S. senator John J. Crittenden, whose son Tom helped fetch the Boones, took the stage. A lean, imposing man of medium build bearing a deeply lined visage, he was a military man's military man, a politician's politician, an orator's orator. His forty-minute discourse on Boone's "fame and deeds" was "interrupted by the prospect of rain and high winds," yet "by the spells of his magic eloquence…he threw around his subject all the fascinations of his peerless fancy and unrivaled oratory," leaving his listeners transfixed.

Leading the last prayer was handsome, wavy-haired Reverend John Joseph Bullock, thirty-three, degreed from Centre College and Princeton, minister for the Presbyterian church. Philip Slater Fall, who cast Daniel's skull in plaster the night before, closed the memorial, his polished English accent coloring his benediction. The ex-Baptist was now a Christian church preacher.

The horde eased up the draw to the stone-lined cairn, where "the remains of the noble Western pioneer and his wife, encased in neat and plain coffins, were lowered into their resting places, side by side." The pallbearers shoveled in dirt and stepped back to let the masses file by, each tossing a handful, until the graves were filled. The parade about-faced, military units keeping to the right as "all returned to the city, glad they had taken part....All have united to do him honor, and generation after generation will make pilgrimages to his tomb."

Their "publicity mission accomplished," the following October the *Commonwealth* announced the FCC's sale of cemetery lots. But other than some boards slammed together for benches, the Boones' grave remained unmarked.

Seventeen years later people were still asking: where was their tomb?

17

Not Withstanding All of Kentucky's Fine Promises, Nothing More Was Done

Thus the Frankfort Cemetery was established with the reburial of the remains of Daniel and Rebecca Boone," reads an 1845 account from the *Commonwealth*. The Boones' graves lacked any hint of permanent markers. (One account Lyman Draper alludes to observes there being by the graves a huge sycamore log sawn with two hewn seats.)

"There lies, unmarked by any slab or monumental inscription, the most remarkable man of his day, by the side of her who shared many of his toils and hardships," decried an editorial in the *Yeoman* three years later; the newspaper was willing to donate advertising space to help raise funds for a fitting Boone memorial. Nothing came of it.

No matter—plots were selling, slowly. Sightseers came daily asking the way to the Boones' graves as the FCC erected monuments and shrines and embarked on expansion.

Robert Carmichael's landscaping was coming along. The grounds were filling in and one hundred acres were added, with terracing and banked carriage lanes fringed by imported trees, manicured hedges and exotic shrubbery hemming its winding, shaded wood and stone paths. Willows eased their boughs to the earth as if in prayer. Canelands edged the walnut fence rows. Carmichael never could keep the pond filled.

On February 11, 1849, Orlando Brown's Boone Monument Assembly tried to gin up aid by collecting "voluntary subscriptions and donations" to beautify the Boones' "final resting place and manifest to the world the respect and gratitude of the descendants of the pioneers of Kentucky, to those who first braved the perils of the dark and bloody ground."

Any sign of respect and gratitude had not occurred by 1855, when Lilian Foster rode a rail in less than "telegraphic speed" to Frankfort, "nestled in the midst of wild and romantic scenery." She roamed the capitol, awed by Gideon Shyrock's suspended staircase that the designer said would collapse if its keystone moved a hairsbreadth. In the chamber she gazed at portraits of George Washington, the Marquis de Layfette and William Henry Harrison.

At the "city of silent inmates," past the "broad avenues" lined with "handsome forest trees," she paused by the state's military tribute to "those who have fallen in defense of the country." The towering marble spire dwarfed the Boones' humble plot nearby, an irony not lost on Foster who realized what everyone knew: Rebecca and Daniel were the cemetery's lure.

Their graves, "pillowed...under the shadow of two fine sycamores," were marked by "a clump of cane" and a "semicircle of rough rocks and stumps promiscuously thrown together" with boards to sit on. Maybe the spare memorial was "appropriate," she wrote, struggling to put a polite face on the FCC's neglect, "as Boone was one whoever flew before civilization."

Still, "there should be some memorial erected by which a stranger would recognize his resting place." Frankfort had forsaken what thousands came to pay homage to. "When you visit other cities and wish to go out for a stroll... you are taken to a park, but in Frankfort you are escorted to the cemetery." And it was the Boones who drew the crowds.

In 1860 John Warner Barber and Henry Howe Jr., in *Our Whole Country*, told of the land they crossed, Howe writing and Barber illustrating one of the nation's first travelogues—think William Least Heat-Moon's *Blue Highways* before any highways. When the Connecticut Yankees arrived at the Boone site, nothing had changed since Foster's visit. "The graves of Boone and his wife are without monument save the forest scene by which they are surrounded. The spot where they were interred is at the foot of the two large trees, around which is a simple board seat."

A couple in Barber's sketch gaze at the river as a lone figure sits watching—it's Barber's selfie, his whimsical signature touch. The amorphous floristic thatch in front bookended by tombstones shows this to be a burial site.

Kentucky's forgotten $10,000 tribute to America's most storied frontier couple may as well have been cobbled from scrap snatched from the town dump. For a legendary huntsman said to flee before civilization, in death Daniel Boone was blazing a profitable new kind of trail and ushering into Frankfort a novel American concept: tourism.

Nearing 1859's end, Samuel Haycraft, the honorable senator from Hardin County, in a speech of "almost matchless beauty, eloquence and patriotism," sponsored "AN ACT authorizing the erection of a Monument over the graves of Daniel Boone and wife." In a day when brilliant elocutionists abounded, and especially so in Kentucky whose native sons spoke music, the bearded and poised Haycraft pushed the rhetorical art higher, trained as he was as a gospel preacher and deacon in the Severns Valley Baptist Church.

At Senator Haycraft's behest, the legislature decreed that: 1) The governor would "cause to be erected" on the Boone's graves "a durable monument… as may appropriately" convey their posterity for all generations and 2) the governor had authority to raise funds privately and as needed from the state's treasury "not to exceed two thousand dollars."

Governor Beriah Magoffin signed the bill on March 2, 1860, tacking on an addendum for ninety dollars to inter Ellison Williamson, the destitute woodsman who walked to Boone's funeral barefoot, beside his old friend—the man's dying request. His body arrived by rail.

Sam Haycraft died eighteen years later and was interred in Elizabethtown. Inscribed on his headstone is "Sponsor of the State Monument to Daniel Boone." He lived to see the shrine's erection. And, its ruination.

The twenty-foot obelisk that Irish sculptor John Haly fashioned, with marble porticos carved by sculptor Robert E. Launitz, depicted the Boones' world: Daniel, the fur-capped hunter in war; Daniel in repose; Rebecca milking a cow, symbolizing domesticity; Daniel near death, telling a Black youth how to bury him (which occurred during an upper Missouri hunt with Derry Coburn, Dan Morgan Boone's slave, when Boone Sr. was severely ill).

Muleskinners wagonned the monument to the graves and tore down the bench, pulling in heavy block-and-tackle hung with thick hempen ropes. Workers dug up the Boones, attracting an onlooker who left a clinician's spin on the spectacle. "The gravedigger shoveled up ribs, tibias, and fibulas, bits of rotten wood, vertebra, cervical, dorsal, and lumbar along with the fossa innominate."

The spectator grabbed a "bit of the coffin" flung from the spade and "one of the lumbar vertebrae." The erstwhile body snatcher soon regretted his bold move; having a chunk of the hunter's "moldy backbone" provoked dreams of Daniel "appearing at his bedside" demanding back his piece of spinal column for the resurrection. Reburying the relic ended the wraith-like hauntings.

By 1862 Daniel and Rebecca Boone's monument was up in time for its virtual demolition during the Civil War's occupation of the capital city.

THE 1860 ELECTION THAT ushered in Abraham Lincoln divided the Bluegrass as Kentuckians grappled with sectional loyalties. John Bell, a constitutional unionist, carried the state as secession talk overrode John J. Crittenden's voice of compromise. With sons on both sides of the issue, the senator's own house was as divided as the nation. In the Union's fifteen states, it was a brother war.

Lincoln's declaring that to lose his native state was "to lose the whole game" was blunted by Governor Beriah Magoffin's vow that he'd invade the South and, by Charles Morehead's public railings against Lincoln's presidency, which landed him in prison. He fled the country after release, returning after the war to his Mississippi plantation that survived it.

More than one hundred thousand Kentuckians donned Yankee blue. Less than forty thousand wore Rebel gray. After the commonwealth's general assembly declared it a Union state, Confederates set up power at Bowling Green, governed by George Johnson (who'd die at Shiloh).

By 1862 John Hunt Morgan convinced Jeff Davis to step up his Kentucky warring. The CSA skirmished in Barbourville and seized the day at Richmond—victory. Rebels grabbed Lexington and Frankfort that September. Union sympathizers fled to Louisville. Johnny Reb celebrated by inaugurating the newly elected Rebel governor.

Union men returned to the capital to run the Johnnys out and then came bloody Perryville—fifty-six miles from Frankfort—on October 8, 1862, finalizing General Braxton Braggs's bluegrass foray with a CSA tactical victory but an ensuing retreat. Kentucky was besieged by bushwhackers from the North and South, like Jesse James's gang and William Quantrill's boys. Hostiles occupied the capital city and vandalized the Boone monument for souvenirs, chipping out its incised porticos and knocking pieces from its base.

ONE COULD NOT MISS seeing Frankfort's postwar scars. Rolling caissons delivered flag-draped coffins to its "City of the Dead."

C.C. Fulton, writer for Baltimore's *American*, toured the necropolis's "imposing monuments" to "distinguished Kentuckians," a site "of more than ordinary elegance and good taste," and marveled at Richard M. Johnson's emblem of him "in the act of shooting Tecumseh." A walk beyond the veteran's spire to the Boone's monolith, once "a beautiful and chaste affair," dismayed him—vandals had "defaced the fine bas reliefs in their greed for mementos."

Defaced Boone monument, Frankfort Cemetery, circa 1900. *Kentucky Historical Society.*

A *Chicago Times* reporter assured readers that it was worth a trip southward "to spend a day in the beautiful cemetery," where "the wild, natural beauty" had been preserved." But alas!, its "most melancholy feature" was its most famous one, the shabby Boone shrine. "Wretches have sadly marred its beauty." In its blemished marble panels Rebecca milked a hornless cow suspended in midair, the Black youth's straw hat was smashed, the Indian's upraised tomahawk and Dan's rifle were gone and a vandal had chiseled out "half the rifle" in the deer slayer scene.

The marring "has been so frequent," reported the *Earlington Bee*, that "little is left of the work of the artist." Most blamed the "Union soldiers," saying that since the Yankees left, "the monument has not been touched." The grave once inspiring veneration now animated "anger and disgust at the lack of decency…by heartless scoundrels." Citizens issued pleas to Pennsylvania, North Carolina, Kentucky and Missouri—the Boones' home states—for funds to right this wrong against the one "who blazed the trail toward the Westward."

Christian County train engineer on the Louisville and Nashville line Warner Campbell ran for office promising to make it a "felony to deface" the shrine. With the Spence Bill passing six years later, the *Bourbon News* reported on February 16, 1906, that Kentucky's general assembly re-created the late Orlando Brown's Boone Monument Commission and set aside $2,000 toward the monolith's refurbishing, matched by private donations. The Rebecca Bryan Boone chapter of the Daughters of the American Revolution donated $500 more.

Cemetery official Henry Craik hired Cincinnati sculptor Leopold Fettweiss to cast what was left of the old plates in plaster to duplicate them. After immersing himself in Boone's world—gazing upon his portraits, studying his life, meditating on the battered cenotaph—Fettwiess incised new panels. Workers dismantling the shrine carted it onto Louisville-bound locomotive flatbeds for redressing.

Episcopal Bishop reverend C.C. Penick led the opening prayer on Saturday, May 26, 1910, at 2:30 p.m., when the shrine returned, the commemoration hosted by the DAR's Rebecca Bryan Boone chapter. After "America the Beautiful," Judge H.V. McChesney read Theodore O'Hara's "The Old Pioneer." O'Hara, buried nearby, walked with Boone's cortege that blustery September 13, 1845, the spectacle inspiring the pale, top-hatted man to pen his paean:

A dirge for the brave old pioneer!
Knight-errant of the wood!
Calmly beneath the green sod here
He rests from field and flood
The war-whoop and the panther's screams
No more his soul shall rouse,
For well the aged hunter dreams
Beside his good old spouse.

Then there were more speeches, poems, presentations and honors before Fannie Belle Bryan, a Bryan descendant, unveiled the restored shrine. The state's anthem, "My Old Kentucky Home," marked the ceremony's end. Workers placed an iron fence around the monolith.

Daniel and Rebecca Boone's monument, Frankfort, Kentucky. *Bob Lanham.*

Kentucky's seventy years of neglect did not go unseen west of the Mississippi. Missourians, roused by Rebecca's death centennial in 1913, two years later unveiled their DAR tribute—a large stone on the Boones' graves fitted with a bronze plaque of Dan in a coonskin cap—to a crowd of two thousand, paralleling in miniature Frankfort's 1845 memorial service.

After a prayer, Judge Huckriede "spoke of what Boone had been to the state and bewailed that his remains had been allowed to be removed." Schoolchildren sang "America." Boone descendant Jesse P. Crump unveiled the Boones' fifth gravestone in under a century—its epitaph getting wrong the couple's days of birth, their birth years and Dan's birth county. Kinfolk like George Chester Bryan came to hear Robert Louis Stevenson's "Requiem" and Lord Bryon's "General Boone, Backwoods Man of Kentucky." As the sun set, the band played "God Be with You."

The Boones at last had a real Missouri marker. David Gardyne had tried before, but Dr. Sylvanus Griswold said no, not "until the people of Kentucky carry out the agreement they made with my father." George Chester Bryan deemed some of these earlier efforts as schemes by publicity seekers "to raise money on the patriotism and loyalty of Boone's descendants" and refused to lend his name or support to them.

STRANGE RUMORS WERE GROWING about Daniel Boone's removal, snickering tales egged on by the embittered Dr. Griswold, who hinted of a "lost grave," bolstering his bizarre tale with a cryptic sketch delineating, supposedly, the Boones' true burials. Other mystics and storytellers began getting their names in print and soliciting funds.

In 1908 Nathanial Gardyne, Charles W. Thompson, Benedict Thoroughman, J.W. Tuttle and Reverend R.E. McQuie launched an "inquest" about Boone's exhumation. On viewing the graveyard and asking locals about Boone's corpse, Marthasville's forensic sleuths concluded that Frankfort's officials "took the wrong body and that Boone lies where he originally was buried." The Kentuckians, "being strangers," bypassed Dan, "there being no tombstone to mark the grave," read the *Mexico Weekly Ledger*, and boxed up Rebecca and "a stranger…as Boone and wife were not buried side by side." In the report, FCC envoys Thomas Crittenden, William Boon and Philip Swigert become "John J. Crittenden, William Boone, and one McSwaggert."

Back in Louisville's Filson Historical Society, Colonel Rueben Durrett, Kentucky's distinguished historian, called the Missourians' theory "incredulous and baseless" and unworthy "of serious consideration." He

DAR 1915 Boone monument in David Bryan Cemetery. In 2008, the stone was vandalized. The bronze was removed and later replaced by a black marble marker. *Historic Daniel Boone Home.*

knocked the tale "into a cocked hat" with contrary evidence, one interviewer said, that "would have convinced Reverend McQuie himself" that such tales about Daniel's remains were "absolute rot."

Unease east and west of the Mississippi grew as the mystery mutated and took form and sprouted legs enough to develop its own warped hermeneutical apologia that swerved into low-simmering, racially toned ridicule indelicately known as the "Negro Story."

18

The Mortal Part of the Old Pioneer Still Sleeps in Missouri Soil

William S. Bryan was born in Warren County in 1846 and was buried ninety-four years later in Franklin County. A self-made writer and publisher, his newspaper was the first to print in color. He edited children's books and history and science compendiums. Aided by Robert Rose, in 1876 he coauthored *Pioneer Families of Missouri*, which became the authoritative chronicle of the Femme Osage's past until the release of Louis Houck's *A History of Missouri* in1908.

Kin to the Boones via Rebecca's line, Bryan wrote on the hunter's life and become a popular Boone lecturer—one of the first. His knowledge came from his father, Elijah, who was twenty-one when his Uncle Dan died. William's lineage gave him credibility and folks accepted his word as gospel. Though his heart was in the right place, his "facts" at times were not, as in his spin on the Boones' exhumation.

"Bryan's descriptions of Daniel and Rebecca in their graves started…a suspicion of a mistake in the disinterring," argues Missourian Ralph Gregory. "Many of the relatives and admirers of Boone were unhappy about the bodies…being moved." In Bryan's reports, some of them saw hints of an alternative explanation.

In *Pioneer Families,* he said that "Mrs. Boone's coffin was found to be perfectly sound, and the workman had but little difficulty removing it; but Colonel Boone's coffin was entirely decayed, and the remains had to be picked out of the dirt by which they were surrounded. One or two of the smaller bones were found afterward, and kept by Griswold as relics."

He embellished his tale thirty-four years later for the *Missouri Historical Review.* "Both the cherry-wood coffin and the body of Boone had entirely decayed, so that the mortal part of the pioneer still sleeps in Missouri soil. Only a few partly decayed bones were taken to Kentucky. Mrs. Boone's coffin…was still sound and whole."

William S. Bryan never saw *any* of this. He hadn't been born. The event of sixty-five years past that he's conjuring occurred at dusk under heavily-canopied trees, a sinking sun and rising moon with three slipshod gravediggers surrounded by a gawking horde in varying stages of sobriety.

Bryan believed the Boones had been moved. He never doubted it but his telling of their unearthed coffins lent to the affair a tinge that something was amiss, an enigma of something not right, birthing a glut of displaced body theories voiced by those with mixed agendas and media access. "Bryan's words," says Gregory, "stimulated some historians and descendants to believe a mistake had been made in digging up Boone. People began looking elsewhere in Missouri for Boone's body."

And look they did, their exploits making headlines. Soon others came forward to tell their stories to the press.

LIKE JOHN S. JONES of Mexico, Missouri, who in 1911 got lots of ink in the *Mexico Evening Leader* and the *Warrenton Banner* to muse on Dan's earthly whereabouts. "There is doubt whether it was Col. Boone's body; it might have been someone else," he told an interviewer, lacing his narrative with facts and flawed excerpts from elsewhere and with snippets from *Pioneer Families.*

Born in Marthasville, Jones was Daniel's great-grandson. His father, Dr. John Jones, was Daniel's physician. His mother was Minerva Callaway, daughter of Flanders and Jemima Boone Callaway. Jones thought Dan was buried by Rebecca but believed their graves at first had no markers—"No stone was erected for many years after the bodies were buried. For sixteen years his body had lain in the old Bryan Cemetery…unmarked." If the Boones' graves were barren from 1820 until 1836, then the tombstones John Wyatt cut and inscribed likely were wrongly set, Jones contended.

Jones depicts Susannah Bryan Shobe, who helped Wyatt set the stones, as a very confused girl. After showing him about her father's cemetery, Susie, says Jones, "after deliberating for some time," finally points to two unmarked graves, saying, "'I believe grandmother and grandfather are buried here.'"

An alternate version adds that the "trees and weeds had grown up thick in the cemetery and there were many graves." Yet another spin inserts dialogue, with Susie saying, "I believe these are grandpa's and grandma's graves, but I am not certain." Thus, Jones concluded, "Whether Susan Bryan had caused the stone to be erected at the head of Col. Boone's grave…is a matter of conjecture."

None of this is true.

From the beginning the Boones' burial sites had head- and toe-stones, monogramed with their initials and cut by Tarleton Goe, commissioned by Daniel himself. Mrs. Shobe, in her thirties, was very familiar with the boneyard two hundred yards from where she was born and raised. As a teen, likely she went to Dan's funeral and burial. She'd just interred her mother, her husband, Archibald, and their child. Soon she'd lay her father to rest by her mother at the foot of the Boones' graves. She knew where everyone important to her was—including Rebecca and Daniel.

Jones and his interviewer log an impressive array of blunders: 1) He names David Bryan as "Davis" Bryan; 2) he says Daniel's 1836 headstone bore his initials, not his full name; 3) he says the exhumation was in 1848, though it was in 1845; 4) his interviewer cites Jones's age as eighty-eight. Jones was eighty-three.

Jones misidentifies Kentucky's emissaries; Crittenden, Boon and Swigert become "John C. Rittenden and Col. Beckham." According to Jones, how do these officials find the graves? "A mulatto Negro slave," he said, "was sent out to show the Kentuckians where Col. Boone and his wife were buried."

Mulatto. Negro. Slave. Let that bit of innuendo sink in.

In truth, Marion McKinney, of Warren County, escorted them to the cemetery less than a mile from Harvey Griswold's home. One suspects Jones (or his amanuensis) lobbed this racialized nugget to sully their mission. They were not the only purveyors of such convoluted Boone burial mythology. Six years later came another, fitted with a second racially infused twist that became known as "the Negro Story."

ON JANUARY 4, 1917, Mexico, Missouri's *Weekly Intelligencer* ran David Gardyne's letter to Jesse P. Crump, a Kansas City politico, banker and Boone descendent, about the Boones' reburial. In it was a bedside confession from a feverish Black man who was once enslaved, now wracked with tuberculosis. The old man with the death rattle summoned his strength. He leaned on his elbow. "They didn't get Boone," Alonzo Callaway snickered, gasping.

Gardyne sat by his bed spellbound, listening, scribbling Alonzo's last words. Alonzo died a few days later.

Gardyne's letter to the newspaper told the strangest of tales, about a "lost grave" next to Rebecca's plot and how the plan to snatch her husband to Frankfort was foiled by the gravediggers. How, twenty-five years earlier when Daniel died and they went to bury him by Rebecca, they unearthed a Black man's bones. To respect the enslaved, the Boones, most of whom at one time had chattel, left him, some say on the left side, others say the right, and put Dan at her feet (or, say some, above her head). As the "lost grave" was a secret, when someone finally got around to marking their graves, they assumed Dan was buried alongside Rebecca and set his stone. Except that it was at the head of the enslaved.

When Frankfort's envoy arrived, the gravediggers slyly dug up Rebecca and the Black man to pawn off to the Kentuckians. Thanks to their cagey skeleton switching, the interlopers steamed off with Dan's wife and who-knows-who, leaving Dan in his unmarked grave above or below or beside where Rebecca once lay. Here was proof positive Dan'l Boone was still in Missouri—Alonzo, based on David Gardyne's unproved words, said so.

On its face, Gardyne's letter is a personal note to Jesse P. Crump. But it's more than that; Gardyne knew he was playing to a naive hometown crowd, saying how "Alonzo became quite enthused when we were talking. Like many others he considered it a smart deception and justifiable." Gardyne didn't elaborate on who deemed packing Mrs. Boone off with an unknown man "smart" and "justifiable"; evidently, he did. Bloviating with sham indignation, he pretends to blame Missourians for mismarking Boone's grave due to their not knowing about the "lost grave."

Adding to his note the yarns of John S. Jones's unmarked graves and William Bryan's "rotting coffins," Gardyne ends his tale by describing his meeting with a "Rev. Mr. Cunningham," who, he says, "preached Boone's and wife's funeral." When Gardyne interrogated the pastor about authenticating Daniel's remains in Kentucky, Cunningham, he said, told him he "didn't know what the Boones' caskets contained."

Here Gardyne's fable implodes. U.S. senator John J. Crittenden was the Boones' eulogizer, and no Cunningham is named on the program. No matter, Jesse Crump, Gardyne's correspondent and soon-to-be Alonzo Callaway's premier booster, passed the memo to St. Charles's chamber of commerce, then to the *Kansas City Star* and to weeklies far and wide. In his lectures and essays he proclaimed the tale's validity.

Kentuckians were outraged. Missourians mocked and tut-tutted. The Bluegrass Boys had it coming. The seed of doubt, now planted, was cultivated as the legend grew to spawn a century's worth of myriad forms, like how Alonzo was one of the gravediggers; he was not, his father, Jefferson, was. An influential Missourian would call Alonzo Dan's pal of camp and trail.

JESSE CRUMP'S COUSIN, GEORGE Chester Bryan, who'd returned from Kentucky to live in Missouri, read one of Jesse's newspaper articles about how "a mistake was made…and that a stranger was taken instead of Boone." On January 6, 1922, in the *Marthasville Record*, he dismantled Crump and Gardyne's tale, calling them out by name. He himself knew where his grandparents' graves were and how his parents, Corelia and Willis, were buried by the Boones near Mary and David Bryan.

"This is the fourth time the thing has been revived," George said, mocking Crump for accepting it, "with all the evidence he has to the contrary. I cannot believe his mind has been so burdened with…this matter that he is led into these insinuations." Crump should "clear his mind of the whole matter or he will soon need a padded cell." Gardyne, Crump and

David Bryan Cemetery, circa 1880. *Missouri Historical Society.*

Jones knew nothing of Boone's burial, he said, offering half-truths to create doubt, as in Alonzo's story.

"I knew old Jeff Callaway. From the time I was a small boy until my father's death...I never heard him intimate there was any doubt the body of both Boone and his wife being removed," George said. Alonzo "was much too young to have been an assistant in removing those bodies." If Dan *was* at Rebecca's feet, he was with Mary and David Bryan, he said. And furthermore, there was plenty of room for more graves on either side of Rebecca.

Susannah Bryan, he said, "was born and reared in a house...within 200 yards to the graveyard." She knew where the bodies were. Besides, the Boones' graves were always marked and there were about twelve graves in the cemetery when their new memorials were placed.

And of the coffins' rates of decaying? Why, timber hewn from winter-felled trees outlasts lumber from summer's sap-filled trees. "Boone's body was buried," said George, whose father attended the Boones' burials and removals, "beside his wife on the left side when facing the east. Bryan and his wife were buried at the feet of Boone and his wife in the place Boone and Bryan had selected. The proper graves were opened."

His vigorous defense made no impact on the mystics. Convoluted iterations of the "Negro Story," "the lost grave" and the "Missing Body" legends surfaced with teasing details, needing the equivalent of a Vatican II–sized papal bull to address the murky permutations—all of which works well to any myth's shelf life. It has for this one.

As Dan's kin met in Frankfort in 1934 for his 200th birthday, Missouri's lieutenant governor Frank Harris called for Rebecca's return, inciting Governor A.B. "Happy" Chandler to deflect their efforts. They tried three years later when John Bakeless's *Daniel Boone: Master of the Wilderness* spun the tale into the woodsman's literary canon: "It has been suspected that the wrong grave was opened and that Daniel Boone still lies in his original grave; but there is no good evidence for this."

St. Charles's chamber of commerce tried to snag Rebecca for Dan—whose grave "had never been opened." Becky will stay, retorted Governor Lawrence Wetherby, the issue settling into restive dormancy. At the Historic Daniel Boone Home, in the 1960s curated by Rolla and Randall Andrae, Louisville reporter Byron Crawford named the patriarch a "chief proponent" of Alonzo Callaway's story. In Rolla's spin, Alonzo (who may not yet have reached his teens when Dan and his wife were dug up) is "one of Boone's friends and hunting companions in later life."

"We like to tell people the facts as best we know them. We tell it here all the time," said Rolla, graciously adding, "We're not trying to hurt Kentucky."

Rolla framed Crump's tale to hang in the home for its 25,000 annual tourists to read and printed it in his gift shop's bio, *A True, Brief History of Daniel Boone*, telling how Dan'l "never cursed, never drank and wouldn't listen to dirty jokes," and how his wizardry was on display throughout the home, like "the hand carving" of its intricate woodwork and how the home was "filled with authentic pieces and documents of Daniel Boone. Almost everything, including the furniture, belonged to Daniel and Rebecca or Boone descendants."

Such reportage promoted tours, sold books and spread the Dan's-still-here gospel. The Andraes, to their credit, sacrificed for years to keep budgets intact to save the Femme Osage's antebellum architectural crown gem. Were it not for them, Francis Curlee and others one shudders to think what might have been the home's fate.

IN 1983 KENTUCKIANS WERE sideswiped by their commonwealth's forensic anthropologist who examined Boone's plaster pate and loosed a stunning report, the news ricocheting from the Associated Press to *National Geographic* magazine. At the storm's eye was an unassuming AP freelancer who'd spotted Daniel's mortar skull in Louisville.

Thomas Shelby Watson reckoned he'd have it checked out.

19

He Gave Me All Kinds of Hell

Sunday noon found me south of Frankfort on the Bluegrass Parkway Springfield/Lebanon exit to Highway 555. Fearing I'd missed my turn I swerved to the shoulder to grab my phone, alternately hammering in Thomas Watson's cell and his landline. There was no answer on either, except for a disembodied computerized lady's voice saying the message recorders were full.

June's humidity was high. There was no breeze. It was in the eighties and mercury rising. Anticipating my tardiness, so was my blood pressure.

The Ohio's flooding forced the barges and their tugboat escorts to tie on to shore. The bluegrass was lush and green, spiked with juniper. The sumac's tasseled spires would soon burst into red berries. Oak, maple, sweet gum, cherry, walnut and hickory crowned the upper story above dogwood, redbud and buckeye. Fence rows sagging with honeysuckle parted tobacco plots between the hills where horses and cattle capered in pastures brightening in the sun. It was not hard to see why colonists east of the Blue Ridge hied with Boone to this isle in the wilderness.

Much of that was lost on me now as I veered onto the parkway, dodging church traffic, golfers and boat-trailer flotillas, barrel-assing through the verdant farmland to Bloomfield, passing through its one stoplight where U.S. Route 62 became Taylorsville Road, to park across from Hometown Pizza. Tom Watson was waiting outside, seated and nursing a cup of coffee with two bulging manila folders piled on his café table.

I was late. He rose from his chair as we shook hands. I offered my apology.

Tom smiled. "This is Bloomfield. You think anyone here cares?" We went in for lunch. He was in a long-sleeved blue shirt, gray slacks and brown shoes and my height, medium build and lean. Seventy-one years ago he was born in nearby Spencer County.

Customers greeted Tom as our server led us to a booth with seats like high-backed church pews. His calling as a reporter began when the Associated Press lured him to Louisville to freelance, leading to induction into Kentucky's Journalism Hall of Fame. Between deadlines Watson plowed the Filson Historical Society's troves to research Civil War guerilla William Quantrill. "I was at the Filson a bunch. They had a cast of Daniel Boone's skull."

The faux skull was in a display case with other alleged Boone relics: a boy's Plains Indian buckskinned shirt, the obligatory flintlock rifle and a wide curl of beech bark carved with the usual misspelled inscription: "D Boon kill A BAR 1775." Alongside hung a handsome oil portrait of Colonel Boone credited to Chester Harding.

Watson was intrigued by the Missouri skeletal switch tale. Was there any truth to it? He contacted commonwealth heavyweights Dr. Thomas D. Clark, University of Kentucky's prolific author and legendary history professor, and J. Winston Coleman Jr., famed photographer and pamphleteer of the common man.

"Well, that's the big question," said Coleman. "There was some doubt if they got the right bones or not. 'Course when they brought him back here they made a cast of the skull."

Could the alleged Boone head have been based on a Black man's skull?

"Well, it could have been," Coleman said. It was all symbolic anyway, helping to fund Frankfort's cemetery. "They got something that stands for him. That's what people go see—the biggest drawing card in the cemetery." That Civil War soldiers hacked up his monument should prove to Kentuckians "how well he was received and still is."

From the beginning Dr. Clark had found the story suspect. "The only way to settle it is to have a reputable anthropologist examine that casting." Whether Boone was buried in Frankfort or Missouri mattered little, as "he was on friendly ground in either place."

Clark's idea was not lost on Watson. "Why had no one ever done this? It seemed like a logical, obvious thing to do." He knew a Frankfort pathologist who might help.

Dr. David J. Wolf had helped establish Frankfort's Medical Examiner Program for crime solving and body identification. Under the auspices of the University of Kentucky's public outreach, he'd assisted in forensic anthropology community courses. Affable with the press and friendly, Wolf was well liked and valued. "Dave's one of those fellows who comes along only once in a lifetime," said Dr. George Nichols, a colleague.

"I had the greatest respect for him," said Tom. "I talked to him all the time in news stories that dealt with death. He was a consummate professional. Never slacked. Never bragged."

In June 1983, Andy Lippman, Louisville's AP chief in Louisville and Watson's boss, told him to "get out there and find something." Watson decided finding out who was buried in Daniel Boone's grave would be a good story.

Wolf already knew the Boone tale's basic storyline. They agreed to meet at the Old State Capitol, home of the Kentucky Historical Society, where Frankfort's skull cast was housed. "I didn't care what the conclusion was," Watson said, pausing for coffee.

Hometown Pizza was Bloomfield's social hub. I devoured a delicious Greek salad and sipped iced tea—unsweetened, special order in these parts. Watson swilled coffee and ate an angus burger garnished with cheese. Finding the din distracting—the bustle of waitresses, kids scampering, chatty customers, iPhones erupting into "Sweet Home Alabama"—I suggested moving outside. We walked to the cash register.

News of our conversation had leaked out. Missy, an attractive blonde in retro Daisy Duke cutoffs, Hometown T-shirt, sneakers and bobby socks stood behind the cashier shuttling pizzas and placing pepperoni, tomato slices, olives and peppers in tomato sauce slathered across a crust. She sprinkled on mozzarella and glanced up. "Daniel Boone died at the Alamo—right?"

Tom looked at me and smiled.

"No ma'am. That was David Crockett from Tennessee," I began, trying not to lapse into professorial mode at its most pedantic awfulness. "Boone and Crockett get confused a lot. The same actor played both of them on TV."

Missy reddened, frowning. Customers in nearby booths ceased talking to listen to the historian.

She lobbed another one. "Well, they lived at the same time, right?"

"They overlapped. Boone was born in Pennsylvania before the Revolutionary War and died in Missouri. Crockett was born after the Revolutionary War."

A partial victory—Missy took a last stab at Frontier History 101. "That movie out a while back, *Last of the Mohicans*, that was the Revolutionary War, right?"

"Well, no. *Mohicans* was about the French and Indian War, twenty years before it. Mel Gibson's movie *The Patriot* was about the Revolution." She hadn't seen *The Patriot*. She didn't care for Mel but liked *The Passion of the Christ*.

"Okay. So, who won the French and Indian War? The French or the Indians?"

"Uh, neither. The British."

"The British? How did they get in on it?"

I wasn't sure how to proceed. Tom's eyes wrinkled at the corners and bored holes in me, his cheeks dimpling under his beard. Missy seemed confused at this over-the-counter blast by a nerdy history professor with wire frames, thin braid and out-of-state accent. The prof, regretting he'd opened his mouth (and making up for it with an inflated tip), and the reporter walked out to settle into black wire chairs fronting a patio table.

Outside, I took in this picturesque town as Tom filled in its history. Platted in 1817 and named for a Dr. Merrifield who married a Miss Bloomer, Bloomfield lists its population at 1,200. Its income is based mostly on an agrarian economy, and unemployment runs high.

A renaissance has come here from an unlikely source: Hollywood. Louisville's Linda Bruckheimer, novelist and wife of film mogul Jerry Bruckheimer, was a trustee of the National Trust for Historic Preservation. She restored an 1820 Greek Revival house, adding a cabin belonging to Abe Lincoln's uncle. One can visit Amy's Florist Shop, get refreshed at Miss Merrifield's Tea Room, shop at Nettie Jarvis Antiques and stroll under Victorian streetlamps lighting redbrick sidewalks. Linda's efforts, says the mayor, "brought people and money here. She's been like a fairy godmother."

Few towns, admittedly, can claim Los Angeles cachet and be where a Yankee sniper popped William Quantrill, the CSA guerilla who sacked Lawrence, Kansas.

WE WERE SEATED TEN yards from Bloomfield's one stoplight which reigns over downtown's NASCAR ambience. As the light switched red, hulking pickups with horse trailers, high-wheeled pesticide sprayers, Harleys with rebel flags, cars, RVs and gravel-laden dump trucks growled and hissed, downshifting to line up in an anxious queue of gunning diesels and revving throttles.

I needed earplugs. Watson's mellifluous baritone rose to a shout. We ceased talking.

The light flashing green galvanized a *whoosh* of exhaust, grit and jake brakes, fluttering Stars and Bars and decibel overload blending Hank

Williams's "I'm so Lonesome I Could Cry" with Jay-Z's throbbing hip-hop and Lady Gaga's guttural rants. Every half hour a gong tolled, backed by "Faith of Our Fathers" in ding-dong chimes blasting from a Baptist steeple.

Bloomfield certainly promoted musical diversity and all at once. As it was Sunday, I caught the religious fervor, praying that my recorder was picking up Tom's voice as he talked about Dr. Wolf's forensic examination of Boone's plaster head.

Watson reminisced between light changes. Wolf was the first to get to the Old Capitol, then housing the Kentucky Historical Society, bringing calipers, scalpel, legal pad and pen. Watson arrived with a writing pad, camera, pen and recorder. Boone's faux skull was out of its case, patiently waiting on the curator's desk.

An old KHS photo of the head's showcase has it next to a powder horn initialed "DB." Bullet molds, spectacles and daguerreotypes sat on a lower shelf with a Bowie knife. Across the front stretched Dan's shooting iron, Tick-Licker—with "DB" gouged on the butt. On the reverse was "BOoNs best FREN." Fifteen notches in the stock marked his grim tally—this from a modest ex-Quaker who killed only in self-defense. The display was a Dark and Bloody Ground take on the Ark of the Covenant.

None of the display's artifacts bore verifiable attribution to Boone. Some—like the absurdly embellished Tick-Licker—were laughable frauds. After scrutiny by long rifle expert John Bivens, he refused to believe that "Boone would have so wretchedly defaced the stock of a rifle in such a manner. To be as succinct as possible, I believe that it is generally understood among students of the American longrifle who are familiar with this

American long rifle, circa 1770s, with leather lock cover, from the McAfee family of Kentucky. *Jim and Carolyn Dresslar Collection.*

particular weapon that the piece is exceedingly unlikely to have enjoyed actual ownership by Daniel Boone. That is certainly my opinion."

The KHS had more "Boone" guns—a caplock shotgun and a small-bore rifle, among others. Just up the hill, Kentucky's Military Museum housed a second Boone arsenal, with a firelock carved "D. Boon. CILLED. BIG / PanTHER. this / Gun. I WAS. 13." The gun's side opposite the lock bears a date meaningful only to the dyslexic fraudster who created this counterfeit. Thumbtacked to the display, a handwritten note covering all the bases reads, "One of these guns may have been Daniel Boone's, but not all, and perhaps none of them were."

"Dr. Wolf was very professional," Watson said. "When I got there, he already had the skull cast out." For twenty minutes, Wolf pored over the cast, measuring and tracing his fingers along its features, taking notes. His concentration fascinated Watson.

"He was objective. I didn't have any preconceived notions of what he was going to find out. I gave him the reins." As he scrutinized the pate, jotting notes and measurements, Watson noticed Wolf's demeanor change. "He became animated, like he seemed to know something."

"I asked him, 'Have you reached a conclusion?'"

"Well, this may have been a Black man after all," Watson paraphrased Wolf's response. "He commented about the muscle that goes down to the back of the skull being so strongly exhibited. That confirmed that this was a person that did a lot of heavy lifting—a lot of heavy work."

"Wolf took into consideration Boone was a powerful man. He never said definitively, though, the individual's race." Watson recalled Wolf saying he wished the cast was intact and not missing its facial features. There was no way to make a sure determination. "The more he looked, the more he thought, 'this could be from a Black man.'"

On June 24, 1983, Watson typed in his byline, "Expert says clues indicate Boone may lie in Missouri, not Kentucky." It appeared on page B1 of the *Louisville Courier-Journal*. "That's pretty good when you make the front page of any section," he told me, smiling. Wolf's jocular, off-handed remarks quoted in the article did not hurt newspaper sales.

> *The old boys in Missouri may have done it.*
> *The general slope of the brow ridges are more black than white.*

Watson's scoop splashed across every commonwealth daily and went national. Kentuckians seethed. Chamber of commerce politicos chided Wolf after he delivered for Rotarians an impromptu talk on the matter. Frankfort's cemetery superintendent Jim Richardson wasn't buying any of it—nada. The pathologist "was a self-promoter," he charged. "He would say controversial things to draw attention to himself." Wolf ignored his critics, infuriating them.

KHS historian Ron Bryant spoke guardedly. "Whether the Missourians could have pulled this one over on Kentucky has been hotly debated ever since that report came out. The official stance is that Daniel and Rebecca are buried here.…It's hard to say you were wrong."

It wasn't hard for Missourians. B.H. Rucker, head of the state's historical sites, couldn't confirm that Boone was not west of the Mississippi. "We really don't know. I could see where it was possible that a mistake was made."

Warren County's chamber of commerce "wanted a slice of the Boone trade." Republican representative Russell G. Brockfield demanded Kentucky house speaker Donald Blandford "admit a mistake was made when the bones were disinterred" and "claim that Boone is still buried in Warren County." He wanted Dan's skull shipped to St. Louis's forensic lab—"tourism dollars were attached to the issue"—and called for Governor John Ashcroft to "issue a proclamation unilaterally declaring Missouri the possessor of Boone's remains." Spokesman Randy Sissel, "advising against it," barely kept Ashcroft out of the fray.

General William R. Buster, decorated World War II vet and the KHS director, phoned Tom Watson. Could he stop by the museum for a chat?

"Buster was really ticked. He gave me all kinds of hell. He told me, 'This kind of thing doesn't help us. It's not good for Kentucky.'" Watson bore up under General Buster's bombast on the sanctity of all things Boone. Boone was in the right grave—drop it.

"He more or less chewed me out," Tom said. Buster retired a few weeks later.

We lingered outside Hometown Pizza Parlor as the sky darkened.

"It would be a modest black eye to Kentuckians if you found out it wasn't Boone buried in Frankfort," Tom said. "But I didn't write the story to create doubt or cause anyone embarrassment. I did the story to find out what I could find out from a scientist. In a story like that, ultimately, you set out to find the truth."

Tom's report of a Boone skull at Louisville's Filson Historical Society intrigued me. I called the Filson. The bemused receptionist, transferring my call to special collections, could not confirm nor deny its existence: "Daniel Boone's head, you say?"

20

More Boone Skullduggery

Jim Holmberg, the Filson's special collections curator, whose writings on William Clark's letters has enriched our sense of the man, his world and his famous trek, took my call about a plaster Boone skull.

"When I came here, it wasn't on display. I'd remember something as ghoulish as that."

As Lavina and I planned to be in Louisville, I told him I'd drop by. In the meantime, he said he'd look for Boone's mortar noggin. "It's probably part of the Rueben Durrett Collection." Lawyer, antiquarian and historian, Colonel Rueben Durrett was the Filson's original leading light.

Weaving through Monday morning's traffic, I hurried along. Passing along downtown Louisville's outskirts bordering the Ohio's south bank and circumambulating the cloverleaf of concrete spirals linking I-64, I-65 and I-71 and then a hard right on I-65 south to exit on St. Catherine and over to Third Street's crossing of Ormsby, I pulled out of traffic, easing right, and into the asphalt parking lot adjoining the stately Ferguson mansion at South 1310.

Exiting, I stepped into a broiling heat wave to search in vain for shade. I thought of Boone's first writer, John Filson, an expat Pennsylvania schoolteacher turned bluegrass real estate agent, authoring Edenic myths about this Elysium that settlers would find in the first Far West, like, "This country is more temperate and healthy than the other settled parts of America. In Summer it wants the sandy heats which Virginia and Carolina experience, and receives a fine air from its rivers. In Winter, which…is but seldom severe, the people are safe in bad houses; and the beasts have a good supply without fodder."

Folks arriving after reading this falderal learned that Kentucky was hot in the summer and cold in the winter, snow drifts crashed through cabins and livestock, like all livestock, had to be fed. A century after the commonwealth's first historian vanished in Indian land, Rueben Durrett and some devoted history aficionados founded the society named for him.

I hugged the lot's edge past a hemlock and ducked beneath a maple; a leafy gingko looming over the curb looked odd among native hardwoods. Wide, long steps across the street led to ten towering columns crowned with a cornice emblazoned "1ST CHURCH OF CHRIST SCIENTIST" shading Mary Baker Eddy's acolytes as I hied onward to cool water, central air, plush couches and musky antiquarian book smells.

The Filson evokes a sense of the sacred that puts me in a mindset akin to Moses before the burning bush. Unlike the Hebrew wanderer in the wilderness, I kept my shoes on, tugged my white sport coat's lapels back from my red vest and white shirt, felt of my blue silk tie knot and stepped over the porch's pastel fresco reminiscent of an Aegean motif lifted from a Dionysian festival cult. Pulling on the brass knob to enter the twin ornate doors and passing the threshold, nodding at the curious faces, I felt myself straighten, inhale deeply and slip into warrior mode.

Here rests Louisville's historical heart—perhaps literally. Completed in 1905, after Edward Hite Ferguson's business failed, he lost his manor which became a funeral parlor until Filsonians claimed it in 1986. The mansion's baronial interior and elegance—wood floors, carved oak and damask paneling, French hand-sculpted mantels—represent a past era's artistic apogee unsullied by Wi-Fi signs and blasting espresso machines and is a refuge for historical literati who have slipped their moorings. If one wants to experience those transcendent ephemeral openings that randomly flash on a sensitive researcher, plowing the Filson's troves will invoke them.

Jim was busy with patrons. I wandered about vintage furniture to read portrait captions; the Filson houses Kentucky's largest collection of antebellum portraiture. A vigorous Alexander Campbell, rendered by Chester Harding, gazed at me. Near the stairs I was startled by a pale, ebony-eyed woman in a long black dress and coifed brunette tresses who looked as if she'd stepped from the Victorian wall-hanging at my elbow. "May I help you?" she asked.

The svelte cameo vanished past a door as Jim called me to his office. I eased into a Windsor under a canvas of Henry Clay—the Great Compromiser

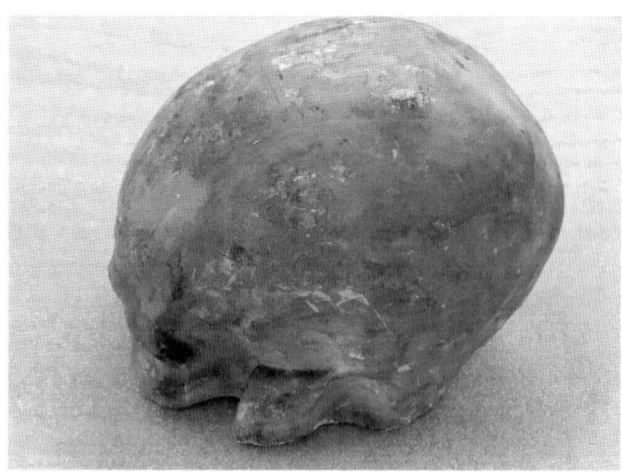

Boone skull cast A. *Filson Historical Society*.

was poised and alert, eloquent repartee on pause. Boone died the year Clay emerged as the Missouri Compromise's voice in the U.S. House, balancing its eleven slave state delegates with its eleven free. The Kansas-Nebraska Act's predictable unraveling of it spawned Bleeding Kansas, Beecher's Bibles and John Brown. Seven years later Confederates fired on Fort Sumter.

Jim's desk was awash in archival flotsam. Two cardboard boxes, corrugated top flaps torn and brown with age, sat on a round table to my right.

"You aren't going to believe this but I found two Boone skull casts," he said, utterly poleaxing me as he exhibited the skulls, dubbed A and B.

Boone skull A was white clear to its eye sockets. We turned to A's enigmatic inscription:

> *Plaster Cast of Daniel Boone Skull*
> *Major General Preston Brown 1885*

Lexington-born Preston Brown was a Yale graduate and World War I army officer who rose to the rank of brigadier general. He was the son of John Mason Brown, a founding Filsonian and son of Liberty Hall's Mason Brown. "Cast of skull of Daniel Boone taken when remains were transferred home to Kentucky" was penciled in cursive on A's right temple.

Perhaps Preston Brown gained ownership of skull cast A in 1885. In April 1939, he gave it to the society. A was chipped at the nape. The chip rattled about the box. On the exterior of A's box was written "1892," the date of Kentucky's centennial.

"The provenance from our records is that it was passed down through the Brown family," Jim said. "Whether this was done from Boone's head or is a cast of a cast I don't know. According to the records it had with it, it would appear to have been cast from the skull itself."

Cast A was part of the Dr. William Durrett Collection inherited from his father, Reuben Durrett. So much for Boone skull cast A.

Boone cast B's was zinc gray. Its shape and surface looked much like cast A, but B's suture seams were, to my untrained eyes, more delineated and deeply etched, providing more of a phrenological relief map. A cryptic note in B's box offered few clues, just "Boone Skull: Human Relic Curio No. 10 B."

Skull B had sustained trauma by an unknown assailant who had drilled a one-fourth-inch hole straight into the top of its cranium. "It appears someone had been trepanning his skull," observed Holmberg, peering. B's path to the Filson reliquary passed through three distinguished owners. Dr. Robert Peter was the first. Dr. Peter, an English-born American medical doctor who joined Transylvania College in Lexington, acquired cast B in September 1845. It was likely a first-run Boone head by sculptor Henry C. Davis. This alone was a remarkable discovery.

George W. Ranck, a Louisville-born reporter and teacher who wrote two of the society's finest books, *Boonesborough* and *The Story of Bryan's Station*, became B's owner. In 1892 he gave B to Rueben Durrett, knowing his love of esoterica. Rueben added B (along with A) to his growing trove of curiosities that he publicized to create interest in the Filson.

Was the 1892 inscribed on A's box flap tied to its donation date to the Filsonians—perhaps timed to Kentucky's centennial? Had the two skulls been switched? How would they compare to each other and to the Boone cranial cast in Frankfort?

Durrett's skulls animated a few quandaries. Early society curators had displayed cast A with a buckskinned fringed coat, rifle and other artifacts attributed to Boone. Pictures of the relics in biographies (like in John Bakeless's *Boone*) have assumed an aura of sacredness not unlike similar dubious relics in other Boone collections. Jim was cautious of such claims. "To our knowledge, none of them had any traceable provenance to Boone," he said.

Durrett, a Kentucky renaissance man, had an oddly paradoxical dualism. As an obsessive antiquarian collector of Kentuckiana, he was indefatigable. His library, which he began as a boy, consisted "of 20,000 volumes, 250 pamphlet boxes, 200 volumes of atlases and maps, hundreds of newspaper titles, and thousands of original manuscripts."

His was the most comprehensive repository in the commonwealth—the envy of Lyman Draper at Wisconsin's State Historical Society. Teddy Roosevelt

Boone skull cast A, with penciled inscription on right temple: "Cast of skull of Daniel Boone taken when remains were transferred home to Kentucky." *Filson Historical Society.*

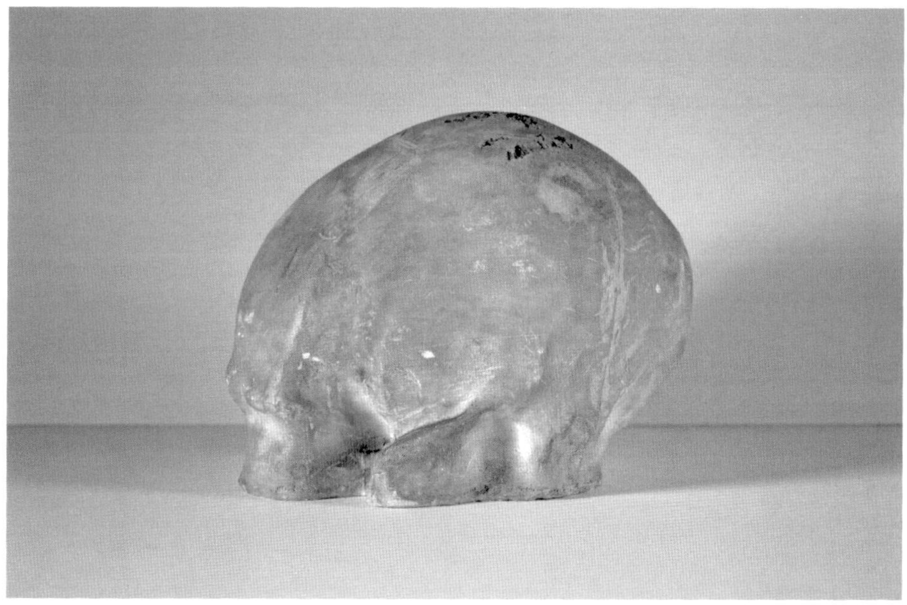

Boone skull cast B. *Filson Historical Society.*

plowed Durrett's stacks while writing his *Winning of the West.* After he died in 1913, the University of Chicago bought his library; Kentucky, it seemed, lacked a fireproof building. That many of Kentucky's treasured archives are in the Windy City is still a sore point among Filsonians.

But the colonel had a creative, malleable streak when it came to material culture. "He liked to dress things up. He liked to help history along," Jim said. He had no qualms about "manufacturing antiques" and tall tales to go with them—either to enhance their value or to make history come alive. "He thought, 'You want to be able to enjoy your treasures.'"

Holmberg paused. "If the facts don't support the story, go with the story. You'll appreciate the items more." One need only count all the Boone guns and accoutrements housed in historical societies, museums, Boone home sites and private collections to sense that he was not alone in this.

"That's a lot of guns," Jim chuckled. "Did Boone get a new long rifle every month?"

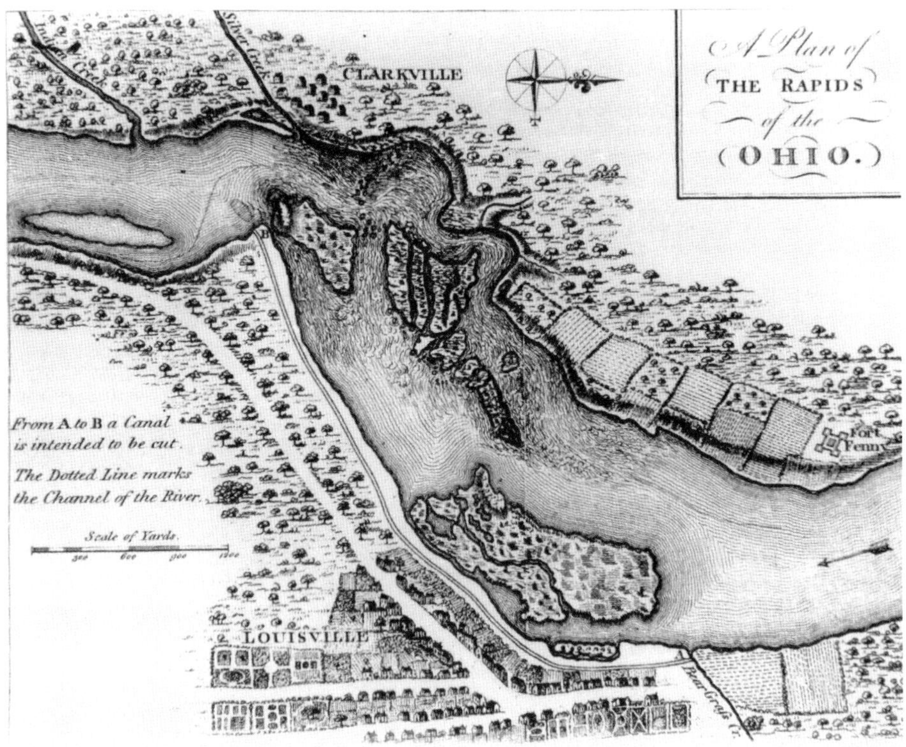

Falls of the Ohio. Gilbert Imlay's Topographical Description of the Western Territory of North America, 1793.

Durrett's "love of the relic," he called it, knew no bounds. On Clark's Point, overlooking the Falls of the Ohio before the U.S. Army Corps of Engineers dynamited the channel for shipping, he commissioned the building of a cabin he touted as owned by the legendary long knife George Rogers Clark. Clark's younger brother William, Durrett claimed, used it "as a base camp" prior to trekking to the Pacific with Meriwether Lewis.

Things got weirder. Durrett added to his collection misshapen "part-human" oddities like Annie the mummy, crafted of wire, cloth, papier-mâché and mismatched bones. Hung on a nearby wall was a grainy black-and-white photo of a Fiji mermaid, sewn and glued together from a mishmash of unknown animal parts.

Jim laughed. "Either he was duped by whoever donated some of the items or he made things up." Either way, the colonel knew how to draw a crowd.

After my Filson visit I called Tom Watson. Along the way we talked about his controversial article on Dr. Wolf and how, two years later, Wolf zoomed back into a bigger spotlight.

National Geographic magazine, the yellow-framed journalistic fortress of all things cutting edge, in December 1985, released "Daniel Boone: First Hero of the Frontier," by Elizabeth A. Moize. It features a smiling Dr. David Wolf peering over Boone's skull, calipers in hand. With a circulation nearing nine million, and printed in thirty-three languages, the magazine's story garnered global publicity, adding scholarly legitimacy to the century-long hullaballoo.

"Easiest lead I ever wrote," Betsy Moize told me. She was born in Virginia on November 2—the same day as Boone, only two hundred years later. (This is by the New Style, Gregorian calendar; Caesar's old Julian calendar makes it October 20, though the British adopted Pope Gregory XIII's calendar in 1752.) A graduate of Columbia, Missouri's Stephens College, she started as a typist in *National Geographic*'s correspondence department. Soon she was writing and running the editorial staff.

Her opener, "Let's get one thing straight from the start: Daniel Boone never wore a coonskin cap," nails the big stereotype. Her essay is a lucid condensed rendering of the frontiersman's life with superb photographs, art and detailed maps. I wondered why she took it on and if she knew the murky issues surrounding Boone's reinterment beforehand.

"Some guy mentioned it when I was in Missouri working on the article. I visited his Missouri grave and heard about the misplaced body story—that when they dug down to bury Daniel beside Rebecca, they discovered a slave already buried there, so they buried Daniel at Rebecca's feet. I went to the Frankfort Boone grave and heard the story as well."

She read Watson's article and asked Wolf to take a fresh look at Boone's pate at the Old State Capitol. With photographer William Strode shooting pictures, Wolf again pored over the gray plaster cranium, his fingers rubbing its sutures, tracing its brows' ridges and bumps to its roundish occipital bun, as he held for the camera and fielded questions. Now was the perfect time to recant his earlier comments—except he didn't.

"I found Dr. Wolf to be modest and even-handed about his opinions regarding Daniel's whereabouts," Moize said. "If I had detected that he had any agenda beyond trying to determine the truth, I would have given him scant space." She devoted three paragraphs to the tale, writing, "There are those in Missouri who say that Kentucky has Rebecca, but not Daniel," believing slave bones "rest in that Kentucky hill." Wolf concluded, "The cast was poorly made and was only of the cranium. But the round forehead and long, narrow head are typical of Negroids, and the apparent young age at death certainly cast doubt that it is Boone."

It wasn't possible, the anthropologist said, to render a final call given the material evidence's limitations. "I remember Dr. Wolf being a little ambivalent about the controversy. So, since he wouldn't say definitively, I and so many others have left the question hanging," Moize said.

Bill Strode, who shot Moize's photos, was one of the *Louisville Courier-Journal*'s stars. His single-lens reflex helped earn the team two Pulitzers and his pictures have appeared in *Time*, *Sports Illustrated*, the *Washington Post* and the *New York Times*. His forebearer John Strode, a Virginia Tory who settled in Clark County, knew Boone. I asked Moize about their relationship.

"Bill worked for *National Geographic*'s illustration department. I think the director of photography hired him. On this article we both pretty much worked on our own."

A soft-spoken man of slight build, owlish eyes and thinning brown hair, Bill was as honest as his pictures. While shooting *Boone*, he'd visited the apartment my wife and I rented while in school; later, I used his Chester Harding Boone portrait as a jacket for my third book, Lyman C. Draper's *The Life of Daniel Boone*. He asked me if I'd ever located any relics with a firm provenance to the woodsman.

Not really, I said, just surveys and letters. Maybe the forged beaver trap Boone allegedly gave Paddy "Daniel" Huddlestone's family when he was trapping below West Virginia's Kanawha Falls. Had he?

Bill laughed. During his investigative treks he'd embarked on a near holy grail search that proved more quixotic than fruitful, studying scrimshawed powder horns, guns, knives and Bibles. He'd peered into rock shelters, hefted rusty salt kettles and tracked down enigmatic carvings—articles all claimed to have been Boone's but weren't. It would have been easier, he concluded, to find Genghis Khan's grave.

He'd done his own research into Boone's reburial and, like Moize, found the data convoluted. So, I put it to Moize who, in her *National Geographic* essay, ends Daniel's body-switch tale vaguely, like most writers and many historians do: "Nobody knows for sure and maybe that's best."

But off the record she was blunter with me: "I don't have a clue where Boone is buried."

Kentucky's official forensic anthropologist, I figured, was burned out on talking about Boone's masonry head and had no wish to rekindle yesteryear's cranial blowback. But I had nothing to lose calling Dr. David Wolf at the medical examiner's office, which doubled as the state morgue.

21

Tales from the Morgue

Dave's gone for the afternoon," the morgue's janitor said. "I'm the only one alive around here this time of the day." On my second phone call to the state's dead house, I was transferred to the man himself. I said I found the Boone reburial tale intriguing. Would he be willing to talk?

Dr. David Wolf could not have been more helpful as he discussed Boone's plaster skull cap in his profession's terms. He was also hilarious, which I hadn't expected from someone in his line of work. My call ended with his impolitic salvo blasted across the bow of two hundred years of Dan'l hagiography: "I'll be blunt, pal. There ain't no way that skull belonged to an eighty-five-year-old white guy."

He laughed uproariously at his one-liner. I winced, jotting down his camera-ready sound bite. He promised to send his notes.

In my mail days later was an official envelope enclosing a photocopied page of handwritten measurements and anatomical terms, with Dr. Wolf's taut cursive above the top line: "Cast of Daniel Boone." Over the months I phoned back asking his thoughts on death miscellany; admittedly, one cannot get this kind of gen just anywhere. I could see how his candor endeared him to colleagues and how his spontaneous irreverence might ruffle feathers.

I found it odd that after Wolf's fifteen minutes of media fame no one followed up. Was it possible to talk in person? "Come on up," he said. My delight vanished as his next words, "I've got cancer," broadsided me. He'd begun treatments. Groping for words but struck by his stark resolution and openhanded generosity, my mission now had a sense of urgency. We set a date.

At 9:00 a.m. on the steely gray morning I entered the medical examiner program building's foyer.

A bleached, bashed-in skull leered hello from a garish display of more skulls small and large—some cracked, their cheeks smashed and missing teeth. The top shelf exhibited leather-handled blackjacks and galvanized pipes, zip guns stuffed with match heads and clubs bristling with nails. Hacksaw knives and filed toothbrushes lay among barbed screwdrivers, straight razors, brass knuckles and switchblades.

Sheesh!

The vestibule's creepy homespun arsenal put me in mind of a medieval torture diorama blended with Appalachia's dark side as I eased past wanted posters to the receptionist. I scanned a bulletin board's murder-mayhem clips of court cases and slayings. Pothunters were unearthing relics from Mississippian mounds in Union County. Grave robbers near Hazard dug up Civil War veterans to rob the skeletonized boys in blue of contraband—Colt revolvers, Bowie knives, rings and buttons—to hawk to unsuspecting reenactors, museums and collectors. The only thing wasted were the vets themselves, who disintegrated when exposed to fresh air.

The petite woman said Dr. Wolf would see me. His cancer was spreading, she said, digging for a tissue. She gazed at her desk. Wolf was forty-nine—my father's age when doctors diagnosed the pancreatic cancer. I was a high school sophomore.

Wolf waved me into his office and motioned to a chair facing his desk. He was not as robust as my clips of him but he was a handsome fellow—big eyes deep set, blondish wavy hair and a sandy mustache over a boyish grin. I stared at his thick hands as he sat, phone stuck under his chin, grinning and winking. Both hands, from wrists to fingers, were freshly chewed and puffy. His knuckles were bleeding as if he had just scaled concertina wire. He hung up.

He and his wife, Judith Ann, had rescued two puppies dumped on I-64. Before work this morning the dogs, now much bigger, were brawling over their food bowls. He'd waded into the fray to yank them apart. Wolf held up his swollen palms, spread his oozing fingers and laughed. He walked to the sink to pour on peroxide, his hands fizzing crimson and white as we segued into Tom Watson phoning about Dan's plaster cranial cast.

"He was making arrangements with the Filson but found out that the Kentucky Historical Society in Frankfort had a copy. It would be easier just to go look at the one that was here."

Confronting him was a gray plaster of Paris orb of "reasonably good quality," considering it was from 1845. "It certainly is not the quality of

Boone skull cast made by Philip Slater Fall. *Kentucky Historical Society*.

casting we are capable of nowadays. It's obvious that whoever did it was not a rank amateur—he had some experience at it."

Plaster three-dimensional spheroids were cast in sections and pieced together. Boone's was a composite. "I'd have to go look at the photographs. It's been years." Why the casters did not mold the face he was not sure, reckoning the day's limited knowhow rendered it difficult or the skull's features were too badly decayed. "Since the cranium's general size and shape are what they were trying to preserve…it makes sense that you do what technically you can do."

"When you looked at the Boone cast, was it a superficial, cursory examination?"

"I got calipers out and took measurements, realizing that there was some error margin because it was not an exact casting. It wasn't a superficial going over." Had the cast been complete, he felt he could have done more.

"What I was interested in, if the error margin was the same in all directions, the proportions would have been the same. Meaning, if the casting was two millimeters bigger than it should have been, it doesn't really matter, because it would be two millimeters in length, in breadth and in height."

"It would be consistent."

"Yeah. So, I made some visual observations and took measurements."

I pulled out my copy of his notes. The first line read, "Cranial length 19.6 cm." He picked up two skulls to show the anatomical landmarks used as reference points. "There's a series of requirements for making comparable measurements on different kinds of skulls so that everybody is measuring the same thing in the same relative position." He traced across a thirty-year-old male Caucasian murder victim's skull. "Cranial length is a measurement in the skull's midline between the eye orbits to the widest dimension back here."

"Cranial breadth 14.6," I read.

"Now, in measuring cranial breadth, these bones right here are the parietal bones. This is the front parotid, the temporal and occipital. The widest point across the parietal bones is the cranial breadth." On Boone's, he was able "to measure the cranial length and cranial breadth…and with some hint of accuracy, the post-orbital constriction," measuring "10.5 centimeters."

He had written "depressed sagittal sut plateau," "sut" meaning "suture," the serrated interlocking lines uniting the skull's bones. Some skulls are flat across. Others are slightly peaked or slightly sunken. Boone's "formed a sort of a flat plateau with a little indention. And that is depending upon the accuracy of the cast itself."

"Could that have been altered then when they made the cast?"

"Not likely. It would have been fairly difficult to distort it."

The forehead was "rounded" when gazed at straight on. Scrutiny revealed a pair of bilateral external sulvices, twin skull grooves to form blood vessels, a normal creation of the skeleton. "It's just there. It isn't detrimental. It isn't beneficial."

Wolf had written "external frontal sulvices: left and _____." There was a blank. Left and what? Puzzled, he peered at my photocopy of his notes and then convulsed with laughter.

"I was intending to write 'right.' Obviously, I left it off. [More laughter.] They were on both sides." I wrote "right" on his note sheet and bracketed it in with an asterisk. Above Boone's eyebrow ridges was written "divided." Divided brow ridges are not uncommon: "The association is with different racial groups….it's not definitive.

"Here is the mastoid process." He traced on a skull where an ear once was, beginning a voluble discourse on zygomatic arches and nuchal muscle mass—nuchal muscles attach at the upper neck—the "scooped-out areas" at the skull's base indicating connective sites. Genetics, gender, size and degree of strength, activity and athleticism influence nuchal development, allowing the inferring of general conclusions on anonymous skulls, but variations exist.

"Grab that skull right behind you. Compare this mastoid process with that one."

"Ok. This one is bigger." Yet my skulls, one in each hand, were about the same size.

"You could take an Olympic athlete, female, and look at her muscle attachment areas and perhaps they would be as rugged and big as some couch potato males of the same size."

On Boone's cast the superior and inferior nuchal lines, mastoid and upper mastoid process were "large and well pronounced," exhibiting traits of an impressively muscled-up male, suggesting the mesomorphic frame of an enslaved male. Wolf had examined many slave skeletons. The Boone skull cast came from a big man. Its nuchal lines, "large relative to the skull," indicated tremendous muscular development and density.

Boone, I said, was a solidly built fellow of five foot eight, weighing about 175 in his prime. Cherokees dubbed him Wide Mouth because of his sturdy features. The Shawnee chieftain Black Fish named him Sheltowee (Big Turtle) due to his stocky frame. Showing off at a rifle frolic, he lifted more than anyone there. Beaver trapping—wading, digging, pounding stakes and lugging rocks and hand-forged traps for sets—is hard work and Boone reveled in it, even naming his favorite traps. Eyewitnesses describe the woodsman as being "stout," "robust," "muscular" and "having thick hips." My point: Boone likely had some pretty dense nuchal lines.

"Yeah." Wolf seemed less than convinced. We went back to his measurements.

"Ectocranial suture," I began.

"*Ectocranial*, 'what you can see from the outside,'" he translated. "In some individuals, depending upon age, the sutures will obliterate." As age indicators, suture lines were "not highly accurate." Twenty-two bones make up a skull, plus three more in each ear. "Sutures" are the interlocking serrated lines delineating several points where skull bones fuse.

As a person ages, suture closure (ossification) begins to occur inside the skull (endocranially), eventually closing on the outside (ectocranially). In old age, sutures tighten and may fuse. Though far from perfect, cranial suture closures remain a popular age indicator in forensic anthropology and archaeology. Still, results can be contradictory.

The deeply serrated suture, the lambdoidal, runs between the parietals and occipital. The lambdoidal bisects, from left to right, the skull's lower half above the neck. The sagittal divides the centerline. The coronal suture, above the skull's forehead, runs temple to temple.

"Ok. So, in the Boone cranial mold, how much of this was open?"

"A bunch. All the coronal was open. The sagittal and lambdoidal was open. If I was to show you a typical eighty-six-year-old man's skull sutures, you would see that most of them are obliterated along most of the length." He found several skulls to prove his point.

"And you didn't see that with…"

"They were all open. That would indicate a much younger person."

Attempting to extrapolate a skull's age from its suture lines is controversial. "Again, there are variations. If you have the sutures and that's all you have, you can make some estimation. But they're not 100 percent reliable."

He reckoned he'd examined about thirty thousand skulls, plus participated in longevity studies of the Abkhazia of Soviet Georgia of people one hundred years or older leading active lives—riding horses, working, fathering children. To quantify morphological changes, he examined Abkhazian skeletons and bones of the elderly.

"I didn't see any of those normal, healthy-aging features in the Boone skull," he said.

We switched to the delicate topic of race. "Most of the characteristics of the Boone skull are seen on skulls of African American origin," he said. "Most of the enslaved in Boone's day would have been predominately of African ancestry." He concluded that this skull may have been molded from an adult male "younger than eighty-six. Most of the neuro-cranium's morphological features suggest African ancestry." I pressed him for a definitive answer.

"My gut feeling is that it was a forty- to sixty-year-old African American male." He said it was better than a "50/50 chance." The way to know would be to check DNA, measure long bones to calculate stature and look for anomalies. "Did Boone ever have a broken arm or anything?" he asked.

"Ankle. He was shot during an Indian raid," I said.

"OK. You could X-ray the ankles and see if you have an old healed fracture." Since Dan's smaller bones were too decayed for recovery, likely his ankles, along with his hands, feet and short ribs, never made it to Kentucky with his head and pelvis, vertebrae, arms and legs.

"In your opinion, is the cast of the alleged Boone skull made from the skull of an eighty-five-year-old male Caucasian that stood five foot eight?" I held my recorder close to his face.

"I tend to think not," he said, grinning and speaking louder in my mic, "I'm shaking my head 'no.' I can't prove it unequivocally. For all I know it may not be a cast of the real thing." This is a good point, considering some casts were molded from an actual skull, and some were molded from copies. A case against body-switching, I argued, lies in its disrespect for the dead.

Not so, he said. "People's bodies are consistently bulldozed out of the ground and destroyed. If it's somebody else, you just turn your back, but if it's your family you'll get upset about it." Looters vandalize burials. Developers encroach on abandoned graveyards. "I can take somebody out in the woods and they'll say, 'This is where so-and-so is buried,' and you're lucky if you get within twenty feet of them."

He worked with law officials in collecting murder victims from shallow graves, under rocks and in rivers. He worked with archaeologists on Native American remains. Families called to find their kin in old graveyards. Body retrieval is rarely without complications.

Indoors, distinct frames of reference exist. A witness to an indoor murder recalls concrete details—rooms, corners, stairways and distance to an object in a hall or furniture. Left undisturbed, such references do not change. Outdoors, lighting changes, trees fall or grow, paths are created, stones are moved, landscapes are destroyed and vandals kick over stones and steal fixtures.

Wolf had accompanied lawmen escorting murderers to forested crime scenes to retrieve victims. The killer will point and say, "'I buried him right next to that rock,' and you dig and there's nothing there. You find the body twenty feet away." Eyewitnesses are not always reliable.

"Without trying to impugn anyone, what was the general reaction to your comments?"

"Let's just say they weren't well received here in Frankfort." At a Rotarian talk he sensed real hostility. After the story broke before his previously scheduled appearance, he was unable to lecture on his original topic. "Everyone wanted to get on with the Boone thing." He obliged them, adlibbing an affable, good-ole-boyish death chat over lunch to a boisterous, less-than-appreciative crowd.

"I received all kinds of negative comments. People got bent out of shape." Attendees publically chastised him—creating doubts would hurt tourism, they declared. Speaking engagements were cancelled. A New York City talk show host invited him up, offering airfare, lodging and a generous check. Wolf demurred.

Boone's descendants called to offer theories and mailed in their genealogical pedigrees. None of them wanted to unearth Dan. Schoolkids came by with a unique fundraising idea: to solicit cash to exhume Boone. Wolf told them to "donate the money to something like the famine in Ethiopia or something that matters."

We toured the lab. An antlered buck lay strewn on the walk-in cooler's floor, its tawny carcass pushed aside. "Out of season," he said. A frozen red-tailed hawk crowded a corner, beak open in a silent scream, yellow talons curved inward and frosty neck feathers ruffled by a shotgun blast. An image flashed in my mind of bloody knuckles and rescued puppies.

He autographed the picture of him hovering over Boone's skull in my *National Geographic* as we sipped coffee in the lab's kitchen. I poured the rest in my thermos and munched a sandwich as he popped in a VHS tape and switched on a TV. A swastika-carved forehead with a scrunched brow and bullet eyes loomed like an evil Oz from a dark lair—*Manson*.

I felt a shiver. I wasn't sure why we were winding down by watching a docudrama about a psycho blathering helter-skelter poetry to his baldheaded hippie harem. I'll admit, viewing *Manson* among the whipped-stitched and toe-tagged and near the morgue's murder and mayhem lobby showcase transported me to a higher plane of enlightened, goose-bumped creepiness.

Dr. Wolf had been more than hospitable. I stopped hours later at Beaver Dam for gas. Under my dome light, I opened my *National Geographic* to read, "Here is to your boon to history, David J. Wolf."

We stayed in touch. He talked about his dogs, investigations, treatments and the long hours he was putting in. Our last call ended much like my first, with his parting shot: "I hope this Boone thing doesn't wind up being a boondoggle for you." Our laughter was less hearty this time.

Still, I was startled afterward when I saw in our newspaper's obits the headline: "Forensic Anthropologist Dr. David Wolf, 49, Dies."

Three years later, his successor did her own inspection of Boone's skull cast as Kentuckians reenacted Frankfort's Boone's sesquicentennial funeral anniversary.

22

He Analyzed His Brain

Houseboats edged nearer to Riverfront Park's shore, sleek double-deckers trimmed in chrome, white and blue and hung with safety floatation throw rings. Pilots in swim trunks, Panamas, Ray-Bans and flip-flops manned helms, the crews' faces planted on PBR cans. Two hours past meridian, Saturday, August 12, 1995, the cheery funeral armada made an amphibious landing as part of Frankfort's Bicentennial-Boone Burial Sesquicentennial. Bare-chested sailors handed off two coffins to sartorially dressed pallbearers beside the horse-drawn, glass-sided hearses.

It was scorching. Brows and lips beaded sweat and faces dripped. Panting horses stomped and pooped in the canvas catch bags hitched under their tails. Ladies in antebellum dresses sported parasols and wide-brim Victorian straw hats with flowers.

War of 1812 reenactors stood at ease with gun butts grounded, their River Raisin "United We Stand" battle standard limp. Red fringe bordered the militiamen's navy hunting shirts. Embossed leather cravats forced all heads forward and haversack and canteen straps bisected their chests. Clergymen for the Presbyterian, Methodist and Christian Churches lay aside doctrinal wrangling to exhibit their piety. Rotund Masons were in shorts, their shirts tucked under mystic aprons cinched below their girths.

Luminaries baked in coaches, drivers snapping the reins, hooves hitting dry and hollow on the road. Nicky Hughes, dressed in wool as John J. Crittenden, walked to the van's left—carpetbag in one hand and cane in the other. Saxton's Cornet Band—in soaked scarlet tunics, black and red visor caps and black pants—struck a dirge, the entourage tromping down Broadway to the Old Capitol. Russ Hatter, opposite Hughes and to the van's far right, portrayed Ben Franklin, the county's namesake (who never visited). Poor Ben was beset with his own tailoring woes.

"I remember wondering if my leotards were going to stay up," Ben told me. "They were slipping below my knees." It was too hot to go to the cemetery. "Mayor Frank Sower nearly passed out. We just walked around the block once."

Nicky Hughes and cemetery supervisor Jim Richardson planned the parade, hiring NASA astronaut Dr. Ronald M. Sega to talk about America's spirit of exploration. It was an apt parallel: how argonaut Daniel Boone was like space pioneer John Glenn, or even Captain James Kirk's brave men and women on the starship *Enterprise*, "going where no man has gone before… the Final Frontier." There were more speakers, heaps of burgoo, a long rifle frolic and a cemetery tour. Hughes, a well-regarded historian and writer, is also a dedicated living history buff and helped secure reenactors.

"Nicky is into authenticity. He tried to do it as much as possible the way they did it," Russ said. Pastors preached on the quad. Hughes channeled Senator Crittenden's oratory. Ben's leotards miraculously clung to his sweaty midriff. And the band played on.

Boone cousins representing six states admired the Kentuckians' stoic solidarity in the face of climatic adversity. "It was really hot for them," Marshall Wilcoxon, a New Yorker whose forebear married into Boone's sister's line, told the *Journal*. "Sweat was pouring off their faces." She was dismayed at the boaters clad as Daytona spring breakers. "It should be a solemn occasion."

Cable 10's Community Television crew on Broadway zoomed in on processional host and hostess Charlie Hinds and Janet Myers. Charlie, past seventy, wore a white, long-sleeved shirt and gray slacks. His necktie knot made an edifice for his moist jawline, horn rims pressed above his nose, gray hair parted and swirled left. An alumnus of University of Kentucky, he was born in Henderson County and fought with General Patton in World War II.

Janet, screened under a wide straw hat, glanced back at the oncoming cavalcade. A flashing police car was nearing. Behind it rolled the hearses. The townsfolk were up for it in spite of the sultry heat. She nodded and smiled at the camera, awaiting her cue. Then she said, "Hello Frankfort. We're here on August the 12th, 1995, a wonderfully hot August Saturday afternoon. We're getting ready for the celebration today of the reenactment of the interment of the bodies of Daniel and Rebecca Boone."

She gazed over at Charlie through her square glasses. His purplish face on the TV monitor was not radiating comfort.

"Hello," he said, squinting. "I'm very much interested in history in the area. I've lived here about forty years. I used to be director of the Kentucky Historical Society. We have Boone's rifle, his original rifle called Tick-Licker, over here in the museum and have other artifacts of Daniel Boone's."

Janet clasped her neck chain and smiled. Charlie, gathering steam, went on.

"In September, this will be the 150th anniversary of the reburial of Daniel Boone, brought in from Missouri. Missouri didn't want to let him go. We talked to 'em. We worked through the family and the family helped us dig him up."

"I'm not so sure that would have been agreeable to him," Janet said. "He had some unpleasant experiences here."

"Well, he left here in 1799, and he died there in 1820. I guess if he wanted to come back, he would have, wouldn't he?"

"You would think so," Janet's brow ruffled, the marching band high-stepping past them.

"I would like to think he would, though," Charlie said, introducing the parade's historical players: preachers and politicos, militiamen and frontiersman Bland Ballard. "Bland Ballard loved to fight Indians. He'd get up before breakfast in the morning to see if he could find any Indians because some of his family was killed by Indians."

Saxton's Cornet Band veered left as horsemen reined in at the Old Capitol. Men, women and children crowded the green under the shade. Pallbearers in coats and top hats unlatched the hearses' rear doors, sliding out the black-draped coffins to lug up to the pavilion.

"When they brought Daniel Boone back, all that was left was his skull," Charlie said. "His skull lay in state up here for two months with his wife—there was more of her. They had a phrenologist come in and examine his skull, and he said, 'You've got the right man, all right!' And he analyzed his brain and showed how clever he was. So, we're fairly satisfied that we got him. There's a story that they dug up somebody else, but I don't believe it one minute. And I don't think Kentuckians do."

"No, but it does make for some good controversy," Janet said. "And goodness knows we enjoy a good controversy."

"We really do," agreed Charlie, smiling.

Jim Richardson really did not enjoy this good controversy. Frankfort's cemetery superintendent was no fan of the hullaballoo surrounding, arguably, the state's most famous historical tiff.

"Daniel Boone is buried in the Frankfort Cemetery. It's a statement of fact. It requires no explanation," he'd told the press before the parade, as rumors ratcheted up about exhuming the frontiersman for DNA testing. "We're not going to dig Daniel up!"

More than twenty years of fielding nagging queries had made the middle-aged superintendent less than patient in dealing with grave-visiting necromancers and letter-writing naysayers. He was critical of the state's past forensic anthropologist Dr. David Wolf for spinning anew the unidentified body myth. The public kerfuffle sent fresh passels of inquiring minds to Daniel and Rebecca's grave site for him and his crew to deal with, often daily.

Richardson had had his fill of it. "The pathologist had a flair for the theatrics and liked to stir up controversy," he told reporters. The superintendent chided folks on all sides of the controversy. Even, seemingly, the FCC's Missouri envoys Thomas Crittenden, Phillip Swigert and William Boon. "They dug them up and got out quickly. They filed a report in the newspaper about it, so it must be true," Jim said.

Nor did he think much of Missouri's marker that the Daughters of the American Revolution placed on the Boones' graves in 1915. "The DAR put a bronze plaque up at the Missouri site saying it was him. If the DAR says it, it must be true." And of the on-going revisionist declarations and rumors about Boone's plaster pate housed at the Old Capitol?

"I went to the historical society, signed out the cast and took it to the state's new forensic pathologist, Emily Craig," Richardson told *Frankfort State Journal*'s Susan Allen. "She took it out and practically burst out laughing. She said there was no way anybody could make any prediction on it. The plaster cast had been rounded and polished. All the bumps were gone."

Richardson said Dr. Craig described the partial cranial cast as "having negligible scientific worth," being only the top of a decidedly male skull. "It was altered," she said. "It was filed down to make it look nice. As a scientist, I can't in good conscience make a determination."

Frankfort's cemetery head was adamant. "The historical record leaves no doubt that the Boones are here," he said, offering his own evidence. "I received a piece of mail from a mass mailing addressed to 'Daniel Boone, director of Grounds and Management, Frankfort Cemetery.'"

AT BUDDY'S PIZZA ACROSS from the Capital City Museum, I ordered a Stromboli hoagie and chips. Jabba, a table over, crammed a monstrous pepperoni and cheese wedge down his pelican gullet and gulped a Bud, between burps lecturing his wife on the dangers of veganism.

Jim Richardson, a squarely built, tall older guy with glasses, sat across from me. Trained "in intelligence and surveillance," after Vietnam, the twenty-year air force vet did tours in Thailand, Tokyo, Philippines and Las Vegas—"the last was the best." After thanking him for his service in the trenches at Harrah's, a No Man's Land of showgirls spilling from skimpy bathing suits festooned with ostrich plumes, I asked about the Frankfort cemetery's original nucleus, Colonel Ambrose W. Dudley's Hunter's Garden.

"It was named for John Hunter, an early settler, who sold it to Isham Talbot, whose daughter Eliza married Dudley. The FCC bought it and renamed it." There was a quid pro quo; Dudley's lots, he said, were partial payment for monies he had advanced for the growth of the cemetery. The Dudleys are buried near the Boones.

"The FCC deeded the site to the state. The Kentucky Veterans War Memorial is also owned by the state," Richardson said, which clinched the deal to get Boone's monument built.

"That's fascinating. How did that come to be? Politics?"

"Politics. Basically. That was how Brown, Crittenden, Swigert and all those guys got involved. You know, 'We'll give you a space here for Daniel Boone to be buried in.' So, the state owns it." I wondered when he was hired on—before or after Wolf's comments hit the news.

"In 1985, just after Dr. Wolf's story was published in *National Geographic*."

"Did the controversy affect tourism at the cemetery? Did it generate interest?"

"Not really. The average person—they don't care. The monument's there. The state has a sign over him. We got him." After being Dan and Rebecca's caretaker for twenty-three years, he seemed to take the Boone burial matter as a personal feud. Kentucky is famous for them.

"Did you ever talk to Dr. Wolf about these things?

"I never knew Dr. Wolf. I never talked to Dr. Wolf. Just read the magazine article."

As the sesquicentennial's events reopened the burial debate, Richardson decided it was time for a second opinion on the skull cast. He called Wolf's successor, Dr. Emily Craig. "I showed it to her. She said, 'All the points that could be used for identification had been sanded off.' Took about five minutes."

"She didn't get out calipers or anything?"

"No. She laughed and said, 'You can't determine it, period!' She looked it over, felt it and within a minute or so, she said 'don't bother with it 'cause it can't be done.'"

Dr. Craig summed up her thoughts on the "model that was reportedly made from a mold of Daniel Boone's cranium" in her letter to Richardson on March 1, 1995. After finding the skull cast "unique and significant" due to its history, she observed that "this is apparently a filed-down plaster model made from a multiple-piece mold of the top of a human male's skull....However, the craniometric analysis...is based upon precise measurements of an actual skull. Variations of a few millimeters here and there can make an enormous difference in the outcome of the analysis. Therefore, I would be very reluctant to base any scientific conclusions regarding race on such an artifact."

I wasn't sure how much Dr. David Wolf's analyses veered from Dr. Emily Craig's. Both forensic experts seemed to concur that the plaster cast was molded from a male's skull. Neither would confirm the relic's race. Both said there wasn't much to go on, readily agreeing that any assumption based solely on this relic would be inconclusive.

When I emailed Dr. Craig about my unearthing two more provenanced Boone plaster skull casts at the Filson, transparently hinting and wondering aloud how skulls A and B might compare to each other and to the Kentucky Historical Society's plaster cranial model in Frankfort, she politely replied, "I would rather not comment on any of the work done related to this particular artifact."

My second inquiry to a University of Louisville–based forensic anthropologist animated another firm demurral along the lines of "I'd rather not get involved. I'm sure you understand." (I did.) A third University of Kentucky forensic pathologist merely ignored my query.

I could go no further.

Honestly, I wanted to send them all thank-you notes for helping bring to an end my odyssey along Daniel Boone's last trail, and in the same year, ironically, plans were underway in Kentucky and Missouri to commemorate his death's bicentennial.

EPILOGUE

My journey on this trail began when the renowned Louisville photographer William Strode, escorted by a Mountain Man friend of mine, Warren "Hawk" Boughton, visited Lavina's and my garage flat while we were poor college students. Bill, on his own quest shooting the Boone story for *National Geographic* magazine, sought any gen I had, which was none. I later scrounged Hawk's *National Geographic*'s December 1985 issue, with "Daniel Boone: First Hero of the Frontier," by Elizabeth Moize (smashingly illustrated with Bill's superb photographs), and eagerly devoured it.

Moize's inclusion of Dr. David J. Wolf's assertions rekindled memories of Hawk's and my July 1982 tour of the Historic Daniel Boone Home, where I first gazed into the colonel's death room and at the gift shop bought the Boone coffee cup I'm drinking from as I write this. In the home's basement, I hand-copied Jesse Crump's 1919 letter, yellowed with age and framed on the wall, about Alonzo Callaway saying Daniel was still in Missouri.

My curiosity whetted after Moize's article, I began collecting historical minutia about the matter and, on December 17, 1991, met with Dr. Wolf. Following his death, I shelved my notes on Boone's plaster head to write on other things and gain my sea legs in my first year as a very unlikely professor at Murray State University's Department of History.

Four books and too many articles later, thumbing through my files for something else, I dug out a faded manila folder marked DAVID WOLF INTERVIEW: BOONE'S SKULL. Intrigued, a muse arising like Lazarus from his deathbed, I read it, puzzling anew over the colonel's bones and again took up his trail, ending this book in the bicentennial year of Daniel Boone's death and two years after my retirement from MSU. It's been a mighty long journey.

NOW, TWO HUNDRED YEARS after Daniel Boone died, I prowled Hunter's Garden near where he and Rebecca are buried. The altitude-defying Cliff Avenue and scenic river walk no longer exist and the hillside's dense scrub obscures the awesome beauty that was once here. Still, taking in this majestic vista makes this adopted son of the Bluegrass feel like a Kentuckian of old. History so pulses from this sacred earth that it makes me tremble.

A spitting rain wetting my straw fedora's brim dripped onto my glasses. Indigo vistas above darken and then clear and return to zinc. Cumulus slip past, hurrying along at Zeus's beckoning, dramatically yielding to a high-arching cumulonimbus's puffy pastels reminiscent of an N.C. Wyeth painting in the 1925 edition of Francis Parkman's *The Oregon Trail.*

The goldenrod's swatches hang heavy and low, teeming with bumblebees packing onto their bowlegged shanks' thick, sticky pollen. Summer's end is a fortnight away. The honeysuckle is spent. Tickweed—yellow, tall, waving, petals cascading—and agrimony and skullcap are giving way to boneset, thoroughwort and brown-eyed Susan. Yucca stilettoes stab past the perimeter's headstones. Hickory and oak mast are heavy—a hard winter is coming. Webworms shroud mulberry and persimmon trees in elaborate silken whorls.

Scottish landscaper Robert Carmichael is buried in Section G near four of Frankfort Cemetery Company's original trustees. Philip "the pope" Swigert rests on the crowded upper ledge. Mason and Orlando Brown are with their brood on the spacious lower deck; dingy mort cloths top a few of the more opulent monuments. Thomas Crittenden's marker on the upper row is hard to read. So too is the Honorable John J. Crittenden's spire (down near the Browns) and his wives'—Sarah, Maria and Elizabeth.

Several of Kentucky's governors are buried near the Revolutionary War soldier ossuary. Ambrose Dudley, Bland Ballard and the Reverend and Mrs. Philip Slater Fall are close to a host of luminaries named on Rebecca and Daniel's 1845 processional program.

Hunter's Garden's lower tier remains a serene, grass-lined walk of the FCC's who's who within stone-bordered plots a baseball's toss from the omnipresent Boones—the barefoot pauper Ellison Williamson off to one side of them. Age has pitted many monuments leaving them illegible. Mason

Brown's truncated obelisk of pinkish-brown granite has been spared this indignity; it's rather plain and hard to read, but it still has a satiny gleam. His is the only one like it. I doubt this is coincidental. Ten yards to its right is Orlando's supine, grayish-white sepulcher. Orlando passed the night before he was to be confirmed as an Episcopalian.

There's a military burial today. Far off, I hear taps and doff my hat in time for the three volleys loosed in perfect sync. I wipe my eyes.

O Death!

A rabbit path cut down the slope behind the Browns to bisect a narrow stagecoach path—marked by ATV tires—that has been here since the site's founding. I crossed it, pushing into a thicket, descending, clinging to tangled vines, eying the swirling Kentucky below and trying to get there. Easing into a copse to relieve myself and eat a pawpaw, I knew I'd never get back up this crag with my shirt and jeans intact and went back past the coach road to sit by Judge Brown's grave.

One can't help but marvel at his prescient creative ingenuity. Embarking on such an expansive project in what little spare time he might have had, sure that his fellow Kentuckians—a curiously unpredictable breed as a rule, even when sober—would see it through. A peculiar quality of his was his phantom-like ability to stay off stage, content to be a judicial Oz behind the curtain, pulling the gears and levers, nudging Orlando to fire off newspaper editorials, while letting others take credit for his gift to his beloved city. One senses an extraordinary genius at work in Liberty Hall plying along on his own journey.

Mr. Brown, in rescuing Mr. and Mrs. Boone materially, kept them safe historically. In July 1845, Messrs. Boon, Crittenden and Swigert warned Mr. Griswold that the Boones would be hard to protect in his remote graveyard. One hundred and seventy-five years later it still has no secure barrier or border plat. Most of its original markers are gone. The Boones' stone has been defaced, its bronze marker obliterated for drug money. Warren County officials referee local squabbles over it. The state, of course, does nothing. One day maybe the old graveyard and those in it will get their due.

But my odyssey ends in the heart of the Bluegrass at the foot of a tall brown monument overlooking the Kentucky River. I have found what I sought. It's taken many years to get here, journeying along the last trail of America's original pathfinder, Daniel Boone.

The End.

Bibliography

For Daniel Boone's post–1799 western years, I consulted Boone's biographies but opted for the original sources from the Draper Manuscripts, mostly the Daniel Boone Papers, 19C, 21C, 23C, 28C, 30C and Draper's Notes, 6S, 22S. I've been the beneficiary of an abiding friendship with Missouri Boone historian Ken Kamper. Ken has performed yeoman's service in tracking down, platting and collating Boone's trans-Mississippian land grants, trails and more. One hopes his indefatigable one-man Dan'l crusade will help correct Missouri's neglect of this unique part of its fur-trade past. His stoically penned newsletters always make for profitable reading. Ken also supplied reams of information and remains a collegial kindred spirit who I hold in brotherly awe.

Primary Sources: Manuscripts

Lyman C. Draper Manuscript Collection. Microfilm ed. Madison: State Historical Society of Wisconsin, 1980.

Series C: Daniel Boone Papers.
Series E: Samuel Brady and Lewis Wetzel Papers.
Series J: George Rogers Clark Papers.
Series NN: Pittsburgh and Northwest Virginia Papers.
Series S: Draper's Notes.
Series BB: Simon Kenton Papers.

Series CC: Kentucky Papers.
Series ZZ: Virginia Papers.

Primary Sources: Articles and Related

American State Papers. Vol. 2, 396.

Clarkson, Thomas. "Quaker Funerals." World Spirituality. http://www.worldspirituality.org.

Coshow, A.J. Letter, March 10, 1894. *Brownsville (TX) Daily Herald*. [Daniel Boone exhibiting cherrywood coffin.]

Johnson, Dave. "Reminiscences from the Life of Col. Cave Johnson." *Register of the Kentucky Historical Society* 20, no. 59 (1922): 207–12.

Landrum, Reverend William B. "Daniel and Rebecca Boone are Reburied in Frankfort." *Kentucky Explorer*, 2001.

"A Letter by Wade Hays from California." *Searching for the Boone Family*. https://www.Saucybookworm13.wordpress.

Nwokebuihe, Stanley Chinedu. *The Use of Ground Penetrating Radar to Locate Unmarked Graves at the Bryan Cemetery Missouri*. Missouri University of Science & Technology. September 2012.

Welch, James E. *Christian Repository*. Louisville, KY, March 1860.

Primary Sources: Books

Barber, John Warner, and Henry Howe. *Our Whole Country*. Cincinnati, OH: C. Tuttle, 1861.

Cresswell, Nicholas. *The Journal of Nicholas Cresswell, 1774–1777*. 2nd ed. New York: Dial Press, 1928.

Devoto, Bernard, ed. *The Journals of Lewis and Clark*. 8 vols. Boston: Houghton Mifflin, 1953.

Filson, John. *The Discovery, Settlement, and Present State of Kentucke*. New York: Corinth Books, 1962. Originally published 1784.

Flint, Timothy. *Life and Exploits of Col. Dan'l Boone.* Philadelphia, PA: H.M. Rulison, 1856.

Foster, Lillian. *Wayside Glimpse, North and South*. New York: Rudd & Carlton, 1860.

Hammon, Neal O., ed. *My Father, Daniel Boone: The Draper Interviews with Nathan Boone*. Lexington: University of Kentucky Press, 1999.

Houston, Peter. *A Sketch in the Life and Character of Daniel Boone*. Edited with an introduction by Ted Franklin Belue. Mechanicsburg, PA: Stackpole Books, 1998.

Peck, John Mason. *Life of Daniel Boone: The Pioneer of Kentucky*. New York: University Society, 1905.

Ted Franklin Belue Interviews

Wheelock Crosby Brown, Bernardo Brunetti, Ralph Gregory, Russ Hatter, James Holmberg, Marc Houseman, Ken Kamper, David Knotts, Grady Manus, Elizabeth Moize, William Ray, Jim Richardson, Thomas Shelby Watson and David Wolf.

Other Interviews

Clark, Thomas D. Interview with Thomas S. Watson. May 22, 1975.

Coleman, J. Winston, Jr. Interview with Thomas S. Watson. May 22, 1975.

Parker, Fess. Interview by Don Carleton. Television Academy, July 24, 2000. https://interviews.televisionacademy.com/interviews/fess-parker.

Tapp, Hambleton. Interview with Thomas S. Watson. May 22, 1975.

Ken Kamper Newsletters

Boone-Duden Historical Review (*BDHR*)

Boone-Duden Historical Society (*DBHS*)

Boone and Frontier Research Letter (BFRL)

History and Genealogy Research Letter (HGRL)

Contemporary Newspapers

Capital Gazette, circa 1880s.

Chicago Globe, circa 1888.

Earlington Kentucky Bee, circa 1890s.

Frankfort Commonwealth, circa 1830s–40.

Franklin County Observer, circa 1911.

Kansas City Times, circa 1911.
Kentucky Yeoman, circa 1840.
Marthasville Record, circa 1915.
Mexico Weekly Ledger, 1908.
St. Louis New Era, circa 1844–45.
St. Louis Reporter, circa 1845.
Warrenton Banner, 1911.
Weekly Enquirer and Messenger, 1844.

Multimedia

Daniel Boone Celebration/Activities/Funeral with Service. FPB-TV-Frankfort, Kentucky. August 12, 1995. DVD.

Secondary Sources: Articles and Related Data

Alirangues, Loretta M. "Funerary Practices in Early and Modern America." *Morbid Outlook*. http://www.morbidoutlook.com.

Allen, Susan Allen. "Mystery Solved," *Frankfort State Journal*, June 2, 2000.

Amyx, Clifford. "The Authentic Image of Daniel Boone." *Missouri Historical Review* 82 (1988): 153–64.

Anderson, Hattie M. "Missouri, 1804–1828: Peopling a Frontier State." *Missouri Historical Review* 30 (1937): 150–80.

Baker, Dave. "Boone Reburial Revisited." *State Journal*. August 13, 1995.

Bell, Ovid. "Missouri History Not Found." *Missouri History Review* (1955): 288–90.

———. "St. Louisan Restoring House Where Daniel Boone Lived." *Missouri Historical Review* 21, no. 2 (1927): 288–90.

Belue, Ted Franklin. "Indian-Influenced Woodsmen of the Cane." In *Book of Buckskinning VII*. ed. William H. Scurlock. Texarkana, TX: Scurlock Publishing, 1995.

Bible passages from King James Version.

Bien, Peter. *The Mystery of Quaker Light*. Pendle Hill Pamphlet, n.d.

Bishop, Julia Truitt. "Old Papers Give Light as to How Daniel Boone Ran His Store." *Kentucky Explorer*, June 1993.

Bloomfield, Kentucky. www.bloomfieldky.com.

Boone Manuscript, vol. 26, no. 67, Wisconsin Historical Society. Archived at the Historic Daniel Boone Home.

Bourbon News, February 16, 1906.

Brown, Preston. "John Mason Brown: One of the Original Founders of the Filson Club." *Filson Club History Quarterly* 13 (1939): 125–134. [For John Mason Brown handling skull of Daniel Boone, see his letter to Lyman. C. Draper, October 4, 1882, in Draper MS. 16C: 82–82.]

Bryan, George Chester. "Favors Boone Monument." *Warrenton Banner*, September 3, 1915.

———. "Marthasville—As the Town Appeared Seventy Years Ago." *Marthasville Record*, July 13, 1923.

———. *Marthasville Record*, January 6, 1922.

———. "Relative of Daniel Boone Tells of the Pioneer's Grave." *Franklin County Observer*, May 26, 1911.

Bryan, Jonathan. Find a Grave. wikitree.com/wiki/Bryan-21.

Bryan, William S. "Daniel Boone Burial Site." *Missouri Historical Review* 4 (1909).

———. "Daniel Boone in Missouri." *Missouri History Review* 3, no. 4 (July 1909): 293–99.

———. "Daniel Boone in Missouri." *Missouri History Review* 4, no. 1 (October 1909): 29–35.

———. "Who's Who in the World, 1912." www.findagrave.com/cgi-bin/fg.cgi?page=gr&GRid=74163020.

Callaway, Bobbie. "Flanders Callaway House, Femme Osage District, St. Charles County, MO." *Callaway Family Association* (*blog*). November 2, 2004. https://callawayfamily.info.

Carmen, Amy. "A Fitting Tribute to the Boones." *State Journal*, August 10, 1995.

———. "The 'reburial' of the Boones." *State Journal*, August 6, 1995. [Contains excerpt from September 16, 1845 account from *Frankfort Commonwealth*.]

"The Cemetery That Was a 19th Century Tourist Attraction." New England Historical Society. www.newenglandhistoricalsociety.com.

Chittenden, Hiram Martin. *History of Early Steamboat Navigation on the Missouri River: Life and Adventure of Joe LaBarge.* New York: Francis P. Harper, 1903.

Cinnamond, Mrs. Alex. "Letter to the Editor." *State Journal*. n.d. [Co-chairperson of Frankfort's Graveyards Committee writing about lost location of 1812 River Raisen soldiers.]

Clark, Rikki. "Bellevue Cemetery." *State Journal*, 2015.

Clift, G. Glenn. "*The Old Master*, Colonel Orlando Brown, 1801–1867." *Register of the Kentucky Historical Society* 49 (January 1951): 5–24.

Coady, Jean Howerton. "Whatever Happened to Idea to Move Graves of Daniel Boone, Wife?" *Louisville Courier-Journal*, August 29, 1977.

Cochran, Rochelle. "Official Statement from the Boone Society About the Sale of Daniel Boone's Missouri Gravesite." *Boone Society*, 2005.

Cole Family Association. https://www.colefamilyassociation.com.

Craig, Emily to Jim Richardson. March 1, 1995.

Craig, Emily email to Ted Franklin Belue. August 2, 1917.

Crawford, Byron. "Daniel Boone's Body Lies A-Mould'ring in Missouri?" *Louisville Courier-Journal*, August 7, 1981.

"Curlee, Col. Francis Marion Curlee." Serling Price Camp No. 145. www.pricecamp.org.

"Daniel Boone's Body Undoubtedly Lies in the Cemetery in Frankfort: Colonel Durrett Says Missouri Story Is Unfounded Rumor." *Kentucky Explorer*, July/August 2009.

"The Daniel Boone Judgement Tree." *Missouri Botanical Garden Bulletin* 10 (1922): 25–26.

Daniel Boone Shrine Association. The Sage of a Man and a House. https://archive.org.

Darnell, Ermina Jett. "*Filling the Chinks*." *Warren County Record*, 1966.

Denn, Charlie. "Man Charged with Plaque Theft." *Warren County Record*, July 17, 2008.

Dyer, Robert L. "A Brief History of Steamboating on the Missouri River with an Emphasis on the Boonslick Region." *Boone's Lick Heritage* 5 (1977). http://www.riverboatdaves.com.

Earlington Kentucky Bee, January 25, 1900:1. [RE: Warner Campbell and defacing of Boone's KY tomb.]

Emmons, Benjamin to Floyd C. Shoemaker. Undated letter. Papers #995. Western Historical Manuscript, vol. 1. University of Missouri, St. Louis.

Emmons, Benjamin to Nettie Beauregard. Undated letter, circa 1928. Missouri Historical Society.

Emmons, Benjamin to Nettie H. Beauregard. Undated letter circa 1928. Western Historical Manuscript, vol. 1. University of Missouri, St. Louis.

Evening Sun, May 27, 1910. [DAR unveiling of redressed Frankfort Boone monument in *Paducah*.]

"Filson Historical Society's Beginnings and Col. Reuben T. Durrett." *Filson Historical Society* (blog). https://filsonhistorical.org.

Flanders Callaway Home. National Register of Historic Places. U.S. Department of Interior. National Park Service. 1968.

"Forensic Anthropology Assitant." Joe Nickell. www.joenickell.com.

Foristell, Jennie Chinn Lewis letters to the *Marthasville Record*, November 15, 1915.

"Former NPPA President William H. Strode, 69." National Press Photographers Association. http://www.nppa.org.

"The Fowler Brothers." Talking Heads. https://www.countway.harvard.edu.

Franke, Dorris Keeven. *Warren County, Missouri*. Charleston, SC: Arcadia Press, 2011.

Frankfort Weekly News and Roundabout, June 25, 1908. [Regarding Louis Fettweis restoring Boone tomb.]

Freeman, Joan E. to Ken Kamper. Letter. August 5, 1991. [Dr. Freeman, curator of collections, Museum Division, of the State Historical Society of Wisconsin, confirming Lyman C. Draper had a plaster Boone skull that deteriorated and was disposed of. Archivist Harold Miller told me the same thing.]

"'French' Jacob Groshong." Washburn University. www.washburn.edu.

Gardyne, David. "Kentuckians Honor Boone and Wife, but Fail to Get Right Bodies." *Weekly Intelligencer*, January 4, 1917.

"Gen. Thomas L. Crittenden's Frankfort." *Random Thoughts on History* (blog). randomthoughtonhistory.blogspot.com.

Gibson, Dan. "Burial Customs and Rituals." Our Ancestor's Way of Life. 2003. www.angelfire.com.

A Grave Interest (blog). agraveinterest.blogspot.com.

"The Grave of Daniel Boone." *St. Louis New Era*, April 30, 1944.

"Griswold, Harvey." Access Geneaology. www.accessgenealogy.com.

Hardin, B. Bayless. "The Brown Family of Liberty Hall." *Filson Club History Quarterly* 16 (1942): 75–87.

———. "Daniel Boone and the Frankfort Cemetery." *Register of the Kentucky Historical Society* 50 (1952): 201–36.

Herron, Ron. "No Owner Can Be Found: From Underground, Graveyard Emerges." *State Journal*, August 1, 1971.

———. "The Underworld: Old Graveyards Continue to Mystify Local Historians." *State Journal*, n.d.

"History and Assessment: Historic Daniel Boone Home." The Historic Daniel Boone Home & Heritage Center Self-Guided Tour. Lindenwood University.

Horsley, McKenna. "War Veteran, Historian and Volunteer Remembered as 'Wonderful Man.'" *State Journal*, August 19, 2019.

Hughes, Nicky, and Russ Hatter. *Frankfort Cemetery: The Westminster Abbey of Kentucky*. Frankfort, KY: Frankfort Heritage Press, 2007.

"Jerry and Linda Bruckheimer to Give Commencement Address." Centre College. http://www.centre.edu.

"John P. Hale." *West Virginia Encyclopedia*. https://www.wvencyclopedia.org.

Jones, Donna Dodd Terrell. "Kentucky's Frontier Moral Code for the Body Retrieval of Indian-Wounded of Indian-Slain Pioneers and for the Subsequent Burial of Indian-Slain Casualties." http://jkhg.org.

Jones, Humphrey, and Susannah Gentry. Isaacs and Related Families of Kentucky. http://janstree.com/.

Jones, John S. *Warrenton Banner*, October 13, 1911.

Kamper, Ken. "The Boone Salt Lick." *Boone-Duden Historical Review*. Paper No. 2-11. (September 1991).

———. "The Booneslick Trail." *Boone-Duden Historical Review*. Paper No. 2-10. (October 1991).

———. "The Burial of Daniel Boone in Missouri and Reburial in Kentucky." *HGRL* 8 (2002): 1–10.

———. "The Daniel Boone Historical Area." *HGRL* 1 (1996): 5–17.

———. "Daniel Boone's Spanish Land Grant and Boone's town of Missouriton." *Boone-Duden Historical Review* 3 (June 1989): 2–6.

———. "Daniel Morgan Boone, Missouri's Pathfinder." *Boone-Duden Historical Review* Paper No. 3-02. (September 1991).

———. "A Fact or Two on Early Missouri History." *Boone-Duden Historical Review* (1989): 5.

———. "A Fact or Two on Early Missouri History." *Boone-Duden Historical Review* 7 (August 1992): 1–4.

———. "History Focal Points—The Boone Spanish Land Grants at Matson. Paper No. 5-01. *Boone-Duden Historical Review* (September 1991).

———. "The History of the Stone House of Nathan Boone." Paper No. P-13, 0910. 9 (2013).

———. "Papers Related to the Factual History of Daniel Boone Including His Twenty-One Years in Missouri." *Boone-Duden Historical Review* (September 1991).

———. "Research Uncovers Three Important Boone Trails in Missouri." *HGRL* 5 (2011): 3–17.

———. "Stone House of Nathan Boone." Paper No. P-13, 0910.

———. "A Tour of the Boone Settlement in Missouri." *Boone-Duden Historical Review* 1 (1993): 3–15.

Kramer, Carl. *Capital on the Kentucky.* Frankfort, KY: Historic Frankfort, 1968.

"Lexington & Ohio Railroad." Lexington History Museum. https://www.lexhistory.org.

Liberty Hall Historic Site. http://libertyhall.org.

Lindenwood University's Historic Daniel Boone Home. One-page tourist leaflet.

Loughborough, Preston Samuel. findagrave.com.

Maret, Colonel Jim. "Boone's Remains Reinterred at Frankfort, Kentucky." *Kentucky Historical Notes*, 1922.

McDaniel, Lyn. "Hannah Cole Exemplified Pioneer Spirit." In *Bicentennial Boonslick History*. N.p.: Boonslick Historical Society, 1976.

McQuie, R.E. *Mexico Weekly Ledger*, August 27, 1908.

McVicker, Mary Ellen Harshberger. "Reflections of Change: Death and Cemeteries in the Boonslick Region." 2 vols. PhD diss., University of Missouri, Columbia, 1989.

Miles, Margie. Friends of Daniel Boone Burial Site in Missouri. facebook.com/DanielBooneCemetery.

———. "Marthasville—Rich in History." City of Marthasville, Missouri. April 2013. https://cityofmarthasvillemo.org.

———. "*Marthasville's Amazing Early History*." City of Marthasville, Missouri. July 2015. https://cityofmarthasvillemo.org.

"Missouri Rhineland, Marthasville to Machen Section." Missouri State Parks. mostateparks.com.

"Missouri's Endangered Glades." Missouri Department of Conservation. https://mdc.mo.gov.

Moize, Elizabeth A. "First Hero of the Frontier." *National Geographic*, 1985.

Moon Phases. Moonconnection.com.

Morrow, Lynn. "Daniel Boone and Slave Derry Coburn." *Boone's Lick Heritage Quarterly* 12 (2013): 4–13.

Morton, Jennie C. "History of the Frankfort Cemetery." *Register of the Kentucky State Historical Society* 7 (1909): 23–34.

Mount Auburn Cemetery. https://www.nps.gov.

1997 Board Meeting. Kentucky Genealogical Society. Franklin County, KY, Bellevue Cemetery.

"OSV Documents—Historical Background on Mourning Rituals in Early 19th Century New England, 2003." Old Sturbridge Village. http://www.osv.org.

Parkman, Francis. "The Works of James Fenimore Cooper." *North American Review* (1851).

Peter, Robert. Letter from Dr. Peter to Rueben Durrett at the Filson Club. December 20, 1889. Rueben Durrett Papers, D 965, FL. 47. [Accompanied by his letter to George C. Ranck on August 18, 1880, describing Henry C. Davis casting in plaster Daniel Boone's skull on September 12, 1845, and phrenology report.]

"Philip Slater Fall." History of the Restoration Movement. https://www.therestorationmovement.com.

"A Place for the Living—Leisure, Learning, and Mourning." www.npc.gov.

Plaster casts of Daniel Boone's skull. Artifact Collection #1939.19 Major Preston Brown. Filson Historical Society.

Pring, G.H. "The Daniel Boone Judgement Tree." *Missouri Botanical Garden Bulletin* 36 (1948): 159–61.

Removal of Daniel Boone's Remains, 1845–1937. Kentucky Historical Society. [Contain Frankfort Cemetery Company letters to Nathan Boone; William Boon correspondence; statement promising to indemnify Harvey Griswold, received from grandson Arnold Griswold; massive file on early beginnings of Frankfort Cemetery, circa 1844; and Kentucky's title to Boone remains.]

Richardson, Jim. "Daniel Boone and Wife Are Buried in Frankfort," *Lexington Herald-Leader*, April 8, 1995.

———. "The Rural Cemetery Movement and the Founding of the Frankfort Cemetery." Circa 1980s.

Richmond Daily Register. "A Day in History–Aug. 30." Fort Boonesborough Supplement. August 27, 1974.

Savage, Sam. "Bloomfield Belle." Red Orbit. February 7, 2005. http://www.redorbit.com.

Schlinkmann, Mark. "Daniel Boone Home Will Become Part of St. Charles County Park System." *St. Louis Dispatch*, April 30, 2016.

Scott, Dawn. "Old Time Burial Customs," Scrapbook Memories. Scott County Historical Society. April 13, 2019. sites.rootsweb.com.

Scott, Joe. "Cemetery Ownership in Dispute: Property Includes Boone Burial Site." *St. Louis Post-Dispatch*, August 12, 2009.

"Sitting Up with the Dead." Josephine's Journal. josephinesjournal.com/sitting.htm.

"Slavery at Liberty Hall." Liberty Hall Historic Site. https://www.libertyhall.org.

Soule, Joshua. Dark Fiber. darkfiber.com.

"State Forensic Anthropologist Dies Saturday of Cancer at 49." *Murray Ledger & Times*, July 13, 1992.

State of the Ozarks. https://stateoftheozarks.net/natural/hill_hollars/glades.php.

Steere, Douglas V. "Friends and Worship." Friends General Conference. http://files.usgwararchives.net.

Talbott, Tim. "Lexington and Ohio Railroad." Kentucky History. explorekyhistory.ky.gov.

Taylor, Philip Fall. "The Plaster Cast of Daniel Boone's Head." *Register of the KY Historical Society* 15 (1907): 22.

Trout, Allan M. "Oh Be Not Deceived—Those 'Bones of Boone' in Missouri Just Ain't." *Lousiville Courier-Journal*, February 2, 1955.

2001 Board Meeting. Kentucky Genealogical Society. Franklin County, KY, Bellevue Cemetery. [Update clarifying Bellevue and Bellfont Cemetery sites. Capital City Museum Collection.]

Van Ravensway, Charles. "A Rare Midwestern Print." *Antiques* 43 (1943): 77, 93.

Vass, Arpad A. "Beyond the Grave—Understanding Human Decomposition." *Microbiology Today* 28 (2001): 190ff.

Walters, Edward M. "Rueben T. Durrett and His Collection." *Filson Club History Quarterly* 56 (1982): 368.

Warranty Deed Abstract. From Walter and Grace Stemme, recorded by Alvin H. Juergensmeter, Warrenton, MO, 1995.

"Washingtonian Gives Description of Impressive Event." *Washington Citizen*, November 5, 1915.

Way, Frederick Jr. *Way's Packet Directory: 1848–1994*. Athens: Ohio University Press, 1983.

Webb, W.L. "Daniel Boone's Body, Believed Removed to Kentucky, Still Rests in Missouri Soil, Says Kansas Relative." *Kansas City Star*, September 25, 1921.

Weich, Susan. "Historian, 101, Still Volunteering at Library Named for Him." *St. Louis Post-Dispatch*.

"Where Is Bellevue Cemetery?" Friends of Daniel Boone Burial Site in Missouri. https://www.ket.org.

"Where Lie the Remains of Daniel Boone, His Wife and Other Noted Kentucky People." *Earlington Kentucky Bee*, May 20, 1897.

Winchester News, December 23, 1908. [Data on restoration of tomb's panels.]

Wolfe, Charles. "Ky. Cemetery Probed for 1812 War Remains."

———. "Unmarked Graves at Building Site Baffle Frankfort. *State Journal*, 2002.

Woodson, Mary Willis. "History of the Lee's of KY, Con't." *Register of the Kentucky Historical Society* 1 (1903): 73–88.

Wyatt, John. "New Dispute Over Boone's Grave Ignores Mystery of His Burial," *Kansas City Times*, October 11, 1937.

Secondary Sources: Books

Andrae, Rolla P. *A True, Brief History of Daniel Boone*. Washington, MO: Miller Publishing Co., 1997.

Aron, Stephen. *American Confluence: The Missouri Frontier from Borderland to Border State*. Bloomington: University of Indiana Press, 2006.

Bakeless, John. *Daniel Boone: Master of the Wilderness*. Harrisburg, PA: Stackpole Books, 1939.

Banta, R.E. *The Ohio*. Lexington: University Press of Kentucky, 1998.

Bass, William M. *Human Osteology: A Laboratory and Field Manuel of the Human Skeleton*. Columbia: University of Missouri, 1971.

Boone, Daniel Morgan. *The United States Biographical Dictionary: Missouri Volume*. 1878.

Brown, Meredith Mason. *Frontiersman: Daniel Boone and the Making of America*. Baton Rouge: Louisiana State University Press, 2008.

Bryan, William C., and Robert Rose. *A History of the Pioneer Families of Missouri*. St. Louis, MO: Bryan, Brand & Co., 1876.

Clark, Thomas D. *A History of Kentucky*. Lexington: John Bradford Press, 1960.

———. *The Kentucky*. Lexington: University Press of Kentucky, 1992.

Collins, Lewis. *History of Kentucky*. Covington, KY: Collins and Company, 1882.

DeVoto, Bernard. *Across the Wide Missouri*. New York, American Legacy Press, 1947.

Draper, Lyman C. *The Life of Daniel Boone*. Edited with an introduction by Ted Franklin Belue. Mechanicsburg, PA: Stackpole Books, 1998.

Ellis, George Edward. *Memoir of Jacob Bigelow*. Cambridge, MA: John Wilson & Son, 1880.

Faragher, John Mack. *Daniel Boone: The Life and Legend of An American Pioneer*. New York: Henry Holt, 1992.

———. "'More Motley than Mackinaw': From Ethnic Mixing to Ethnic Cleansing on the Frontier of the Lower Missouri, 1783–1833." In *Contact Points: American Frontiers from the Mohawk Valley to the Mississippi, 1750–1830*, 304–26. Edited by Andrew R.L. Cayton and Fredrika J. Teute. Chapel Hill: University of North Carolina Press, 1998.

Ganey, Terry. "Location of Daniel Boone's Grave Becomes Bone of Contention." *St. Louis Dispatch*, September 13, 1987.

Gregory, Ralph. *The Graves of Daniel and Rebecca Boone*. Washington, MO: Self-published, 2007.

Hafen, LeRoy R., ed. *The Mountain Men and the Fur Trade of the Far West*. 10 vols. Glendale, CA: Arthur H. Clark Company, 1972.

Harper, Josephine L. *Guide to the Draper Manuscripts*. Madison: State Historical Society of Wisconsin, 1983.

Harrison, Lowell H., and James C. Klotter. *A New History of Kentucky*. Lexington: University Press of Kentucky, 1997.

Hatter, Russ, and Gene Burch. *A Walking Tour of Historic Frankfort*. Cincinnati, OH: Paul Neff, 2002.

Horan, James. *The McKenney-Hall Portrait Gallery of North American Indians*. New York: Bramhall House, 1972.

Houck, Louis. *The History of Missouri*. 2 Vols. St. Louis, MO: R.R. Donnelley & Sons Company, 1908.

Hurt, R. Douglas. *Nathan Boone and the American Frontier*. Columbia: University of Missouri Press, 1998.

Johnson, Lewis Franklin. *History of the Frankfort Cemetery*. London: Andesite Press, 2017.

———. *The History of Franklin County, Ky*. London: Forgotten Books, 2015.

Kleber, John, ed. *The Kentucky Encyclopedia*. Lexington: University Press of Kentucky, 1992.

Kukay, Madonna. "Some Still Claim Kentuckians Left Boone's Bones Behind." *State Journal*, January 18, 1988.

Lipton, Leah. *A Truthful Likeness: Chester Harding and His Portraits*. Washington, D.C.: National Portrait Gallery, Smithsonian Institution, 1985.

Nickell, Joe. *Ambrose Bierce Is Missing and Other Historical Mysteries*. Lexington: University Press of Kentucky, 1992.

O'Hara, Theodore. "The Old Pioneer." http://www.poetry-archive.com.

Oliver, Lilian Hays. *Some Boone Descendants and Kindred of the St. Charles District*. Rancho Cordova, CA: N.p., 1984.

Olivier, Georges. *Practical Anthropology*. Springfield, IL: Charles C. Thomas, n.d.

Peattie, Donald Culross. *A Natural History of Trees of Eastern and Central North America*. New York: Bonanza Books, 1965.

———. *A Natural History of Western Trees*. New York: Bonanza Books, 1965.

Pollack, David A., Gwynn Henderson and Peter Killoran. *Frankfort's Forgotten Cemetery*. Education Series Number 10. Frankfort: Kentucky Heritage Council, 2009.

Prichard, James M. *Embattled Capital: Frankfort Kentucky in the Civil War*. Frankfort, KY: Frankfort Heritage Press, 2014.

Schake, Lowell M. *La Charette: A History of the Village Gateway to the American Frontier Visited by Lewis and Clark, Daniel Boone, Zebulon Pike*. New York: iUniverse Star, 2003.

Slotkin, Richard. *Regeneration through Violence: The Mythology of the American Frontier 1600–1860*. 2nd ed. New York: Harper Perennial, 1996.

Spraker, Hazel Atterbury. *The Boone Family*. Baltimore, MD: Genealogical Publishing Co., 1999.

Stewart, C.W. *The Daniel Boone Home*. St. Charles, MO: Lindenwood University, n.d.

Taylor, Richard. *Girty*. With an introduction by Ted Franklin Belue. Frankfort, KY: Wind Publications, 2006.

Wood, Raymond W. *Prologue to Lewis & Clark: The Mackay Evans Expedition*. Foreward by James P. Ronda. Norman: University of Oklahoma Press, 2003.

Skull Sutures Age Data

Forensic Anthropology, The Case Report. http://www.anthro4n6.net. 2004.

Kirk, Jason Dale. "Cranial Suture Closure: A Quantitative Method for Age Estimation Using Laser Instrumentation," Thesis Abstract, Wichita State University, December 2007. http://soar.witchita.edu.

Sabini, Rosanna C., and David E. Elkowitz. "Significance of Differences in Patency Among Cranial Sutures." *Journal of the American Osteopathic Association* 106 (Summer 2006): 600–4. http://www.jaoa.org.

T.G. O'Brien. "On the Effect of Cranial Deformation in Determining Age from Ectocranial Suture Closure." *Growth Developmental Aging* Summer 71 (2008): 23–33. http://www.ncbi.nlm.nih.gov.

Index

A

B

C

D

F

G

H

J

K

L

M

T

V

W

About the Author

Ted Franklin Belue is the author of *The Hunters of Kentucky: A Narrative History of America's First Far West* and *The Long Hunt: Death of the Buffalo East of the Mississippi* and has edited two Daniel Boone biographies. Belue is heavily published in trade and academic press; served as consultant and commentator for the History Channel and advisor for A&E, BBC and NBC; and survived the French and Indian War as a Hollywood extra in *The Last of the Mohicans*. He lives in Kentucky with his wife, Lavina, and a horde of dogs, cats and guitars.